Building With Ethereum

Products, Protocols, and Platforms

Jamie Rumbelow

Apress®

Building With Ethereum: Products, Protocols, and Platforms

Jamie Rumbelow
London, UK

ISBN-13 (pbk): 978-1-4842-9044-6
https://doi.org/10.1007/978-1-4842-9045-3

ISBN-13 (electronic): 978-1-4842-9045-3

Managing Director, Apress Media LLC: Welmoed Spahr
Acquisitions Editor: Celestin Suresh John
Development Editor: Laura Berendson
Coordinating Editor: Mark Powers

Cover designed by eStudioCalamar

Cover image by Jessica Rumbelow

Distributed to the book trade worldwide by Apress Media, LLC, 1 New York Plaza, New York, NY 10004, U.S.A. Phone 1-800-SPRINGER, fax (201) 348-4505, e-mail orders-ny@springer-sbm.com, or visit www.springeronline.com. Apress Media, LLC is a California LLC and the sole member (owner) is Springer Science + Business Media Finance Inc (SSBM Finance Inc). SSBM Finance Inc is a **Delaware** corporation.

For information on translations, please e-mail booktranslations@springernature.com; for reprint, paperback, or audio rights, please e-mail bookpermissions@springernature.com.

Apress titles may be purchased in bulk for academic, corporate, or promotional use. eBook versions and licenses are also available for most titles. For more information, reference our Print and eBook Bulk Sales web page at http://www.apress.com/bulk-sales.

Any source code or other supplementary material referenced by the author in this book is available to readers on GitHub (https://github.com/Apress). For more detailed information, please visit http://www.apress.com/source-code.

Printed on acid-free paper

To Rich, for giving me Ethereum; and to Jessica, for giving me everything that truly matters.

Table of Contents

About the Author

Jamie Rumbelow is a software engineer who lives in London. He was formerly a product engineer at Fei Labs, a major Ethereum protocol, where he built products around Fei's core protocol. Previously, he worked as a founding engineer and senior software engineer in startups, responsible for training and mentoring as well as writing code. In his prior capacity as a software engineering consultant, he got to see organizations at varying levels of scale and the sorts of ways that teams and technologies get shaped by product decisions. As might be obvious from his prose, he also has a philosophy degree. Over the past few years, he has built up a set of principles and opinions on what makes for great software and a great engineering culture.

About the Technical Reviewer

Tom Waite is a software engineer with several years of experience working in the Ethereum ecosystem. Previously, he was at Aztec Protocol, a privacy and scaling Ethereum technology company; contributed to the Fei stablecoin; and studied physics at Imperial College London.

Acknowledgments

This is the sort of book that has taken me a couple of months to write and a couple of years to be ready to write. There are many, many people who have made those years rich, full, and instructive and to whom I give my sincerest thanks.

In particular, and in no particular order, I'd like to thank Arnaud Schenk, Abel Tedros, Jack Jeffrey, Camin McCluskey, Cameron Whitehead, Artur Begyan, Max Glaisher, Neil Davidson, Nathan Young, Lachy Groom, Hannah Chelkowski, Elliot Haughin, Jonny Corrie, JS Denain, Andrew Jordan, Lukas Wahden, Róisín Hannon, Masud Ally, Matthew Batstone, Jake Rozin, James Moore, Iris Lambert, Andreas Sorger, Peter King, Matthew Green, Joshua Kelsall, Jessica Johnston, Tim O'Shea, Jugal Patel, Eric Heimark, Lorenzo Foglianti, Will Porcellino, Lamis Mukta, Jonny and Matthew Clifford, and my parents – all three of them! – for many deep, valuable conversations, emotional support, and the insights on crypto, politics, economics, and programming that they've shared and helped shape.

I'd also like to thank the entire team from Fei Labs for making my time in crypto such a valuable one: Joey, Seb, Storm, Caleb, Erwan, Adam, Brianna, Chris, and Pia, it was a pleasure working with you.

Further thanks go to audiences at the Brighton Blockchain Meetup, ETH Denver, ETH Gathering Barcelona, and various Interintellect salons for feedback on talks that turned into various sections of this book.

Thanks also to the team at Apress – Mark, Celestin, and Laura – for all their help and support bringing this book to life.

Like everyone else in crypto, I owe a huge debt of gratitude to Vitalik Buterin and the Ethereum founding team for designing the original protocol and shepherding it into its teens. Vitalik is among the most interesting thinkers in technology and economics around today, and without his work, I would have very little to say and no easy way to say it.

Special thanks go to Tom Waite, my superlative technical reviewer, colleague, and friend. Without his feedback, arguments, and deep technical expertise, this would be a very, very bad piece of writing.

ACKNOWLEDGMENTS

I'd also like to note my deepest thanks to Richard Burton, the person who gave me my first ether and has been a dear friend and source of constant inspiration (and consternation). You have seen round every corner I haven't, been ahead of every trend. You have supported me for as long as I have known you, and for that I will always be grateful – even if you hate this book.

Finally, I owe my greatest debt of gratitude to my wonderful wife, Jessica. You have made me a better person, a better thinker, and, most of all, happier than I ever imagined I could be. You have read and commented on every word of this book and made it so much more beautiful with your fantastic cover art and illustrations. A big, crashing wave of love for you. No sharks.

Preface

In the chapters that follow, I argue for two main points:

1. Product engineering on Ethereum is a distinct discipline, with its own set of challenges and constraints that make it an interesting and worthwhile endeavor – and one worthy of higher status than it currently enjoys.

2. Decentralization involves trade-offs, and sometimes these are trade-offs that aren't worth making.

This is an opinionated book, which presents a vision for Ethereum – and a style of building products on it – that will be at odds with many current Ethereum developers. That's okay: it's up to you to decide whether my arguments are good and whether the vision I present is one you think is attractive. I don't expect everybody to agree.

But, I hope, it's also an informative book, an introduction for technical people on how Ethereum works and why building products on top of it is challenging and rewarding.

Much technical writing is focused on the practical, with explicit instructions on how to build such and such an application or how to use this or that library. In an ecosystem like crypto, where the core technologies and best practices change and develop every day, this sort of writing has an expiry date little longer than a pint of warm milk kept in a trench-coat pocket. Tutorials are important and can often be helpful, but my goal here is to write something with a little more longevity.

This book therefore tries to walk a delicate tightrope: rich with examples and trade-offs, but also conceptual and philosophically minded. In all cases, I try to be pragmatic. I interweave code examples using various libraries, but the emphasis is on React frontend applications and the *ethers.js* and *wagmi* libraries that can power them. While the details of existing protocols and libraries will change, and the code may sour, the advice and mode of thinking will, I hope, remain cool and fresh.

My writing style here is that of a friend in the pub, talking through some interesting technology; I can therefore be a *little* verbose, sometimes. To remedy that, each main section of each chapter starts with a short summary in italics. If you're completely new to Ethereum and would like a friendly intro to the core concepts, "The Lifecycle of an Ethereum Request" section in Chapter 2 walks you through the basics by taking you on a tour, from start to finish, of how a transaction gets made and ends up in the network. If you're unfamiliar with crypto more generally, then I highly recommend the Matt Levine Bloomberg article "The Crypto Story."[1]

Crypto is full of strange memes and indecipherable acronyms, but I'll try to keep them to a minimum. I also use a few terms interchangeably, unless I make the distinction explicit: "crypto" and "web3"; "account" and "wallet" (see the section "Accounts and Wallets" in Chapter 2 for some disambiguations here); I use "companies" and "DAOs" to refer more generally to organizations that build in the space; and, somewhat awkwardly, "web2" is a convenient shorthand for noncrypto Internet technology and its businesses, culture, norms, and processes.

And since this is a book about Ethereum, any generalizations I make about crypto apply only to this platform.

This book is not intended for beginners to programming or web development, so I will assume knowledge of terms like "state," "interface," and other common computer science terminology. I will assume that you are a mid- to senior-level engineer looking to understand the sorts of constraints Ethereum can put on your products. I won't spend much time talking about how, for instance, it's best to write a React component.

As I said at the beginning of this preface, this book also presents a new(ish) vision for crypto: one grounded in solving real problems, for real people, in real companies. It welcomes regulation, because regulation makes it possible for crypto to grow. I see the future of crypto's growth at the intersection between traditional institutions and these new technologies, not as a disruption, but as a complement. It is a pragmatic vision, grounded in a belief in technology, not in memes or the ill-defined art of community building.

The longer I've been in the orbit of crypto, the greater I've seen the need for a culture of pragmatism, not idealism. This book is my small contribution toward that goal.

---

[1] www.bloomberg.com/features/2022-the-crypto-story

CHAPTER 1

Introduction

Lots of attention in the Ethereum ecosystem is paid to smart contracts: how to write them well, how to design their mechanisms, and how to deploy and manage them safely. These are important tasks, but they only express the responsibilities of one role: the protocol engineer. There are other roles that are equally important, and, in this chapter, we'll look at these roles and how their relative status may change. Understanding the role of the product engineer, especially, will help frame the rest of the book. We'll also look at an important principle that motivates much of the subsequent discussion: the Principle of Trust.

Products, Protocols, and Platforms

The frontend and backend dichotomy should be replaced by a product, protocol, and platform trichotomy. Protocol engineering is important, interesting, and high status. Product and platform engineering are equally important, but less high status; both are becoming more so. When you separate out these roles clearly, and consider how they are integrated within a team, it becomes much easier to focus on solving customer problems. Crypto businesses are still businesses, and businesses should build products that solve problems for their customers.

I'll start this book with a complaint: we should retire the terms "frontend" and "backend" engineer. They create an outmoded division of labor inside software companies that doesn't map well to how software actually gets built. This is increasingly true in crypto, where computation is either hosted on-chain or (often) on some serverless platform.

These arbitrary titles also make hiring more difficult. Candidates with certain job titles on their CVs get pigeonholed into specific functions. "Frontend," in particular, is often used snidely, as a pejorative, diminishing the responsibility of the engineer to "a mere pixel pusher," leaving the more serious work to the *proper* programmers.

J. Rumbelow, *Building With Ethereum*, https://doi.org/10.1007/978-1-4842-9045-3_1

They also make flourishing *within* roles more difficult. The glutinous, sticky contempt held by many "backend" engineers for the "frontend" means that talented programmers, with sophisticated and nuanced understandings of computer science, who write clean and reliable code, are either passed over or find themselves ossified, unable to be taken seriously, unable to grow.

Moreover, these terms refer only to structures internal to the company, structures that are completely irrelevant to customers and completely irrelevant to the products that we build for them.

In my opinion, a much better division is between *product, protocol, and platform*.

A product, protocol, and platform trichotomy could be similarly reductive to the frontend/backend dichotomy; as we'll see, both "product" and "protocol" can mean a wide range of things and subdivide into more specialized roles. There are also parts of each role that overlap. But my contention here is not that it's perfect: it's that product, protocol, and platform is a more useful framing – a more effective way of structuring teams and a better way to think about building on Ethereum.

This distinction better defines where the shift in responsibility from outward-looking (products, tooling, marketing, user interfaces, and experiences) to inward-looking (APIs, internal tools, infrastructure) occurs.

It better explains where the focus of these engineers lies. It doesn't get hung up on technological choices or prejudge abilities. And, as we'll discuss more, it helps integrate these areas properly, in a way that emphasizes customer happiness.

Most of all, it helps put each of these functions on an equal footing – one team working together to build delightful and essential services.

In this section, we'll discuss the product, protocol, platform trichotomy. We'll introduce some of the themes of this book. And we'll argue that crypto teams – and their customers – are better off when they conceive of what they're doing as no different from any other business: building products for customers that give those customers value.

Protocol Engineering

Let's start by looking at protocol engineering and how it fits into the product development story.

Protocol engineers build the smart contracts that provide the core functionality for a crypto protocol. They are an essential part of any company that is building on top of a decentralized platform such as Ethereum. For a certain sort of programmer, protocol engineering is among the most attractive roles in crypto.

Protocol engineering is intellectually challenging and complex, with many distinctive problems:

- Protocols need to be **designed and verified**.

- Protocols need to be **modeled** under both **macro-** and **micro-economic variations**.

- Protocols need to be **tested against real data**, **real money**, and **real behavior** and the insights from such testing integrated.

- At the same time, contracts are generally **immutable**, so getting it wrong early and iterating quickly is more difficult and requires more planning and forethought.

- Smart contracts need to be **audited** and are subject to fierce internal scrutiny and code review.

These are just some of the crucial tasks at which a protocol engineer needs to be competent to do their job well. And these are *new* constraints that typically don't hold when building traditional software.

Protocol engineering is also *fun* and *urgent*. The environment is hugely adversarial: often within milliseconds of deploying a contract, there will be hundreds of bots (and humans) racing to find one of thousands of possible errors in your code or loopholes in your logic. And the results – millions of dollars of value running through your system; the mechanics of the protocol behaving *just* right; your code withstanding thousands of attacks and black swan events – can be very satisfying.

So it's difficult and enjoyable, and it takes dedication and patience. The community is still nascent, grasping in the dark for the right tooling.

Protocol engineering feels like a *new* discipline; writing smart contracts feels like building at the frontier. We're still figuring out how to do it.

All of this combines to make it an incredibly alluring profession. (Not to mention the constrained supply, high demand, and therefore high price that a competent protocol engineer can charge! At the time of writing, the average base salary for a Solidity developer, globally, is $101k per year.)

No wonder it is a high-status job.

Product Engineering

Product engineering is equally challenging and complex. It is, however, not as highly paid or high status.

Product engineers work across the stack, but always with an emphasis on the user's experience and the user's needs.

This, first and foremost, means the UI, the frontends that the user sees and interacts with, the user's portal into the protocol. But it also means answering practical questions about the UX and broader questions about the information architecture:

- How does the **user flow** through the product; how do they **achieve the goals** that they set out to achieve?

- Indeed, **what are their goals**?

- At what point do we need the user to **connect their wallet**?

- What **information do they need** and when?

- What happens when **something goes wrong**?

- How can we **communicate gas fees** in the most useful way?

- How much can we rely on **the security posture** of the wallet, and how much trust engineering – see the next section "Crypto Engineering Is Trust Engineering" for more – do we need to do in our own application?

- Does the application work on **mobile**? Does it need to?

Aside from these more conceptual questions about UX and UI, product engineers are also responsible for making technical decisions that affect the product:

- Should the data be **indexed** or **read live**?

- What kind of a **refresh rate** does indexed data need?

- How should we **transform** and **validate user inputs**?

- How much responsibility for **input validation** should we delegate to the protocol?

Most of all, it means understanding the user's problem and working with protocol and platform to both integrate the stack of existing technologies and develop new technologies in service of solving it.

It is important that these questions – and the actual coding work that falls out of answering them – are squarely within the purview of the product engineering team. These questions have a direct impact on the user and their experience. They have a direct impact on what the user sees, touches, and feels and the psycho-emotional relationship that they have with the product and the broader brand.

The product engineer is responsible for the majority of the contact between the user and the protocol. This means that *security is as important for the product engineer as for the smart contract engineer*. The stakes are similarly high.

Therefore, teams need to place a significant focus on the user – the customer – and what they experience. This usually means a dedicated team, or a dedicated person, who considers these technical decisions always with the user's experience in mind.

Platform Engineering

Platform engineers play a crucial ancillary role in a crypto company, building tooling and infrastructure for the product and protocol to talk, both to the world and to each other.

Products need hosting, and that hosting needs to be designed and maintained. Hosting in crypto can be a lot more complicated than "chuck it on GitHub Pages and forget about it" – although that *can* be the best solution! – for several reasons:

- There may be **auxiliary processes** to run, such as **indexers** or **relayers** or **bots**.

- You may want to **decentralize your frontend**, either in part or entirely (see the section "Hosting" in Chapter 5 for an exploration of these issues).

- Being reactive to users is incredibly important, so you may need to integrate solid **error logging** and **audibility** and **monitoring**.

And it's not just hosting and devops. All engineers – including protocol and product engineers – need good tooling. Software engineering is one of the few disciplines where it's normal to build your own tools. But this is often itself a full-time job! Platform engineering teams can build such tools both for themselves and for the product and protocol teams.

This is an especially important function and contributes significantly to overall product quality, because developer experience is causally prior to user experience. If the developer is having a horrible time, it usually shows in the quality of the product. Good tooling, while not sufficient for good products, is almost always necessary.

Many crypto teams avoid having separate platform engineers and integrate the work into their product and protocol teams. This is absolutely fine, but it's useful to consider the platform role as a separate role nonetheless. Why?

Firstly, the shipping cycle for internal tools is often very different from that of product: how you structure your sprints, how you understand the problem space, and what solutions and trade-offs are acceptable can be wildly different for internal tools than for external products.

Secondly, the testing and audit requirements are generally much less strict: so you can afford to iterate more quickly, to follow the infamous move-fast-and-break-things model much more often.

Thirdly, you likely understand your "internal customers" much better than your "external customers." This cuts both ways: as we've said already, you can spend less time and energy on user research and iterate more quickly; but it's also important to treat the product and platform disciplines as separate precisely so that you don't allow your platform mode to pollute your product mode, precisely so that you stay focused on understanding the user when you're working on the product.

The Ethereum community has made many strides in the right direction, but at least at the time of writing, the quality of the tooling available for product and protocol engineers in crypto is still quite poor:

- Smart contracts are, quite rightly, considered to be APIs – see the section "Contracts Are APIs" in Chapter 4 – but **the tooling for retrieving and updating** and building against the interfaces of these APIs is **still a mess**. I discuss these problems in more detail in the section "Application Binary Interfaces," also in Chapter 4; lots of work can be done here to improve, work for which platform engineers are essential.

- Tools for **automated testing**, especially automated integration testing between the various parts of a full-stack crypto application, are still nascent. Testing infrastructure for smart contracts themselves is getting better; teams such as Paradigm are making good progress with tools like Foundry.[1] But developing a full testing stack still requires a lot of code and a lot of awkward maneuvering.[2]

- **Formal verification** of crypto protocols is inaccessible and complex.

- **DAO governance** is still fundamentally broken, communities torn between the ideals of distribution and the prudence and necessity of effective governance. Token allocations are weighted toward a small cadre of teams, investors, and whales; at the same time, most DAOs preach democratic values such as broad-based consent and inclusivity. There are experiments to improve the quality and participation levels of voting, to pull back from a directly democratic mechanism and toward something more representative, but many more cycles of iteration are needed. Much communication happens principally through Discord, always a good example of the medium introducing noise into the message.

Solving these problems in a general way is the responsibility of the community at large. And a lot of the correct solutions are hard to predict a priori. They will emerge in path-dependent ways, incrementally, which is why it's especially important to dedicate resources internally to solving local problems specific to your team.

Finally, platform engineers can also be responsible for a range of intermediary technical decisions, such as node hosting providers. There are significant technical complexities to building smart contracts and running products on top of them, and it can be useful to treat these complexities as a distinctive source of work for a distinctive team, rather than palming them off on product and protocol.

Crypto Businesses

So we've outlined the roles that product, protocol, and platform engineers fulfill. Many teams will need to do all three, even if they carve up the responsibilities and job titles differently. How does this shake up in your actual hiring practices and in your team structure?

---

[1] https://github.com/foundry-rs/foundry
[2] We'll talk about how to test the products you create in Chapter 5.

Firstly, it's important to understand them as three different functions. These are three different roles for which you are hiring and for which the balance must be carefully calibrated. A team with no protocol engineer lacks the ability to change the underlying data storage and computation; a team with no product engineer lacks the ability to build frontends for customers to use; a team with no platform engineer lacks the ability to host and monitor the product and build tooling to support the other functions. There may be separate people filling these roles or one person doing all three. But be under no illusion: they are different roles!

Secondly, these roles, while all crucial, have different *relative* importance. Many teams will need to do all three and will want to hire separately. But the relative ubiquitousness of product engineering with respect to the other roles offers a good reason for why it is *especially* important.

There are many crypto companies that don't really need protocol engineering. Companies building frontends for existing protocols, for instance, won't need dedicated protocol resources. Similarly, companies building wallet software, or some other user-facing application with no smart contract component, probably won't need a protocol engineer.

There are some crypto companies that don't really need platform engineering – or at least can minimize it and integrate it into other functions. If their hosting requirements are small, and their existing tools are sufficient to support their development efforts, the platform role might be less important.

But in almost every case, there is a *product* component. Crypto companies still need to *sell* something, and there are few instances where selling something means launching a protocol and not building a frontend for it. The only condition under which product engineering is not important per se is when you're building a protocol that is immutable, with a minimal surface area of governance, which provides a service only to other protocols. In these cases, it is unlikely you'll need to hire an engineer to focus on product engineering alone.

But these cases are few and far between. And they are getting fewer. Product engineering is going to become more important over the next few years, not less.

Why? Two reasons:

1. **The core technologies of crypto are beginning to settle**: The core DeFi primitives – token standards, AMMs, lending markets, options, futures, derivatives – are becoming well established. The basic standards around NFTs and ownership are now reasonably

well understood. Efficiency improvements to the Ethereum blockchain and scaling technologies such as layer 2s are known quantities. This is not to say that the foundations are set: there can and should be much more innovation at the protocol level. But the basics are there. The concrete is still soft, but the foundations have been poured.

2. **Fuelling the industry through the returns on token speculation is a haphazard, broken, and damaging model**: It encourages mercenary capital and fragile communities and zero-sum value extraction. We should be building institutions that endure through legitimate defensibility, not institutions whose lives are snuffed out by a sudden drop in an illiquid token's value. As crypto matures and regulation hardens, the ability to meme yourself into economic relevance will become more and more difficult.

And once the basics are there, what is next? *Solving problems for customers.* Creating products that people actually want to use, which suggests that the next stage of crypto's development will be building out user-facing applications and improving user experiences around the primitives that exist today. This has a natural consequence: product engineering is going to increase in both absolute and relative importance.

Note   This book was written during the 2022 bear market. One useful function of bear markets is a renewed emphasis on products that solve problems and drive meaningful revenue – another reason to think that the product role will increase in importance!

Finally, this renewed emphasis on product and user experience means that *product engineering needs to be a part of the story from the very beginning*. Smart contracts should be designed in collaboration with product engineers so they expose the right methods and emit the most useful events. Tooling should be evaluated based on how significantly – even if indirectly – it improves the end-user experience. Innovations at the protocol level should be viewed through a prism of the functionality they unlock, not merely the elegance of their design. I'll bang on this drum a lot throughout this book.

This section has sketched out the three key engineering roles that exist when building complex crypto products. The trichotomy is neither exclusive nor exhaustive:

there is overlap, and there are other important engineering functions that mature businesses need. But if there is one role among the three that does, and will continue to matter most, my money is on product.

We're here to solve problems and serve customers. If we're not, we're not building businesses: we're just building technology.

Crypto Engineering Is Trust Engineering

The psychology of users matters, especially in crypto. Crypto teams can think of their job in terms of trust engineering: making product decisions to increase a user's confidence in the product. Don't move fast or break things; it is more rational to move slow and protect things. Trust engineering means changing your process as well as your product. Trust is built over time. Crypto needs more grown-ups.

Products and Users

As we discussed in the previous section ("Products, Protocols, and Platforms"), most crypto teams are building companies. They exist to serve customers and capture a small part of the value that they create for those customers. This is why product engineering is especially important: product engineers are focused on building experiences for users, with a relentless focus on the user experience. This commitment to user experience and delight, I've argued, is crucial – and becoming more so.

One point I try to make in this book is that crypto companies aren't at all that different from regular software companies. What I've said earlier is true of all software businesses, all businesses in general.

But there are important ways in which crypto companies *are* different, if not in kind certainly in degree.

The product experiences we are building have an altogether different flavor from what you might be used to. The stakes are so much higher. Potentially millions – or even billions – of dollars of value will flow through the products that you build.

This changes things. This changes the focus of your team. It changes your pace. It changes your temperament.

You are no longer just engineering a solution to a narrowly defined problem: you are engineering *trust*.

The Psychology of the User

Let's start by considering the psychology of the user – not just the users we have today but also the users we hope to reach. As the tombstones in the graveyard of abandoned and sabotaged projects attest, in crypto, mistakes have truly significant consequences.

A common refrain in crypto is "not your keys, not your coins." A purely custodial system is not a decentralized one, since it offers a single and vulnerable point of failure or attack. Crypto users, so the refrain goes, need to own their private keys outright.

But this generates serious usability problems. The basic wallet infrastructure is still so weak. The median user is not going to want to store 64 hexadecimal characters somewhere and take on the infosec risk attached. Swapping "64 hexadecimal characters" for "12 random words," as in the case of seed phrases, is hardly better. It is not just awkward from a UX standpoint: it creates stress. Users have been given structural assurances from regulation, insurance, as well as common patterns of account recovery such as "reset password" functionality. They are psychologically unprepared and unwilling to take full control over private keys or private key analogues. Doing it safely, securing yourself from the barrage of technical and social attack vectors that exist in the adversarial environment, is an extremely tough job.

There seems to be a general presumption that there is some form of asset recovery available to users who lose their keys or general apathy toward those who do, expressed by the resigned and lazy epithet "with great power comes great responsibility." In isolated cases, this might be true. But customers deserve better than that; as the user base shifts away from early adopters, they will *demand* better than that, and these handy libertarian dismissals do nothing to help promote the industry or the products we create. The asset recovery mechanisms that do exist are principally on-chain (e.g., smart contract wallets) and often inadequate or incomplete.[3] And on-chain solutions can impose significant user experience burdens that make these products that much less attractive.

Furthermore, the mechanisms for asset recovery via off-chain legal structures are yet to be fully developed and will take time to mature and integrate properly. There are not

---

[3] Vitalik Buterin discusses some technical issues with implementing social recovery for on-chain smart contract accounts here: `https://vitalik.ca/general/2021/01/11/recovery.html`. This sort of approach feels directionally correct, but it addresses only a small part of what "asset recovery" requires.

a lot of options of on-chain insurance – despite the laudable work of teams like Nexus Mutual[4] – and the regulatory game is yet to be played.

There is an underlying point here: crypto is scary because generations of people have relied on trusted third parties to outsource their personal security posture. And as the dollar amount stored gets bigger, it gets scarier.

Crypto is also scary because the environment of crypto is one that breeds reasons to be fearful. It is foundationally adversarial. The financial incentives to play foul and act with malfeasance are obvious. What is less obvious is that one of the core goals of web3 – transparent and permissionless access – serves to double down on these incentives, attracting more foul play and minimizing its risks. Crypto *feels* a certain way, and it doesn't take many rounds in a Discord chat room before realizing that the feeling, in large part, is one of "everybody is trying to scam you, all of the time." Even battle-hardened hedge fund managers and organized criminals – people who work in highly adversarial environments – have, over time, evolved systems of trust and centralization that allow the median participant to be able to operate psychologically and to therefore allow institutions to flourish. Crypto is yet to evolve such comprehensive systems, and the challenge of doing so while remaining faithful to the movement's core vision is great.

The design space for attacks is always increasing as crypto systems become even more complicated. The more mechanisms a protocol introduces to lower the psychological burden of using it, the more complexity and therefore the more opportunities there are to attack it. The core problem is the parameters and bounds of trust haven't been set yet. Users rely often on shaky intuitions: a product "looks a bit off," or a conversation "feels fishy." There isn't a good vocabulary for describing these intuitions. Most of all, there has been insufficient attention paid to how important it is to build products in a way that bolsters user trust and minimizes user risk.

Trust Engineering

So one essential task for the product engineer – working in tandem with protocol and product – is to give the user as many reasons as possible to trust their product. And, usually, the best way to convince someone that something is safer is to actually make it safer.

---

[4] https://nexusmutual.io

Given these general concerns about the adversarial environment, then, what sorts of levers does the product engineer have to generate trust and reduce risk in their products?

One important place where teams sometimes begin is with the Silicon Valley mantra, "move fast and break things." No! When you are dealing with millions of dollars, you should, in the words of my friend Ric Burton, "move carefully and check things."[5] This means a lot of practical things, the details of which we'll discuss later. But the most important of these entails an emphasis on product quality and slowing down to ensure it.

Crypto might move fast – and it does – but this needn't frighten you into cutting corners in order to get to market quicker. There are rational reasons to reduce your product velocity in service of greater attention to security and quality: the expected value of not messing up far dwarfs the benefit of being a few days earlier to market.

This suggests a cardinal rule, something that should always be in the back of your mind when building products in the Ethereum ecosystem:

The Principle of Trust

Each interaction a user has with your product, whether positive or negative, should increase their trust in it.

If you are fighting in a competitive space for user attention, you needn't worry. Competition should be no reason to abandon the Principle of Trust. The core principle of permissionless access means that user lock-in is lower. It is harder for companies in DeFi to build a moat from user lock-in (such as network effects). Indeed, reliability and trust can make up for all manner of sins. There are teams in crypto building poor quality products, or lending protocols offering relatively less interest on deposits, that still maintain large user bases, because of the reliability of the platform. Trust can be a moat, too![6]

So we can, and should, focus rigorously on the quality of our products. We can pay attention to aspects of design and development that are often overlooked by

---

[5] https://twitter.com/ricburton/status/1219962369989758977

[6] The idea of a business's "moat" is generally attributed to Warren Buffett. I like the model put forward by Hamilton Helmer in his *7 Powers: The Foundations of Business Strategy*, which describes a moat as a set of powers that provide persistent, differential returns in the face of competition. Applying Helmer's framework to crypto companies is an interesting project, regrettably outside the scope of this book.

overstretched teams looking to ship quickly. One example: Emphasize information architecture during design. What information does the user need, and what do they expect? How is this information revealed hierarchically? How is it auditable? User interfaces should provide information about where data comes from and justification for its calculations. This can be as simple as a link to the relevant transaction on Etherscan or as complex as a custom UI containing dynamic explanations of some specific, calculated number found in your app. Focus on clarity of information, and trust will follow.

Another important lever is error handling. Some errors that a normal user will face are deeply technical, such as an invalid nonce, which may not even be the fault of the user. Some errors are due to incorrect user input. Some errors are due to the dynamical properties of crypto: the prices of assets and gas rates will change between a first attempt and a retry, further compounding user stress and confusion and violating the Principle of Trust. The most important thing is to communicate errors to the user, simply and effectively. Spend time thinking about wording and integrating documentation into your product. Also, spend time thinking about how to engineer out errors through the UI or its behavior. If an underlying price has changed, can you detect it and reveal it to the user in a humane way? Even sophisticated users will need guidance. And all users deserve it.

Finally, aesthetics matter too. Products that are enjoyable to use and beautiful create more trust, as well as happier users.

A fourth way we can engineer more trust is to focus on the full user experience, from marketing to product to documentation to customer service. Tony Fadell makes this point well in his book *Build*:

> *[W]hen you're creating a new product, regardless of whether it's made of atoms or electrons, for businesses or consumers, the actual thing you're building is only one tiny part of a vast, intangible, overlooked user journey that starts long before a customer ever gets their hands on your product and ends long after.*

—Tony Fadell, *Build* (Chapter 3.1)

Fadell's suggestion is that every touch point – every time your customers interact with your company – matters. Any chance you get to increase trust, you should take it. Trust, like respect, is built over years and destroyed in an instant. That's why the Principle of Trust is framed in universal terms.

Be responsive to requests and problems. If something goes wrong with your restaurant meal, your confidence in the restaurant increases *beyond* the baseline when the problem is fixed expediently and professionally. Companies get in trouble, not when they make mistakes, but when their processes and procedures are of an insufficient quality that they can't correct those mistakes. Errors will happen. Get really good at fixing them, and you'll get really good at engineering more trust.

Excellence starts long before a customer uses your product. Code review and external audits are essential for systems dealing with money and even more so for systems that operate in adversarial environments. Code review is important for the obvious reasons: it produces better code quality; it helps identify and fix smaller issues you would otherwise miss; it helps you when considering larger refactorings or alternative approaches; it helps you see the wood for the trees (and the trees for the wood). But it's also important for less obvious reasons: it is a form of knowledge transfer. It gets more eyes on more parts of the system and helps reduce the bus quotient (the number of people who could be hit by a bus before the company is in danger). It is good for the robustness and antifragility of your team as well as the robustness and antifragility of the products you're building.

External audits are important for similar sorts of reasons. But the other thing that audits provide is an *artifact that signals trustworthiness*. Auditors often provide a report. You can publish this report and show that you've addressed the issues within it. You can, and should, comment on the report and link to the commits and describe the changes you've made. Even the act of commissioning an audit is a good signal. Audits aren't cheap; but neither are hacks.

Perhaps the most important thing you can do when trying to engineer trust is to always bias toward transparency.

One of the easiest ways to increase trust among a certain user base – that is, the current user base of tech-savvy crypto-natives – is to open source your code, to show to others that your code quality is high and to allow unaffiliated individuals to inspect and audit your code for you.

But transparency extends far beyond the code you write. You should be transparent with your errors: publish post-mortems when things go wrong, demonstrating that you understand the reasons and that you are working to fix them. You should be transparent with your reasoning: publish justifications for your product decisions and product strategy. This doesn't mean you need to delegate these decisions out to others, but it does mean you need to communicate in a clear and considered way the inputs into your decision-making processes and the ways you evaluate the possible outcomes.

Finally, and I want to underline this point, trust is built over time, and habits aimed at increasing trust need to be continuously renewed. It's worth considering whether you can include certain indicators of trust in your internal metrics: Have we communicated with our users more than average this month? How easy is it for somebody to complain and feel as though the complaint has been heard? How reliable is our product? How reliable are the ancillary services such as customer support that go around our product? Constantly measuring and attending to indicators of trust is difficult, but extremely valuable.

Professional Arbitrage

I hope that the preceding considerations are both sobering and invigorating: sobering so the importance of what we are building is not lost, and so the consequences of getting it wrong are not forgotten, and invigorating because the importance of what we are building means we can have a renewed sense of care and craftsmanship in how we build. We can afford to emphasize excellence.

Web2 engineers, with experience and focus and care, can do excellent work in web3, especially as product engineers. Understanding your discipline as trust engineering, considering user trust and confidence in everything we do, is a great way to differentiate yourself from the crowd. And none of it relies on skills idiosyncratic to crypto.

I'd like to underline this point again: *none of this is crypto-specific*. Many of the problems you face are crypto-flavored. But few of the solutions have to be! There have been reams written on how to write code well, how to write code in teams, how to respect your teammates and your users, how to understand your users' problems, how to design your solutions so that they solve these problems effectively, how to revisit and revise your solutions to ensure that when the problems shift the solutions do too, and how to scale your solutions so that they continue to work when crossing over various memory and time boundaries. This is all work you have done in web2 and should continue to do in web3.

Finally, in the web3 world of incomprehensible memes and devastating hacks, all set in the tenor of cultural anarchy, your existing expertise is a form of superpower. Web2 engineers moving into web3 are primed, perfectly, to take advantage of a rare form of *professional arbitrage*.

We can be the grown-ups in the room.

What's Next

This chapter has introduced the notion of product engineering, distinguished it from the other roles in Ethereum engineering, laid out my basic reasons for why product engineering is important, and described the sorts of things that product engineers actually do. With that in mind, the chapters that follow are a deep dive into what this all looks like in practice.

In Chapter 2 ("Requests, Networks, and Accounts"), we'll look at notions of *identity*. We'll see how a user's intentions are represented, how the user themselves is represented, and how the network is represented. More precisely, we'll see how an Ethereum request gets from a user's head to the blockchain and back again, and we'll start to think about the various UX and product patterns that help make that happen.

In Chapter 3 ("Transactions"), we'll build upon these core concepts, adding flesh to the bones. We'll look at transactions in greater detail and consider how we should represent them in our UI. We'll also think about how they can fail and how to build experiences that understand and can react to these failure modes.

Chapter 4 ("Contracts") begins by discussing what smart contracts actually are and how they are programmed and executed on the EVM (Ethereum Virtual Machine). We'll introduce a basic conceptual model for contracts – contracts as APIs – and see where this model breaks down. We'll talk about the sorts of data that are available to product engineers, how smart contracts are constrained, and how we can work around these constraints using various indexing techniques.

In Chapter 5 ("Infrastructure"), we'll see how we can ensure our applications are doing what we need them to do and where to put them when we want to get people using them. We'll talk about decentralization in this context, too, looking at some of the difficulties of decentralized hosting and the centralized tendencies of the existing Internet infrastructure.

The penultimate Chapter 6 ("Decentralization") takes a step back from the technical heart of the book, considering various memes and organizational structures that are currently in vogue. We'll look at standards setting in the Ethereum ecosystem. We'll consider how frontends might be decentralized and whether this is even desirable. And we'll challenge whether decentralization should be the central meme in web3.

Finally, in Chapter 7 ("Conclusion"), we'll talk about how crypto sits within broader patterns of technological change and what a world where crypto is essential might look like. This is the least technical of the chapters and the most speculative. I hope that, by the end of this book, you'll agree with me on the big things. But if you don't, I hope that you'll have a clear sense of what I am trying to say, and be eager to start a career in crypto in order to prove me wrong.

Summary

In this chapter, we began by talking about the product, protocol, and platform dichotomy, motivating why each role is relevant and important. We also gave some reasons why product and platform roles deserve higher relative status than they currently enjoy. We then discussed the various psychological features of interacting with crypto products today and how the most important job of the product engineer is to engineer trust. Finally, we sketched out the rest of this book.

CHAPTER 2

Requests, Networks, and Accounts

Requests are the messages, the bits of information which move state and intent around the system. Networks are the channels over which messages are sent. Accounts are the entities that send and sign those messages. In this chapter, we'll develop a foundational understanding of these three central parts of the Ethereum design. We'll look at how these concepts intertwine and how they affect the products we build.

The Lifecycle of an Ethereum Request

Understanding the full lifecycle of an Ethereum request is an excellent way to introduce the platform's core concepts. Transactions are state changers. Requests begin in a user's head and are turned into a transaction by the app. They are signed and verified by wallet software and sent to a node. One node is selected as a block proposer, which is responsible for selecting, executing, and organizing transactions. Several other nodes are chosen to check the work of the block proposer. Once consensus is achieved, the transaction is considered confirmed, and the app can update its state.

The story of how an Ethereum request is made is far from straightforward: a request is born, lives, and resolves in a complex, path-dependent, and sometimes inscrutable way. It is not just complex at one level, but fractally so: every time you zoom in to one small piece of the network, more complexity emerges.

Understanding it fully could be the subject of several PhD theses. Its mechanisms sit at the intersection of advanced computer science, microeconomics, information theory, as well as practical matters of web application development, the infrastructure of the Internet, and systems engineering. But it's helpful to see the story at the highest level – to get a sense of the broad integrative picture and to see how it all fits together.

© Jamie Rumbelow 2023
J. Rumbelow, *Building With Ethereum*, https://doi.org/10.1007/978-1-4842-9045-3_2

To that end, in this section, we'll walk through the entire lifecycle of an Ethereum request. You'll see **NOTE** blocks and footnotes, which nod toward the subtleties and complexities that I'll otherwise pretend aren't there. I also reference other chapters and sections of this book, which will discuss many of these ideas in a lot more detail.

In the next part, I'll summarize the basics; the rest of the section will drill further into the details. So, if you're in a hurry, you should be able to get a good grasp of the fundamentals by reading this list and skimming the sections that are interesting.

But before we begin on our journey, there are two important caveats to make.

Firstly, this chapter describes how transactions work under the *Proof of Stake* consensus mechanism. Secondly, there are two sorts of requests one might make to the Ethereum network: writes and reads. Writes cause changes to the global state; reads simply return values (or derivatives of values) from it. Reads are considerably simpler, so I won't spend much time on them, though I'll highlight in the text where the read path diverges. This section will focus on write requests.

The Basic Story

Requests begin in the user's head and end by effecting a change to the Ethereum global state. Each step between these two is designed to spread the responsibility between multiple, noncolluding parties, ensure the security and historical immutability of the system, and do so in a power- and resource-efficient way via its "Proof of Stake" consensus system.

Note   These properties might seem purely technical. But blockchain design is not merely a technical problem: since blockchains are also social systems, it is also a *political* problem; constraints on, for example, transaction power usage are driven, in part, by exogenous social and political demands.

There are a handful of standard actors in the story of how a request goes from, some with already familiar names, others more obscure, all with specific roles to play. These actors are as follows:

- A **User**, who wants to achieve some goal and is relying on you to help make it happen

- Your **App**, the frontend in which the User interacts with your system

- The user's **Wallet**, the piece of software they use to manage their Ethereum account(s) and sign transactions

- A **Node**, a copy of the Ethereum network software, connected to the wider network and exposing an HTTP RPC endpoint

- The **Network**, the set of all the nodes running on Ethereum and the emergent properties that exist through their interactions

- A **Validator**, a special type of node which can be chosen to construct, verify, confirm, or challenge the current block

- A **Block proposer**, a validator which is chosen to construct the current block

This is a simple cast and represents a simplified model. But these various actors combine and interact to shepherd a request from conception to completion. The basic story is straightforward:

1. The user signals their intent to do something, usually by triggering some sort of user interface event (e.g., clicking a button).

2. The app handles the event and constructs a transaction.

3. The user goes to their wallet to verify and sign the transaction.

4. The wallet – or sometimes the app[1] – submits the transaction to the node.

5. The node verifies the transaction, and the app goes into a waiting state.

6. The node broadcasts the transaction to its peers on the network, the transaction being stored in the mempool of each node.

7. A single validator is assigned as the block proposer, responsible for selecting and executing the block and computing the next system state.

---

[1] Once a request has been signed by the wallet, there is nothing stopping it being submitted to a node by some other party: the app's frontend, some backend service, or some sort of relayer. Hardware wallets, for instance, sign the transaction on the hardware device and then pass the signed transaction payload back to the software wallet or app.

8. A group of other validators are assigned to the validation committee.

9. The block proposer selects the transactions from the mempool and executes the requests.

10. Once the validators agree upon the contents of the next system state, the block is considered confirmed.

11. When the app sees the transaction is included in a confirmed block, it pulls any data needed, informs the user, and updates its state to reflect the new state of the network.

Truncated like this, it seems straightforward enough. Of course though, as ever, the devil is in the details. This list will form the basis of the rest of this section. Let's dive in.

Where Requests Originate

One crucial and often overlooked insight to building on Ethereum: All requests begin off-chain. Ethereum does not support autonomous contracts; requests are always initiated by an externally owned account (EOA).[2] This means that every request comes from either a user or a user-like entity (e.g., a bot). All requests issue in some way from an intention to do something, rather than from the autonomous workings of a protocol itself.

This is a book about building products for users, so we'll be thinking about it in user-only terms. (There is of course an important role for bots too, but we'll generally steer clear of these complications.) In most cases, this means that the user needs to initiate a request through some user interface. We'll discuss how this happens in much more detail in other chapters and in a later section of this chapter. But the core idea is that the user interacts with the app, the app figures out the user's intention, and the app pulls its data from and submits transactions to some node connected to the network, as shown in Figure 2-1.

---

[2] In the early days of Ethereum, there were discussions of an ALARM opcode to trigger contracts at some later time, but it never made it into the protocol (https://github.com/ethereum/go-ethereum/issues/117).

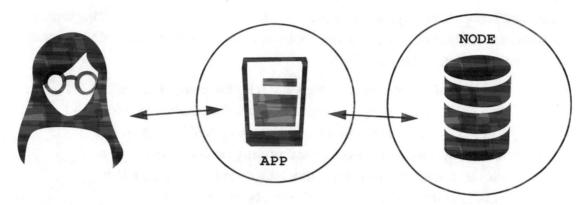

Figure 2-1. *All requests begin with a user wanting something. Data flows from the node to the user via the app, and intention flows from the user to the node via the app*

For frontends, this communication from the app to the node is usually done with the window.ethereum object, typically via a higher-level library like *ethers.js*.[3] But as we'll discuss later (sections "Contracts Are APIs" and "Indexing" in Chapter 4), the node can be treated as a general-purpose API interface, and so there are different approaches to getting data in and out of the blockchain.

In the case of read requests, this is all that needs to be done: the request needs no signing or confirmation, and the node can process the request and return the result to the user. In the case of write requests, it gets a little more complicated.

A write request involves a function call to the network that *gives rise to some state change*. Consensus needs to be reached over the new state, and the network needs to decide how to deal with the various competing requests vying for slot and block space. Moreover, the history of the blockchain needs to be agreed upon and secured. So the user needs to commit to paying something to the network both for its computational power and to sustain the incentive structure necessary for security. (There are still costs associated with fulfilling read requests – bandwidth, computation – but these are borne by the node provider rather than by the network.)

Ethereum uses a mechanism to gas to help price the work required to execute and confirm the transaction. The total amount of gas is determined by the complexity of the transaction: each EVM opcode has an amount of gas attached to it. Certain activities that cost more, like writing to permanent state, consume a higher amount of gas. Each unit

---

[3] ethers.js is a popular, TypeScript-friendly library for interacting with Ethereum smart contracts: https://docs.ethers.io/v5/

of gas then costs a certain gas amount that the wallet software can specify. This creates a market, driven by supply and demand, for computation on the network. Gas therefore serves two important functions:

- Gas is used as **a mechanism for paying for the computational resources required** by a given transaction. Transactions provide a per-gas amount that they are willing to pay, including a base gas fee (set by the network) as well as a priority fee that can be used to incentivize validators to select one transaction over another. If the network is busy, then the gas price will be higher.

- Gas is used to **solve the denial-of-service problem** present in public networks like Ethereum. If submitting requests to the network is free, then this opens the door for a malicious actor to spam the network. If the user has to pay based on a market price, then the marginal next transaction in a block becomes more expensive, eventually pricing out a spammer.

Gas is thus an elegant solution to the problem of pricing network usage. High gas fees, often used as a criticism of Ethereum, are actually a symptom of its success: there is high demand for transaction space, and supply is limited. Attempts to scale Ethereum are concerned with moving this demand around (usually to layer 2s, which we'll talk about in the section "Network and Account Switching" later in this chapter) and increasing the supply capacity (through upcoming network upgrades like sharding).

Anyway, the user is sent to their wallet software to sign and verify the transaction. At this point, they may need to make some meta-level decisions, especially around how much they are willing to pay for gas. Some wallets abstract this complexity away, showing only a price in USD or ETH. Others provide more configuration, allowing the user to specify max gas amounts and prices per gas unit. The wallet will also do its own checks, often verifying lower-level pieces of the transaction that are necessary for the effective functioning of the network. Some wallets will even simulate the transaction in memory and block the transaction if it believes it will revert.

If there are errors with the transaction construction, then the transaction is rejected. Once configured and confirmed, however, the wallet then produces a *transaction hash*, returns it to the app, and submits the transaction into the network, as shown in Figure 2-2.

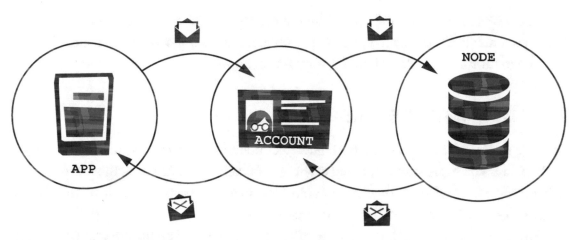

Figure 2-2. *If a transaction is valid, it is confirmed in the wallet software and sent to the node. If it isn't, it gets bounced back to the app*

Transaction hashes are unique identifiers, built by combining all the various properties of the transaction, including who is sending it and what its content contains – as well as when and in what sequence it appears in the account's transactions – and getting the user to *sign* it. (See the section "What Does a Transaction Look Like?" in Chapter 3 for more on the properties of an individual transaction.)

When signing a transaction, the user applies their private key to the transaction details, which allows them to say that they do indeed wish to issue this transaction and that it is them issuing it. The signature and transaction details are then combined and sent into the *keccak256* hashing algorithm.

Note   What is a hashing function? A hashing function is a cryptographic mechanism for producing a fixed-length string from some input. Secure hashing functions have three important properties. They are deterministic, which means that the same input will always produce the same output. This allows them to be verified at some point in the future. They are irreversible, which means that there is no better way to determine the input from the output than by guessing at random. This allows them to be used in contexts where security matters. And they minimize collisions, which means that it is very unlikely that two different inputs produce the same output. This allows hashes to be used to indicate identity. Ethereum uses *keccak256*, which satisfies each of these properties.

Keccak256 produces a 32-byte hexadecimal string, which is prepended with 0x to indicate that it is a hexadecimal. The app then records the transaction hash locally, so that it can monitor the blockchain for transaction approval.

How Requests Are Confirmed

So, let's recap. We have a transaction that describes a function call requesting a change to the state. The transaction is signed cryptographically to confirm that these are indeed the user's wishes. The transaction is identified by a transaction hash. And the transaction is submitted by the node to the network.

Since this book is about users, we won't spend much time on how the network processes these transactions. The Ethereum docs have some good content on Ethereum's original validation mechanism, Proof of Work, and its newer, more computationally efficient mechanism, Proof of Stake.[4] For our purposes, all we need to know is that there is a gap between submitting a transaction and that transaction being included in a block. Often transactions are included directly in the current block; in other cases, the transaction may take more blocks to be included. We'll talk more about this in a moment.

The user's wallet submits an HTTP request to a node's RPC endpoint (cf. "Contracts Are APIs" in Chapter 4). The node takes this request, verifies it, and broadcasts it to its peers. Who are its peers? Its peers are just the other nodes it knows about; this is, in practice, always a small subset of the total nodes on the network (its "neighbors") that it happens to be connected to.

Every node[5] on the network contains a list of pending transactions. This list is called the *mempool*, a liminal space where new transactions await inclusion in a block. Figure 2-3 indicates that a transaction propagates to the mempools of every node when submitted.

---

[4] https://ethereum.org/en/developers/docs/consensus-mechanisms/pow/ and https://ethereum.org/en/developers/docs/consensus-mechanisms/pos, respectively.

[5] Well, not quite every node: only nodes that are participating in validation this *epoch* (a grouping of 32 *slots*/blocks). Participating nodes are reshuffled each epoch.

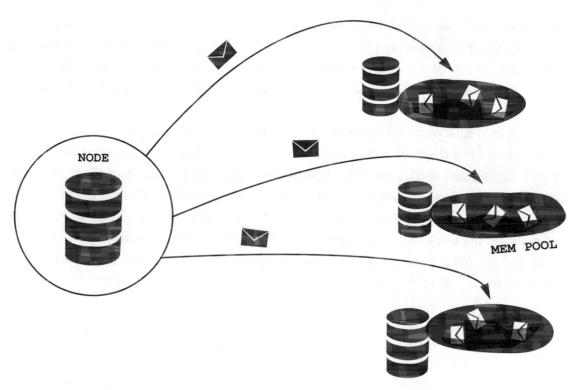

Figure 2-3. *Every node in the network has their own copy of the mempool, a list of pending transactions*

A validator node then is assigned, at random,[6] as a block proposer. This validator chooses which transactions to select from the mempool (or elsewhere), based on the gas price and gas limit remaining in the block that the validator is constructing. Transactions can be left in the mempool for some time before they are verified. If gas fees suddenly spike and the submitted transaction is bidding too low, then the transaction will be left pending until fees are lowered. Transactions can also be dropped outright from the mempool if they are left too long; nodes have finite memory, and removing pending transactions from the mempool is one mechanism by which the nodes achieve reliable, sustained functioning.[7] Similarly, if a transaction takes up a lot of total gas and there isn't

---

[6] Well, not quite at random: there's a weighting relative to the total ownership share of staked ETH among those validators participating in an epoch.

[7] See, e.g., https://ethereum.stackexchange.com/questions/31303/when-are-pending-transactions-dropped-from-the-blockchain for more details.

enough space left in the current block, it might not be included in the next slot or two. In fact, block proposers have unilateral control over what gets added to the block and in what order, and so they are able to construct their own transactions to extract value from the network; the economics are more complex than just "pick the transaction with the highest gas bid."[8]

Once the block proposer has selected and executed the transactions – in other words, once it has derived the new state – it then proposes the block to a committee of other validator nodes. This committee is selected, again, at random. The validators in the committee then each execute the transactions, comparing their results to the proposed block. They submit *attestations*: agreements with the block proposer that the result is indeed what the transaction code said it should be. This allows the validators as a group to reach consensus on the proposed block. Once consensus is reached, the block is considered confirmed (*"finalized"*). This flow is shown visually in Figure 2-4.

---

[8] In the first draft of Chapter 6, I included a detailed discussion of Maximal Extractable Value (MEV), where validators add transactions to or reorganize blocks in order to perform various economic attacks on other transactions. This section was, I think, interesting, but felt like a bit too much of a tangent to the main thrust of the book. So here's the short version: MEV arises because block validators have control over which transactions go into the block and in what order. So, for instance, a validator can evaluate what will happen to the price of a token after a swap and then arbitrage on the transaction by buying the token up to the price that the attacked transaction is willing to pay, then selling immediately afterward and pocketing the difference. These sorts of attacks – and they are attacks – are also a part of traditional markets (see, e.g., Michael Lewis's *Flash Boys*, which explores the frontrunning of stock orders by high-frequency traders), so are not unique to crypto. But they represent serious amounts of money: some ~$300m was extracted by miners in 2021. What is unique to crypto, however, is that in crypto MEV extraction seems unavoidable. Projects such as Flashbots (`www.flashbots.net`) are building important parts of infrastructure to help identify, democratize, and limit the value extracted.

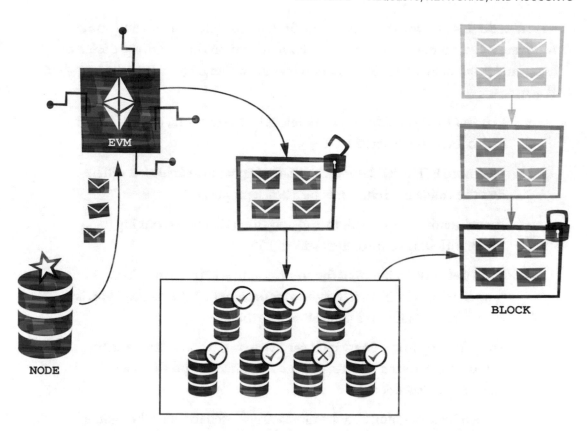

Figure 2-4. *A transaction is submitted by the node on the left. The node executes the transaction to check its validity before sending it to the network for consensus. Block proposers select and execute the transactions; a committee of validators confirms the results. Only then is the block considered "added" to the chain*

Much of the complexity in understanding this flow comes from the inaccessibility of the underlying networking principles and peer-to-peer communication. But the actual mechanism of consensus is relatively straightforward: do the work a few times by a few different people, calculate the new state, and ensure that the proposed block's results do in fact follow from the code that the block is supposed to execute.

How to do this in a way that ensures no foul play or collusion is a little more complicated. But there are some economic considerations built into the design of Ethereum's Proof of Stake implementation that are designed to reduce the impact of bad actors:

- In order to be considered as validators by the network, each validator has to lock up at least 32 ETH.

- The more ETH a validator locks up, the higher the likelihood will be that the validator is chosen to be a block proposer.

- If a validator contests a block's results, the validator is running the risk of forfeiting some of their staked ETH.

- If the network decides that the contestation is correct, the block proposer loses its ETH; if the network decides that the contestation is incorrect, the validators contesting lose theirs.

- Therefore, there is a financial incentive to reach consensus, and the penalty for cheating increases in proportion to the power that they have in the network.

Anybody can be a validator, and the randomness used to select the validator committee makes participating in the consensus layer accessible. In the case that a block is contested successfully, the canonical chain will be reverted, and the state of the blockchain will be updated. These reorganizations happen frequently on Proof of Stake Ethereum, since even when acting in good faith the decentralized nature of the network can mean that it takes a while to propagate, and block proposers can "miss" their slot. Slots might be constant, but arrival times are not. And sometimes there can be discrepancies between the logic run on some nodes and the logic run on others.[9] When the chain is reorganized, blocks may go missing, which you'll want to bear in mind when building products that require strong data freshness.

---

[9] If proposer A is scheduled to build block 101 off block 100, and proposer B is scheduled to build off block 101, and the block doesn't reach proposer B in time, then proposer B will assume that block 101 was missed and base their block 102 off block 100. Some nodes might have received block 101, so the network will need to reach consensus about which fork is the canonical one. This seems to be the most common reason for reorgs and why we see one-block reorgs quite regularly on mainnet Ethereum. Sam Lewis has a good blog post on investigating this phenomenon (www.samlewis.me/2022/03/beacon-chain-reorgs/).

The fact that the chain is reorganized and that consensus is reached based on the attestations of a cohort of validators, who themselves are chosen based on their economic might, changes the trust dynamics of Proof of Stake from those of Proof of Work. Proof of Stake recognizes that there needs to be *some* level of trust. In a world where not everybody is building their own node, you need some trusted sources regardless – the makers of the node software – to provide bug fixes and efficiency improvements. You also need some trusted source of the rules of the network, and the history of the network, itself. There has to be some canonical form of the network, and this puts a requirement of trust on the existing network to provide it. The older Proof of Work mechanism provides these rules by redoing all the prior work and using that to get to the canonical form of the network. Proof of Stake sees this as an unnecessary source of inefficiency and looks to get the same level of security with fewer ongoing costs.[10]

Anyway, enough details, this simple microeconomic design helps underwrite trust in the network and keep it fair while giving it some major efficiency benefits over Proof of Work. Our transaction goes from mempool to the block proposer to the validator committee. Once these steps are complete, and enough time has passed to ensure there are no impending reorgs, the block is considered finalized.

Once a Block Is Finalized

Once a block is finalized, it is then broadcast back through the network. At some point, it reaches the node that the app is listening to, often the original node from which the request was submitted.

Remember the transaction hash we stored earlier? This is where it comes back into play. For each new finalized block, the app checks the block to see whether the transaction has been included. Sometimes, this is direct: by listening for new blocks and running the check. Other times, this might be via a webhook or some other notification mechanism, where an app will register the transaction hash and say "tell me when this block is confirmed."

Once the transaction is confirmed and the app finds out about it, the app parses the transaction results, pulling out any events that have been issued and any results that the transaction code itself might return.

---

[10] For a more technical comparison of the trade-offs between the two mechanisms, read `https://vitalik.ca/general/2020/11/06/pos2020.html`

At this point, the app can then update its state accordingly. It does this by retrieving the relevant information it needs through direct read requests to the blockchain or via some sort of indexer (see the section "Indexing" in Chapter 4 for a detailed discussion of how these approaches work in practice).

And that is essentially it: the story of how a request originates, flows through the network, is selected, and is executed and its changes to the state confirmed and displayed.

Understanding how a request filters through the network is of crucial importance to anybody building with Ethereum. I hope this section has shown that it is also quite legible. The basic concepts are simple, and the tooling and infrastructure that supports the network is getting more sophisticated, robust, and developer-friendly every day.

The Ethereum ecosystem has evolved to a set of trade-offs, some explicit and some implicit in other technology choices. These trade-offs form the subject matter of most of the rest of this book, and each of the chapters that follow is, in one way or another, a discussion of these trade-offs and how they affect building further up the stack.

Accounts and Wallets

"Wallet" is not a useful metaphor for Ethereum accounts nor for the software used to invoke them. Accounts don't hold things, which obscures the mechanism of on-chain ledgers of record. Accounts don't hold merely financial things, which constrains the imaginative power of what tokenized ownership claims can represent. Accounts aren't physical, which means they can be represented in context-specific ways. Accounts, instead, are an identity.

As I'll mention later (in Chapter 7), technologists use metaphors to make *skeuomorphic links* to bridge the old paradigm to the new. One of the most common examples of this in crypto is the concept of the "wallet." This chapter argues that it's also one of the most misleading.

Metaphors work by implying certain things about the subject based on the object. Good metaphors also have the nice property of illuminating the subject of the metaphor in ways that the reader doesn't expect. A good metaphor can help reveal the shapes and contours of a subject by making us consider the subject from a new angle.

What, then, does the metaphor of "wallet" imply? It suggests a few features:

1. A wallet **holds things**.

2. A wallet holds a specific sort of thing, namely, **financial things** (such as credit cards and cash).

3. A wallet is a **physical item** and plays the various roles that physical items do, such as signaling style, wealth, and status.

Crypto wallets have none of these features.

When people speak of "wallets," they are usually conflating two distinct and different things: "wallet software," which provides a user interface to blockchain and any integrated dapps, and "accounts," which are the entity that represents identity on the blockchain.

Accounts are not wallets, and nor do they function like them. Accounts don't hold things: accounts represent identity. Accounts aren't limited to interacting with financial products: they interact with anything representable on the blockchain. Accounts, of course, aren't physical items: they are an abstraction over an individual on a ledger.

Wallet software are not wallets, and nor do they function like them. Wallet software doesn't hold things: it sits on the "many" side of a one-to-many relationship between accounts and their user interfaces. Wallet software isn't limited to interacting with financial products for the same reason as accounts. And, like accounts, they are not physical or physically constrained.

It's worth stopping at this point and asking why any of this matters. Isn't it just a shallow, semantic dispute? No. Because as well as being illuminating about the subject, a metaphor can often constrain our understanding of the subject, especially if it becomes the primary mechanism through which the subject is known.

This has happened with the wallet metaphor in crypto, which is why I believe it's especially important to pay attention to what wallets actually are, how the metaphor shapes our thinking, and how it limits our thinking too.

Accounts Don't Hold Things

An account is a pair of public and private keys. A private key is used to generate a public key, and the public key is used to generate an address. So when you see account addresses such as 0xd8da...6045 (one of Vitalik Buterin's accounts), what you're really seeing is the result of passing Vitalik's private key through the set of cryptographic functions that produce these addresses.

The details of how this works are interesting, but out of the scope of this book. All we need to know for now is that this process is *deterministic*, in the sense that it returns the same value for the same input, no matter how often you run it, and *irreversible*, in the sense that it's very, very hard to get the private key from the account address.

Note   How hard? There's no better way than guessing at random. Ethereum private keys are 256 bits. Since a bit has two possible states, guessing a 256 bit sequence correctly at random has a chance of $1/2^{256}$. There are $\sim 10^{78}$ atoms in the observable universe, which is roughly 2^{260}. Account addresses are only 160 bits long, which means that there are multiple possible private keys, but 2^{160} is still a very big number, equivalent to a little bit less than the total number of atoms on Earth.

So if you know the private key, then you can generate the public key, but you can't (easily) go in the other direction. This is one of the reasons why it's so important to keep your private key private: your private key is the one piece of information somebody needs to get access to your account. Fortunately, most users don't have to worry about the content of the private key at all: they can use wallet software that holds the private key in a secure way. But when building products you'll *always* need to keep in mind that the private key is sacred.

How does this link to the wallet metaphor?

Well, I lied a little: accounts do "hold" something. They hold ether, the native token of the Ethereum blockchain. But this is by communal assent: a group of people, incentivized to follow the same set of rules, collectively agree that a certain amount of ether is owned by a specific account, and another amount of ether is owned by a different account. It's the collective assent that underwrites the ownership claim, not the account itself.

If you've got cash in your wallet, you actually do have cash in your wallet. The state is in your pocket. If you've got ether in your account, you've got a claim on the group for the amount of that ether. It's a guarantee, secured by cryptography and incentives, that when you decide you want to do something with that ether, we'll all agree that you can.

So I'm also telling the truth: accounts don't really hold that much at all, and the notion of "holding" your ether and your tokens is a euphemism. Your account is the mechanism of a record of ownership. The state is not in your pocket, it's "over there."

This might seem a little opaque, so let's consider some code. One of the clearest examples of how accounts don't actually hold anything is the ERC-20 token standard.

This standard is the core primitive in DeFi, the simple brick from which we build this cathedral. It offers a consistent interface for smart contracts that behave as a record of ownership. Contracts have to choose to implement it – that's why it's a standard, not a rule; see the section "Standards" in Chapter 6 for more – but those that do share the same methods.

We can distill the essence of ERC-20 down to only two function signatures:[11]

```
function balanceOf
      (address owner)
      public returns (uint256 balance);

function transferFrom
      (address from, address to, uint256 value)
      public returns (bool success);
```

(The actual standard contains more than these two methods, but the rest are for convenience, expedience, and extensions to the functionality, rather than being central to the model of how tokens are represented by contracts that implement it. Most notably, missing from this definition is the notion of token approvals, which stipulate permissions around who can transfer the token and how many tokens they can transfer.)

These two functions tell us everything we need to know about a particular piece of state. What is that piece of state? It's a mapping from an address to the number of tokens owned by that address:

```
mapping(address => uint256) private _balances;
```

_balances is a map – also known as a dictionary or an associative array – from an owner to the total amount owned. The total amount owned of what? The token that the contract represents.

---

[11] These signatures are adapted from the OpenZeppelin ERC-20 contract, a commonly used implementation of the ERC-20 spec. I've taken out some noise, such as the `virtually` keyword, not relevant to the discussion.

If we want to find out how much of the token we own, we call `balanceOf`, passing our address. If we want to send our tokens to somebody else, we call `transferFrom`, passing our address, the recipient's address, and the amount we wish to send. The token contract does the work updating the list that it holds.

Think about this carefully: a token is just a smart contract that holds a list of who owns the token, plus a bit of metadata (such as the token's name and symbol). The token contract code then specifies the rules around how that ownership list changes.

Your account doesn't "hold" anything. It doesn't know anything about the token, per se. It just gives you a way to identify a key in a mapping from accounts to a quantity. And a token is just a piece of code that understands how to update this map.

This is a very simple and powerful idea, because the token contract is able to stipulate its own rules and policies around who can transfer, who can be transferred, and what the balance is.

You could stipulate that only a specific whitelist of addresses should be able to receive the token, for instance, by restricting ownership of the token to a known set of individuals. You could exclude certain addresses. You could require a certain amount of ether in exchange for the token or even a certain amount of another token in exchange for the token. You could even change the amount transferred when somebody transfers it, deducting a fee. In other words, you can implement a monetary policy, controlling how the token enters the market, how it leaves it, and how it flows around between participants.

Accounts Aren't Limited

Since the token contract is the mechanism for recording who owns what, and stipulating the rules that govern that ownership, your account isn't limited to holding financial instruments like cash or credit cards. Tokens can be used to represent basically anything.

Some tokens represent nonfungible assets, things that can't be exchanged for another asset just like it. You will have heard of NFTs, and NFTs are token contracts much like the ERC-20 contract we just discussed. The biggest difference between ERC-20 and ERC-721 – the basic standard for representing NFTs – is that the parameters of the function are slightly different:

```
function transferFrom
        (address from, address to, uint256 id)
        public virtual;
```

An ERC-721 contract introduces the notion of an id and requires that the (owner, id) pair is globally unique. So a specific token – that is described by the contract and the specific ID the contract defines – is owned by one and only one person.

NFTs are often used for digital art or collectibles, but they can be used to represent ownership of lots more. In time, they may be used to represent ownership of real-world assets: houses, cars, paintings, bottles of wine.

NFTs can also be used for interesting, crypto-native use cases: Uniswap v3, for instance, mints an NFT that represents a deposit to a specific pool within a specific price range. This allows there to be a claim of ownership over a unique liquidity position.

Fungible tokens, too, can be used to represent many more types of things than just those that map to financial value. They can represent governance rights, as they do with the MKR token, which grants the right to vote on proposals of the Maker DAO. (At the time of writing, most governance tokens grant voting rights on a quantity basis: if you have more tokens, your vote represents a larger share of the voting power. But this isn't the only model for governance designs made possible by the ERC-20 token standard.) They can also represent other sorts of values, such as carbon credits, or reputation, or points accumulated in a game.

The point is that the "wallet" metaphor suggests a constraint on the sorts of things that can be "held." Since accounts don't "hold" things, the design space for what sorts of ownership and participation claims they can represent is much, much bigger.

Accounts Aren't Physical Items

Finally, our third feature, accounts aren't physical. This might seem like a silly point to make, but the fact that accounts aren't physical items runs a little deeper than the obvious. Accounts aren't physical items: they are abstractions over an individual, a face you can show to the blockchain.

And this means that your accounts aren't tied to one place. If you know your private key, you can use your account in whatever interface you want.

This means that different interfaces can display different aspects of the same account. Some interfaces, such as the Rainbow wallet,[12] put an emphasis on NFT collectibles, a kind of gallery or showcase. Others might focus on the purely financial aspects of the account, its deposits, loans, and investments. Perhaps an interface could

---

[12] https://rainbow.me

be built around governance, showing the proposals and votes and engagements with protocols. Perhaps another could be built around whatever gaming tokens to which the account has claims. And so on.

When you start to consider these sorts of product implications of the fact that accounts aren't physical items, it makes you realize that the design space for account interfaces is coextensive – overlapping – with the design space for tokens themselves. This "unbundling" of wallet experiences is made possible by the existence of this account abstraction. (Whether this actually happens is a different matter, but it's a useful way of illustrating the flexibility of the account-as-identity model.)

It also pushes the sorts of signaling properties we mentioned earlier elsewhere. Perhaps people do signal with their wallet software – that is, their account interfaces – a little, using a newer or more feature-complete piece of software to indicate the sort of user they are and the sorts of things they are interested in. But the account itself is a very lightweight thing. The account is not the wallet software you use to interact with the account. And in this distinction lies the true power of the account abstraction.

This lack of physicality – this sense of account as an abstraction over an individual – also allows for another crucial feature of accounts, one we've not mentioned yet. *Accounts don't even need to be people.* Many accounts on Ethereum are externally owned accounts (EOAs), which are the accounts we've been discussing. But many others are *smart contract accounts* (SCAs), accounts that are owned and operated by smart contracts themselves. In fact, as we'll discuss in future chapters, contracts are deployed to account addresses. When you interact with a contract, then, you're interacting with an account whose management is handled purely by code executed by the account itself.

Accounts Are Identity

So what is an account, then, if not a wallet?

My answer: An account is an identity. It is a way of informing other participants that you are who you say you are. It is a username and password; it is a mechanism to authenticate yourself. It's also a way of a smart contract identifying itself, a mechanism to authenticate the smart contract as the thing it says it is.

If accounts are identity, then it means you can separate out your identities depending on different contexts of usage. You might use an account to trade, another account to represent your investments, and a third to hold your claims to any artwork or collectibles. You might use accounts for different platforms with different risk profiles or with different privacy considerations. You can separate out your identities in whatever way you choose, isolating your public, on-chain behavior into different categories. The ownership of a private key gives you full control over what aspect of yourself you wish to show to the world.

This use case of separating one's identity into different public-facing accounts, differing aspects, is something that itself has been standardized by the Ethereum (and, before that, Bitcoin) communities. *Hierarchical Deterministic (HD)* accounts take the basic account derivation mechanism and encode structure into it. The core private key – a "master password" – is combined with a *path*. This path is an instance of an *a priori* agreed-upon schema that allows us to generate multiple accounts. This schema is based on the Bitcoin standard BIP-44[13] and gives us a tree-like structure (*"hierarchical"*) that allows us to generate in a predictable fashion (*"deterministic"*) multiple accounts from the same private key, as in Figure 2-5.

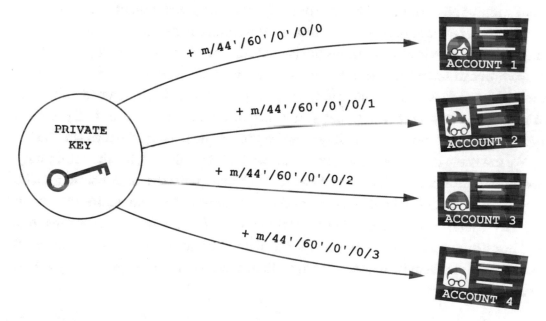

Figure 2-5. *A private key is combined with a path to produce a new public key/ account. This allows the same user to generate multiple, apparently unrelated, accounts in a predictable way*

---

[13] https://github.com/bitcoin/bips/blob/master/bip-0044.mediawiki

Because the derivation method follows the same mechanism as the standard private key ➤ public key ➤ account route, it has the same properties of being deterministic and irreversible, which means that *generated accounts will appear to be unrelated*, offering the privacy and isolation benefits I mentioned earlier.[14]

This multiplicity of identities is essential to product building on Ethereum – it is one of its superpowers – and products should implement support for it in a deep way. Consider this: your identity goes with you wherever you take it. And where your identity goes, so do your claims of ownership. An Ethereum account, then, gives you a login system for free.[15]

This, combined with the standardization of interfaces such as ERC-20 and ERC-721, increases the power of the interfaces we can build substantially. To take a simple example, a tool for listing whatever ERC-20-compatible tokens are "held" by an account will work with any token that meets the requirements of that interface. It's as if PayPal could support all currencies from day one, with no extra development work.

The wallet metaphor is generally broken, then, and can severely constrain your imagination vis-à-vis what accounts are capable of. For sure, there are ways in which an account can seem like a wallet: when you lose your account, just like your wallet, you lose the money in it; to that extent, the metaphor is true. But it's true for different reasons. If you lose a physical wallet, you've actually lost the cash inside it. If you lose a crypto wallet, you've lost your ability to prove you are the person who owns the cash.

We are likely to continue using the term "wallet," since that's what the community uses, and there's not much marginal benefit in changing this sort of heavily entrenched meme. Throughout this book, I try to use the term "account" to refer to the account and the term "wallet" to refer to the interface within which the account and user can interact. But I hope this section has given you a sense of how accounts actually work and why the design space for them is an awful lot bigger than a piece of folded leather that you keep in your pocket.

---

[14] Most wallets support one version or another of HD derivation paths: see my "HD wallets and network switching" blog post for more (`https://jamieonsoftware.com/2022/04/02/hd-wallets-and-network-switching.html`).

[15] This approach is being standardized in EIP-4361 (`https://eips.ethereum.org/EIPS/eip-4361`). Read `https://login.xyz` for more on how this can be integrated in your products.

Network and Account Switching

There are different sorts of networks: layer 1s and layer 2s. Layer 1s are the layer at which the blockchain reaches ultimate consensus. Layer 2s inherit the consensus properties of their layer 1 and provide scalability and additional functionality on top of it. Many products will need to support switching multiple networks. Products will need to handle various cases where the user's wallet and the application are connected to different, or incompatible, networks. Managing your state centrally is a useful way to handle these cases. Products will also need to handle switching between different accounts.

This chapter is entitled "Requests, Networks, and Accounts." So far, we've looked at requests and accounts and at the Ethereum network as a whole. In this section, we'll discuss the proliferation of alternative Ethereum networks that you may come across when building. And we'll start to bring these concepts together, seeing how accounts relate to networks, how your UI relates to an account, and the UX issues that these relationships can cause.

Layers 1 and 2

It's time to introduce some new vocabulary: layer 1 and layer 2. These terms are thrown around in Ethereum discourse very regularly, so it's unfortunate that there isn't complete consensus over their meaning. I'll define them in the way I usually think about them here. There may be some subtle disagreements with my definitions. But these are mostly semantic disputes.

Layer 1 is the Ethereum mainnet network and any other network that operates at the same level. We can think of layer 1s as the base layer that provides the essential consensus mechanism of the blockchain. Other layer 1s include Bitcoin and Celo, as well as other EVM-compatible layer 1s, such as the public testnets (Görli and Rinkeby are two popular public testnets). Finally, a local fork of the mainnet is also considered a layer 1, since that's where the consensus mechanism for your blockchain instance is running.

The benefit to using a public testnet over a local fork is small. Because it's public, it gives you the ability to share the state between users, which is helpful when testing between multiple people. But because it's public, you don't have much control over the token allocations or smart contract state. If you're running a local fork, you can control all of this. We'll discuss this in more detail in Chapter 5. But remember that you can share your local fork quite easily with tools like ngrok.

Layer 2 is slightly more troublesome to define. Vitalik Buterin and the Ethereum Foundation put "scalability" at the heart of their definition of layer 2s: "their purpose is to increase scalability."[16] But layer 2 developers have realized that separating their computational layer from that of the mainnet gives them the opportunity to introduce new functionality too. Aztec[17] wraps up their layer 2 transactions in a Merkle tree, allowing users to transact between each other without revealing to the rest of the world the details of the transaction. The Boba Network[18] goes even further, introducing cross-chain messaging primitives and a natty off-chain computing platform.

So we can broaden the definition of layer 2: layer 2s extend the functionality of layer 1 in some way, either by adding additional features (such as private transactions) or by making the existing functionality faster, more efficient, or more scalable – or, in the case of many layer 2s, by doing both.

While layer 2s are still in their infancy, there are meaningful applications that run on them. QuickSwap[19] began as a fork of the Uniswap codebase, deployed on Polygon. Lyra[20] provides options trading on Optimism. Angle Protocol[21] issues their stablecoins on the Optimism and Ethereum mainnet. The popular 1inch[22] trading router supports all of the preceding layer 2s and more. And in some cases, the functionality of a protocol is split between layers 1 and 2. In Chapter 4, we'll talk about The Graph, a decentralized indexing protocol. The Graph uses Polygon to handle its payments and billing, while the core functionality of the network rests on the mainnet.

As I hope the previous few paragraphs have demonstrated, there are a lot of different layer 2s and even different and competing layer 1s. If you're building an application against a local fork of the mainnet, your products will need to query against your own instance of the Ethereum blockchain. If you deploy beta features to a testnet, to allow

---

[16] https://vitalik.ca/general/2022/09/17/layer_3.htm

[17] https://aztec.network/

[18] https://boba.network

[19] https://quickswap.exchange/

[20] https://app.lyra.finance

[21] https://app.angle.money/

[22] https://app.1inch.io

your more zealous fans to try out the functionality before you publish the work to the world at large, your products will need to query against the testnet. If you deploy contracts on one or several layer 2s, your products will need to query against whichever layer 2s you support. This means that your products will need to support multiple networks.

How are layer 2s distinguished at the protocol level? Wallet software and node software discriminate via the `chainId` and `networkId` parameters. The `networkId` parameter protects nodes from connecting to nodes on other networks. It is used at the networking layer of the protocol and isn't something that product engineers typically need to worry about. `chainId`, introduced in EIP-155, operates at the transaction layer: it is used by wallets and apps to sign a transaction. This prevents a form of replay attack, where a transaction intended for one chain is submitted to another chain. You may need to think about the chainId parameter when connecting to the network, but most frontend tools (such as *ethers.js*) will read the `chainId` from the node provider, so it's rare you'll have to specify it explicitly.

Products will generally need to support multiple networks. However, there are actually *two* cross-cutting dimensions that we will need to consider. As we discussed earlier in this chapter, users can have multiple accounts in the same wallet software. These accounts provide for a multiplicity of identities on-chain. But accounts can also exist on multiple networks at once – a private key is a private key and will produce deterministically the same account identifier wherever it is used (and wherever the standard account ID generation algorithm is used). So you can expect a user to have multiple accounts *within and across* multiple networks. Your UI will need to handle this.

Switching Between Networks

It is a frustrating limitation of most (all?) wallet software that the wallet can only be connected to one network at a time. It is also a frustrating limitation of most (all?) frontend libraries that the library can only be connected to one network at a time. One day, this may change, but for now, it's an awkward constraint that our wallet software places on our libraries and our libraries place on our UIs. Your UI will almost always need to be able to switch between multiple networks:

- Almost always the **Ethereum mainnet**, since most smart contracts are deployed there.

- Often **other layer 1s**, such as **testnets** or **local forks**. This is important for development purposes.

- One or several **layer 2s**, which users may wish to use for their lower transaction fees, scalability, or because of liquidity constraints.

Keeping multiple connections running at the same time is awkward and can make certain use cases (e.g., bridging tokens between two networks) difficult to build. To make matters worse, many wallets don't persist network switches between tabs. Switching between networks and persisting the necessary application state is the current approach, although, as we'll see shortly, it's far from straightforward. There are, however, some simple tasks we can focus on.

Provide a Mechanism to Switch Networks Inside Your UI

You don't have control over the user's wallet software, and users often may not check which network they're connected to when they load your application. At the very least, you need to indicate the current network to the user, even if you don't allow the user to switch networks. But if you're showing the current network clearly, you'll also want to indicate *how* the user can switch, at which point you might as well add a switcher yourself.

Uniswap handles this reasonably well, as shown in Figure 2-6.

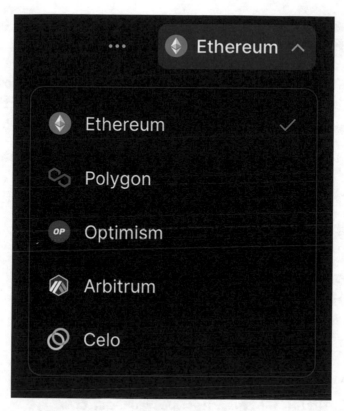

Figure 2-6. *If you click the network name at the top right in the Uniswap UI, you see the network selector*

They've also added a nice touch: the app's background color changes to help indicate which network the wallet is connected to. Try switching between wallets and see what happens to the background. These sorts of small, subtle cues can add helpful, subconscious context to a user trying to navigate between different networks. And another thing to consider is you may want to add support for a custom network, which, at the very least, will allow you to connect to local networks easily. It will also allow your more advanced users to run your UI on their own nodes.[23]

---

[23] Since these are more advanced features, it might be worth enabling it based on your app's environment. Production might not need custom networks, but staging and development almost certainly will.

Handle the Case Where Your User's Wallet Software and Your UI Are Set to Different Networks

This interaction works in two directions. Your users can change their network in your application's UI. In this case, then you'll need to trigger a `wallet_addEthereumChain` event on your user's wallet via a suitable provider. To request Polygon, for instance:

```
const provider = new ethers.providers.Web3Provider(window.ethereum, "any");

await provider.send("wallet_addEthereumChain", [
  {
    chainId: "0x89", // chain ID 137
    chainName: "Polygon Mainnet",
    nativeCurrency: {
      name: "MATIC",
      symbol: "MATIC",
      decimals: 18,
    },
    rpcUrls: ["https://polygon-rpc.com"],
    blockExplorerUrls: ["https://www.polygonscan.com/"],
  },
]);
```

This code will tell the user's wallet to issue an add chain request, via the `window.ethereum` object. Some wallets, such as MetaMask, support arbitrary chains in this way.

Note   Notice that the provider is the type of `ethers.providers.Web3Provider`. Elsewhere, we use `AlchemyProvider`. The former points to the Ethereum object injected by our in-browser wallet. The latter points to the Alchemy node that we use to query the blockchain.

Other wallets, such as Argent, only support a limited subset, and for these wallets, `wallet_addEthereumChain` simply won't work. Wagmi makes it even easier:

```
const network = useSwitchNetwork({
  chainId: 137
})
```

While the basic code is straightforward, you'll need to pay attention to the case where the user rejects the add chain request. There is a gap between what you want the user's wallet to do and when it gets done: so you'll need some sort of a "pending approval" state in your UI. And you'll need to make sure you test it rigorously!

In the other direction, you can listen to the network event on the *ethers.js* provider, which will be triggered when the network is updated in the user's wallet:

```
const provider = new ethers.providers.Web3Provider(window.ethereum, "any");

provider.on("network", (newNetwork, oldNetwork) => {
  if (!oldNetwork) return;
  // handle network change
})
```

This event wraps the chainChanged event emitted by the underlying provider (usually injected by wallet software such as MetaMask). This sort of code is best put somewhere high level in your frontend application. Wrapping the ethers setup in a React Provider, which then supplies the provider to downstream components using a React context, is quite straightforward. If you're using wagmi, it's even easier, since you can inject the provider directly into the WagmiConfig component and then use wagmi's useProvider hook to pull it out in your application code as needed. Wagmi will then cause the relevant components to retrigger when the network changes at the wallet level.

Handle the Case Where Either Your App or the User's Wallet Doesn't Support the Other Network

If your user's wallet is set to Arbitrum, but your application doesn't support it, you'll need to disable the UI and show a modal. This modal should tell the user what has happened and give them instructions for how to get the application back in a usable state. Even if you do display a modal, you should probably still disable the UI until the problem is fixed. Modals can behave in funny ways, and the last thing you want to do is allow a bug in your modal code to cause a user to submit an incorrect transaction. Adding friction, creating redundant systems of protection, can be very useful in keeping your users safe and happy.

State Management

Finally, you'll need to reset the relevant parts of the user interface and update the data you use and display. Gas fees, token prices, and token ownership levels will look different on different chains. The *ethers.js* documentation recommends a full-page reload.[24] This is sometimes the easiest way to handle the behavior, but it's not the most user-friendly, and you'll still need to worry about persisting the chosen network between pages. An alternative approach is to use a state management container such as Redux[25], Recoil,[26] or native React contexts. These tools separate out your state from the components that use it, allowing state to traverse down the component hierarchy. When a network change occurs, you can issue an event that clears and reloads the relevant state, allowing the downstream components to rerender. This has a centralizing effect on your state management logic. You'll generally want to put your contract read calls and indexer queries into a high-level wrapper component that loads the relevant state from the relevant place and puts it into your state management system. This has the handy benefit of putting everything in one place, which can often simplify the code and make it easier to refactor, but it's not a panacea: if you query a smart contract using values that your user provides – such as a token quantity they wish to trade or the token for which they wish to swap it – then you'll need to pass that state back up the hierarchy somehow. This can make things a little more complicated to reason about, but with some thoughtful design, tools like Redux can make this much easier. At any rate, this isn't a React + Ethereum problem: it's a React problem.

You can also use a centralized state store to make it easier to disable the UI. Putting a uiEnabled boolean in your store and then wrapping your inputs and buttons with a component that reads from this store (and disables the input if uiEnabled = true) is very useful for cases where the wallet's capabilities and the UI's capabilities clash.

---

[24] https://docs.ethers.io/v5/concepts/best-practices/

[25] https://redux.js.org

[26] https://recoiljs.org

What is essential to remember is that the erroneous data brought about by a network change can constitute a clear violation of the Principle of Trust. Whichever state management approach you take, keep it simple and be as consistent as you can with its application.[27]

Switching Between Accounts

We've spoken about switching between networks. But there's another dimension that is important: switching between accounts. This only happens in one direction – from the user's wallet to your application – and is therefore more straightforward.

In the case that the user's account changes at the wallet level, your wallet software will usually trigger an event on your provider. Like the chainChanged event we saw earlier, there's an equivalent accountsChanged event that will trigger when the user connects one (or even several) of their accounts to your application.

Note   While it's theoretically possible to connect more than one account to a frontend, in practice this rarely happens. Most wallets provide restricted, or even no, support for this functionality; very few UIs do. There is no expectation that the UI will support more than one account, and doing so will involve rethinking a lot of the basic interactions that your application provides.

The most recently connected account will generally be the only element of the accounts array that the event provides. So you can destructure it quite safely:

```
provider.on("accountsChanged", ([account]) => {
  if (!account) return;
  updateConnectedAccount(account);
})
```

And, of course, tools like wagmi will abstract this away from you entirely. If the account changes in the user's wallet, your components will rerender as you'd expect.

---

[27] Using a separate state management library, and consolidating your state logic into one or a few places, can also make it easier to unit test. In many cases, you can move the bulk of your state logic outside the React component tree entirely, which means you can write standard JS unit tests to ensure that the logic behaves itself.

Your app will only have access to the accounts that the user has connected, so you won't be able to request a switch to a different account directly. Using the wallet as the source of truth is the best – and the only – option you have. This is a good thing: there's only one place the user can change their connected account, and there's only one place you need to look for it.

This doesn't absolve you of all responsibility: you'll still need to reset the state if the user changes their connected account. But this can be done with the same general logic, ideally with a centralized state provider, that we used for handling network changes.

Summary

In this chapter, we've discussed how requests originate and propagate through the Ethereum network, which eventually reaches consensus over their effects on the shared global state. We've discussed the notion of an account and how it is different in important respects from the "wallet" metaphor that is used in common parlance. Importantly, accounts are a form of identity, and this means that users may have multiple accounts. We've also seen how there are multiple networks that perform this consensus-building role and multiple layer 2s that provide additional functionality and scalability benefits. Your products will need to handle users switching between networks and switching between accounts.

In the next chapter, we'll look at transactions in much more detail. What are transactions, and how are they structured? Transactions go through a variety of states during their lifecycle: How should these states be exposed to the user? What sort of contextual information should you display? How should you handle transaction errors?

CHAPTER 3

Transactions

Ethereum is both a platform and a protocol: it is a place where something (accounts, code, state) is hosted and a set of rules for communicating between those things. Smart contracts are to Ethereum the platform as transactions are to Ethereum the protocol.

Transactions therefore sit at the very core of the conceptual model. They have some important properties:

- They **compute values**, normally **based on state**. A read transaction encodes a set of instructions to derive values from state. A write transaction encodes a set of instructions to modify that state. Smart contracts express the logic; transactions express the demand.

- They are **public**. Transactions are included in a block through a consensus mechanism that gains its decentralization and security from the fact that many unrelated people verify the inputs and outputs, and *anybody* can contest them. Transactions therefore have to be public.

- They are **external**: as was discussed in Chapter 2's "The Lifecycle of an Ethereum Request" section, there is no such thing as an autonomous transaction.

- They carry **user intention**: since transactions are external, this also means that they are the result of something (or someone) outside the system *wishing to interact* with something inside the system. They *relate to goals* that users have.

These properties give a sense of both the centrality and the content of the role that transactions play in the Ethereum protocol.

© Jamie Rumbelow 2023
J. Rumbelow, *Building With Ethereum*, https://doi.org/10.1007/978-1-4842-9045-3_3

Note   Sometimes, you'll need to trigger a transaction at some regular interval. One easy way is to write a script to run the transaction whenever required and then schedule it using some other tool. There are also some hosted services that perform this sort of function, such as OpenZeppelin's *Defender*.[1] There are attempts to move this logic on-chain; see, for instance, *Gelato*.[2] Another way of doing it: Some protocols, especially those that integrate a token, can incentivize others to do the work for them, by paying users. This approach exchanges some reasonable amount of a protocol's token for the assurance that the work will be done and the gas fees that performing this work will incur.

If Ethereum is a state machine, then transactions are what make it tick. This chapter takes a detailed look at this role, the structure of transactions, and some of the product implications.

What Does a Transaction Look Like?

Transactions are the language of the Ethereum protocol. There are three types of transactions: transfers, contract calls, and contract creation calls. Transactions can be represented with a simple JSON structure. Transaction signatures provide assurances about the provenance and content of the transaction. Gas fees are payments for work and have interesting dynamics that can affect product experiences in interesting ways. Nonces solve the replay problem but create several others. Once submitted and included in a block, the status of a transaction can be inspected in the transaction receipt.

Transactions can be grouped, roughly, into three categories:

1. ETH transfers

2. Smart contract invocation

3. Contract deployments

---

[1] www.openzeppelin.com/defender

[2] http://gelato.network

In this chapter, we'll focus on (1) and (2); for more information on (3), see the next chapter. We use a transaction object to represent the transaction's properties, and we can disambiguate between these different types of transactions based on whether certain properties have values. This is a bit vague, so see an example of what a low-level transaction looks like:[3]

```
{
  "chainId": 1,
  "to": "0xd8dA6BF26964aF9D7eEd9e03E53415D37aA96045",
  "value": 1000000000000000000,
  "gasLimit": 30000,
  "maxFeePerGas": 30,
  "maxPriorityFeePerGas": 1000,
  "nonce": 0,
  "data": null
}
```

This transaction payload is *raw*: there is no signature. We can also see that it's in our first category of transaction. There is a to address and a value, but no data. This transaction therefore sends 1000000000000000000 worth of wei (1 eth) to the address 0xd8d...045.

A transaction with no data is a simple transfer (category 1). If the transaction uses the zero address for to, but some data, then the EVM treats it as a contract deployment (category 3).

If the transaction has a nonzero to address and some data, then whether the transaction is considered to be a smart contract invocation depends on whether to refers to an EOA or a deployed contract. If the latter, the transaction is treated as an invocation. If the former, the transaction is treated as a transfer (with some general-purpose data attached; this can be used for, e.g., messaging). Smart contract invocations can also be combined with a value, in which case the value is transferred over to the contract.[4]

---

[3] Ethereum actually reads transactions as an RLP-encoded array of values, but I've wrapped some JSON around it and represented the "raw" values to make things clearer.

[4] This is true at the EVM level: compiled contracts using higher-level languages such as Solidity may (and, in fact, do) have subtly different semantics around payment.

The raw transaction can give us more information beyond disambiguating the category. The `chainId` key, included in the transaction to prevent replaying transactions cross-chain, allows us to specify the chain (e.g., mainnet, one of the various public testnets, an EVM-compatible layer 2, a local testnet, etc.). The `nonce` prevents another class of replay attacks; the final part of this section considers nonces in more detail. The gas keys, `gasLimit`, `maxPriorityFeePerGas`, and `maxFeePerGas`, carry the user's desired gas parameters, which we'll discuss shortly.

Of course, most of these details are usually abstracted away by the wallet software. This is a very low-level representation of a transaction, and it's quite possible you'll ever need to worry about these properties or how they're implemented. But the details are fascinating and reveal important structural features of Ethereum that bear upon products built on top of it.

Once a raw transaction has been constructed, it needs to be *signed*. It is to transaction signing that we now turn.

Transaction Signing

Describing what a transaction is supposed to *do* is important. But transactions are being issued on a public network and are implicated in state changes of privately owned resources. It's therefore imperative that there is some way of authorizing these transactions.

If you are writing a smart contract, then authorization is a matter of your contract's code, its business logic. Contract authors can stipulate that only some addresses can interact with some methods and revert if the transaction sender isn't on some whitelist. But this requires a `msg.sender`, a known transaction author. Contract-level code must be underwritten by some mechanism for securing the transaction itself. This is what signatures are designed to do.

A digital signature is an application of asymmetric cryptography that allows a message to be signed by a private key and then later verified by the corresponding public key. This sort of scheme provides two important checks:

1. The **provenance** of the message can be verified; it demonstrates that the holder of the private key really did wish to write the message.

2. The **content** of the message can be verified; it demonstrates that the message was not changed in transit.

Being able to verify both provenance and content is incredibly important for Ethereum, because it means that transactions can be posted publicly and verified by any participant without any special centralized authentication scheme.

The mathematics of asymmetric cryptography are rather beautiful and absolutely worth the time to read about, but outside the scope of this book.[5] For our current purposes, however, all we need to know is that there is an algorithm with which can use a public key to verify that a signature was generated with the message and corresponding private key, *without the private key ever having to be revealed*. This remarkably beautiful innovation allows us to publish our transactions publicly – required for peer-to-peer, decentralized communication – and those transactions be verifiable quickly. Signatures give us guarantees of provenance and guarantees of content.

This has a significant consequence: *one of the most important aspects of your user's journey will happen elsewhere*, on some software that you don't control. We'll talk more about the UI implications of transaction signing, connecting to wallet software, etc., later in this chapter. But this sort of constraint is not typical for most software, which can carefully guide the user through the desired flow. Ethereum apps (normally) don't have that privilege. Transaction signing is one of the most important flows in your product engineering, where your job as a software designer becomes a matter of integration rather than creation.

Gas Fees

In Chapter 2, we introduced the notion of *gas* as a mechanism for paying for the computational resources required by a given transaction and to solve the denial-of-service problem present for systems like Ethereum. Let's recap our understanding of gas and consider how it might affect the products we build.

Gas is a unit of work. In the same way that burning a gallon of gasoline will allow your car to drive a certain distance, a unit of gas will allow the EVM to perform a certain amount of computation. Gas is how Ethereum meters computation.

---

[5] A good StackExchange thread here explains Diffie-Hellman Key Exchange, a similar form of asymmetric cryptography, which is good for understanding the basic mathematical intuition: https://security.stackexchange.com/questions/45963/diffie-hellman-key-exchange-in-plain-english

Each EVM opcode has a different amount of gas required to perform it. This means that as a contract becomes more complex, performing more and more sophisticated functionality, a transaction becomes more expensive. The gasLimit and maxFeePerGas properties, then, allow the sender of the transaction to decide (a) how many units of work they wish to commit to spending and (b) how much they are willing to pay for each unit of work.

The gasLimit is somewhat analogous to how much gasoline you can fit in your car's tank; the maxFeePerGas is analogous to the price per gallon or liter. The relationship between gas and transactions is a little fiddly, but there are some useful rules of thumb to remember. If a transaction reverts, the *unspent* gas will usually be refunded. But the user will still pay some gas, proportional to how much computation the block proposer has had to do so far.

Similarly, if the transaction is completed successfully before the gasLimit is reached, the remaining gas will be refunded. It is worth thinking about this in more detail for a moment. If a transaction is successful, how can there be *unspent* gas? Contracts can contain complex, Turing-complete logic dependent on state that might not be easily accessible to the account constructing the transaction. The scope and computational requirements of a transaction are often not necessarily knowable *a priori*; you don't always know how much gas a given transaction is going to use. But this also means the EVM doesn't know. And that means if you submit a transaction and don't provide *enough* gas, the EVM will eat whatever you give it attempting to fulfill the transaction. If you provide 25,000 gas for a 30,000 job, the transaction will revert and you'll get nothing back. It's therefore usually a good idea to err on the side of more gas than you think you'll need.

Besides being interesting per se, this discussion of gas has some important lessons for those building products:

1. ***You don't always know how much a transaction is going to cost.***
   The market dynamics, along with the ever-changing interplay of transactions and state, means that both the price per unit of work and how much work needs to be done can be hard to predict. Ethereum has some interesting – and flawed – mechanisms for estimating gas. When building products, it's your responsibility to think about how to communicate these variable costs to the user, either by integrating it directly into your apps or allowing the wallet software to handle it.

2. ***Transaction cost varies with time as well as with transaction complexity.*** A transaction submitted at one time might be more expensive than at another: if the *aims* of the transaction are not especially time dependent, then it might not need to be this expensive. If the transaction cost is high, and the user can delay, it might be good to communicate this to the user or perhaps even defer the transaction automatically.

3. ***You can make transactions cheaper by doing some computation off-chain.*** This is a controversial approach, not often appreciated by the decentralization maximalists, but there are many occasions where performing work off-chain can be done without sacrificing the benefits of decentralization. (See Chapter 6 for a bigger discussion of moving computation off-chain.)

Gas is a dynamic market, and its effect on product quality and user experience shouldn't be ignored: it can add friction and confuse even the most technical of users, in ways that are hard to predict ahead of time. Gas is one unique dimension that builders on Ethereum need to consider and *build around.*

The gas values that users input when submitting a transaction are an *upper limit*: the per unit price multiplied by the gas limit tells the user how much at most they are willing to pay for the transaction. But how much they actually pay is a function of whether the transaction succeeds, how much computation the network needed to do, and whether any remaining gas is returned.

Determining an accurate amount of gas to be consumed is, for reasons we've already discussed, not that straightforward. Smart contract functionality cannot easily be predicted ahead of time. Smart contracts often contain functions with loops, functions with stochastic behavior, and functions that rely on runtime state to determine control flow. The current state of the blockchain can change as validators add and remove transactions from the current block. And EIP-114 adds an invariant to certain EVM opcodes such that they withhold 1/64th of the remaining gas once they reach a stack depth of 1024.[6] In short, it can get messy.[7]

---

[6] For more, see https://github.com/ethereum/EIPs/issues/114

[7] For a flavor of quite *how* messy, accurate Ethereum gas estimation is the subject of at least one PhD thesis: https://ieeexplore.ieee.org/document/9678932

There are, however, techniques that can be used, and these techniques are generally already implemented in geth and other Ethereum node software. The approach is essentially a binary search: execute the bytecode with varying amounts of gas, from zero to the block's maximum remaining gas, finding the midpoint on each iteration, and thereby return the minimum amount of gas required to let the transaction run without returning an out of gas error. This is effective, and fairly quick, but the returned value still comes with some wide error bars. This is how most nodes generate gas estimates, and they expose this functionality with the `eth_estimateGas` RPC method.

`eth_estimateGas` takes roughly the same parameters as `eth_call`: the `from` and `to` addresses, any ether `value` sent with the transaction, and the `data` string (as well as the standard gas parameters). It won't consume any gas when running, but it will estimate the gas using the preceding mechanism and return the rough gas amount.

Note   You may notice that *ethers.js* throws up "cannot estimate gas" errors when you try to submit an invalid transaction. Internally, ethers make two RPC calls: one to estimate the gas quantity, which calls `eth_estimateGas`, and one to actually send the transaction. If the transaction fails at the first step, ethers will throw a "cannot estimate gas" error with a contract error included elsewhere in the exception. You might want to parse this error and display something more useful to the user.

So `eth_estimateGas` will give you a rough estimate of the *gas quantity* required. You may want to add some buffer to this gas amount, perhaps 10%, to ensure that your users submit a high enough gas limit to cover any uncertainty in the estimate. Tools like *ethers. js*, if not provided with explicit gas parameters, will calculate the gas upper limit using this sort of technique.

The gas equation contains two terms: the gas quantity and the per-unit price. We've just described how you can estimate the gas quantity; what about the price?

Gas price is also not that straightforward to estimate. As we've already described, gas is a dynamic market, so what you're actually trying to do is figure out what price is both high enough to incentivize somebody to include the transaction in a block and not so high that you spend money you don't need to. This is ultimately something that your user will have to decide: How eager are they to get this transaction confirmed? How much would they pay to have it executed right now; or, alternatively, how much money are they willing to trade off for time?

But, most of the time, most users won't be that discriminating. A lot of the time, gas prices are low enough that the marginal increase or decrease won't affect their demand. In this case, we can take the average of the last few blocks' median gas price. *ethers.js* has a getFeeData() function that returns sensible gas and priority fee values that you can use as a default.

Finally, it's worth considering how you should display this information to your users. The vocabulary is technical, and the ideas are not straightforward. Does the user need to know about gas? Or can your user interface make these decisions automatically, wrap it up in a "transaction fee," and ignore the gas market entirely? We'll discuss this a little more in the "Transaction UX" section of this chapter.

Nonces and Replay Attacks

A foreseeable attack vector in decentralized networks that publish transactions publicly is to take a user's transaction from some time t and to play it again at time t+1, allowing the attacker to essentially hijack the user's signature. If A sends 1 eth to B, B could resubmit the previous transaction again and again, draining A's account. One potential solution is to add a timestamp, but this would require clock synchronization across all participants. A simpler solution is to use an incremental integer and enforce an invariant such that the next transaction requires a higher integer than the current transaction. This integer is called a *nonce*, and it is included in the raw transaction. Signing the transaction, therefore, is also signing the nonce, and thus changing the nonce requires a new transaction signature.

Consider another problem: an account signs two transactions at a similar time. Both are submitted into the mempool within a few milliseconds of one another, during the same slot. Transaction 1 sends 20 eth somewhere; transaction 2 sends 15 eth somewhere else. The account has 30 eth. If transaction 1 is executed first, the account will have 10 eth remaining, and transaction 2 will revert. If transaction 2 is executed first, the account will have 15 eth remaining, and transaction 1 will revert. Under such circumstances, there is no principled way for the block proposer to select whether transaction 1 or 2 should be executed. The block proposer, in effect, gets to decide who receives the eth and who doesn't. A nonce invariant, as described earlier, forces the transactions into a sequence decided by the agent making those transactions.

Nonces are a simple solution to these important problems, and the implementation complexity is much less than an equivalent timestamp implementation would be. However, nonces put a reasonably strong constraint on transactions and can cause problems when the rules are not respected.

Firstly, Ethereum will require that *the nonce increments strictly by one each time*. If, for whatever reason, there is a gap between the account's current nonce and the submitted nonce – even if the latter is higher than the former – the transaction will be left in the mempool until the gap is filled.[8] Transactions also can't be revoked: the purpose of the signature, in part, is to make a claim *irrevocable*. Managing revocations in a general way across a decentralized system is a difficult problem and is best handled at the application layer. The only way to override a currently pending transaction is to submit another transaction with the same nonce, providing a higher priority fee, in an attempt to convince validators to choose the overriding transaction over the pending one.

Secondly, it can create testing problems. If you are running a local fork of the mainnet and perform some transactions using, for instance, your local MetaMask, your wallet will increase and store the nonce. You then need to manually reset your wallet each time you reset the local testing environment. It is a small inconvenience, but it definitely is an inconvenience and can easily dissuade a tired developer from testing a full range of scenarios locally.

Thirdly, it creates concurrency issues. If submitting multiple transactions asynchronously, you will need to create some way to manage nonce assignment, perhaps by centralizing transaction construction within your codebase. Centralizing transaction construction also needs to be done with care, since transactions effect state changes and therefore often need to be submitted and confirmed in sequence.

---

[8] It isn't clear to me why this requirement was stipulated, and I can't think of any backward compatibility issues that would arise from simply removing it. If you know why, I'd love to hear from you.

Transaction Receipts

Once a transaction has been successfully broadcast to the network, the node will return a transaction receipt. We've already mentioned how the transaction will undergo state changes while it's being processed. The transaction receipt allows you to request the transaction's status at the current time and therefore periodically check to see whether it has been processed.

The transaction receipt also contains some useful information that is generated during, and because of, the execution process. Let's look at the receipt for the transaction 0xad2...98d[9]:

```
{
  to: null,
  from: '0x490...E8C',
  contractAddress: '0xcAf…dE5',
  transactionIndex: 29,
  gasUsed: BigNumber { _hex: '0x2ba042', _isBigNumber: true },
  blockHash: '0x6c0...160',
  transactionHash: '0xad2...98d',
  blockNumber: 13619386,
  confirmations: 2213039,
  cumulativeGasUsed: BigNumber { _hex: '0x449c13', _isBigNumber: true },
  effectiveGasPrice: BigNumber { _hex: '0x1a1b952fda', _
  isBigNumber: true },
  status: 1,
  type: 2,
  ...
}
```

(I retrieved this receipt by running provider.getTransactionReceipt against an Alchemy node, using *ethers.js*; you may see a different format if using a different tool. I have also shortened some of the hex data fields and removed the logs entries for the purpose of readability. We'll talk about logs in more detail in the next chapter.)

---

[9] 0xad25be756c3dc12db179548dee5f7dbb07d4c763aa5d30d60db44e34ccef798d, which deployed ParaSwap's PSP token to the Ethereum mainnet.

The definition of each of the fields is quite straightforward:

- The `blockHash` and `blockNumber` fields tell us which block the transaction was included in.

- The `to` and `from` fields are from the transaction payload: a `null` value in the `to` field means that this transaction is a contract deployment.

- `gasUsed` and `effectiveGasPrice` tell us the gas quantity and unit price consumed for this *transaction*; `cumulativeGasUsed` tells us how much gas has been consumed as of this transaction within this *block*.

- The `transactionHash` is the unique identifier for this transaction; the `transactionIndex` tells us where this transaction sits within this block's transaction ordering.

- `confirmations` gives us the number of blocks in the current chain since the block in which the transaction was verified, which can be used as a measure of *confidence* that the chain won't be reordered.

- `type`, a property introduced in EIP-2718, allows for nodes to implement different types of transactions – a type of 2 indicates this is a transaction following EIP-1559 semantics.

- And `status` tells us whether the transaction failed (0) or succeeded (1).

So if we want to check our transaction's status while it's still pending, we'll need to use the `transactionHash` from the receipt, query the current receipt, and check the `status` property. Most frontend tools will abstract away this complexity, but it can be helpful to understand what's happening underneath. If a transaction has a receipt at all, that means it's been included in a block: `status` then tells you whether the execution was successful or not. Depending on the confidence requirements of your application, you may also want to wait for a specific number of confirmations before you display the transaction as confirmed in your UI.

It is a bit peculiar, isn't it? The conventional idea of a "confirmed" is a binary state: either something is confirmed or it isn't. In the strange land of Ethereum, where the guarantees of history are given by consensus over facts rather than the facts themselves, confirmation is a matter of *confidence*: confidence that this block won't be challenged, rearranged, or dropped entirely. It means the reporting of the transaction's status is a matter of judgment for the product engineer, something relative to the demands of the specific product and its users.

Transaction UX

Ethereum puts lots of constraints on the UX of your product, but many of these constraints can be worked around. Transaction construction should always be framed in terms of the user's model, rather than crypto's model. Progressive expansion can be used to hide complexities and reveal them as the user needs to know. Blocking the UI and forcing the user through a single flow can be much simpler than handling everything asynchronously. All transactions should be validated as much as possible before they reach the blockchain; all errors should be surfaced as soon as possible. Transactions can be represented in code as an object separate from the UI used to implement it, which has numerous benefits. The status of a transaction requires paying attention to block confirmations and data updates, not just what the network reports; the status of the system should always be visible to the user. Crypto products don't need to be educational about crypto, and crypto products don't need to be single-page apps.

Transactions are a leaky form of abstraction. On the one hand, the natural inclination is to hide as much as possible from the user: a user doesn't want to submit a transaction, they want to swap some tokens, or buy an NFT, or vote on a governance issue. It's tempting to think that you can sweep away the transaction mechanism entirely. On the other hand, submitting a transaction is a fundamentally technical action, one that requires not just a sensible UI but an integration of the frontend with the wallet software, the node, any indexing service, and, most importantly, the user's intentions and desires. Users may want to adjust the gas prices they pay, and they may wish to verify the transaction data before it is committed on-chain. The Principle of Trust hangs in the balance: if too much of the technical details are displayed, you risk alienating nontechnical users; if too little, you risk obfuscating the details and complicating verification.

The core problem is that the user's wallet will inevitably display the transaction details in a more general-purpose way than your frontend. When designing products around Ethereum transactions, you'll need to understand the user's context and mental states – the fuzzier psychosocial elements of design – as well as the actual mechanics of how a user goes from intention to action.

And the stakes here are high. Transactions are painful: and I mean this literally. Psychological research has shown that people experience stress and pain when spending money due to loss aversion.[10] Priming the user to expect a transaction, clarifying the consequences, and minimizing the number of decisions they need to make can help reduce this stress. This all comes down to the UX and UI decisions you make around your transaction interface.

Alas, very little about the broader Ethereum user experience has been designed with this stress in mind. Every year, the Ethereum community has to solve challenging computer science problems just to make the thing continue to function and grow. Ethereum has thus attracted many incredibly bright, quantitatively minded engineers from the cryptography, programming, and economics worlds. Protocol- and network-level decisions are made based on these sorts of constraints, working up to the application level, rather than thinking about the application level and working down to the network. The job of the product designer and the product engineer is to bridge this gap.

If you ask several designers what the core problems with Ethereum UX are, you'll see common pain points emerge very quickly:

- **The terminology is overly technical.** Gas, priority fees, transaction hashes, calldata, hex data, blocks. These are not things normal people should have to care about.

- **Account addresses are 42-character long strings of alphanumeric nonsense.** Protocols like ENS aim to address this, but abstracting addresses away entirely is essentially impossible.

- **There are different *levels* of concerns – data, protocol, application, wallet, network, and more – all of which impact the user's experience.** One example is not many UIs tell their users that the network is congested. Some wallet software will warn you when the network is congested, when gas fees are high: Argent, for instance, throws up a warning when the current gas fees are large relative to the transaction's dollar value. Informing the user over this wide variety of dimensions makes it challenging to create consistent experiences.

---

[10] Zellermayer, O. (1996). *The pain of paying.*

- **Connecting wallets to the right network**, as we've already discussed, is fraught with UX challenges.

- **The responsibility for transaction construction is split between wallets and dapps.** The wallet software can override the products' values, and the product usually can't control how the wallet software will display the transaction details.

- **Most dapps don't work on mobile** or only work on specific browsers. Even dapps that nominally work on mobile devices aren't designed for those devices, and the UX is degraded accordingly.

The scale of the UX problems in crypto is so vast, an entire book could – and should! – be written about it. In this section, however, we're going to focus on the UI surrounding transactions specifically and explore some of the basic constraints, problems, and potential solutions that you can use. More generally, I hope this section gives you some intuition pumps for topics around user experience, as well as cue up the sorts of questions you might ask yourself when designing and building products on Ethereum.

All this should, under no circumstances, be considered an indictment of the ecosystem. There are lots of very smart product people working with Ethereum, thinking deeply and pushing far to reform, improve, and innovate. It's also very early: what applications are popular and useful are constantly changing; the underlying technology is being built bottom-up by a community, and many standards are still being worked out; the cultural properties of Ethereum that sit underneath it all are in rapid flux. But there is a lot of bad UX in crypto, and doing it well is another form of professional arbitrage: it signals care, thought, and attention. It is also the only hope of scaling crypto to normal consumers.

I'll break the discussion up into three categories:

- **Clarification**: How to communicate properties of the transaction

- **Control**: How to allow users to adjust those properties before they submit the transaction

- **Confirmation**: How to reveal the status and effects of transactions once submitted

What follows is neither exhaustive nor relevant for every application nor even especially novel. (Most of the examples I give are taken from decentralized token swap providers, because the basic user flows are simple and well known.) Rather, it's a starting point: an initial set of thoughts and examples of how Ethereum's idiosyncratic computation model affects a UI and an illustration of the sort of things you can think about.

Clarification

We'll start by considering how our products can communicate the properties and behaviors of a transaction. As we've mentioned several times already, transactions are a result of a user's *intention*. Users want to achieve a goal by submitting a transaction; the transaction is not the territory! Explaining what a transaction aims to do is a central part of aligning the user's intentions with the actual mechanics of interacting with the protocol.

Understanding this intention, then, is at the heart of designing intuitive interfaces for what the user actually wants to do. And understanding this begins with understanding how the user thinks about what they're trying to do. What is their model of the world? What is their model of transacting? Once we understand the answers to those questions, we can see how it diverges from the model of the world – and, *a fortiori*, of transactions – that crypto suggests to our designs.

How do we understand our users' worldviews? We talk to them. We observe them using our applications. We develop user profiles and design with those profiles in mind. In short, we do all the same sorts of things that we do when designing products not intended to run on Ethereum!

The User's Model

One place where this schism between crypto's model and our user's model becomes clear is in the *units* that we use to represent the transaction. Gas fees are always paid in ether, whereas many transactions implicate other ERC-20 tokens (or, indeed, nontoken actions) to power their behavior. The problem is that users – even advanced users – don't have a good sense for *how much one ether actually costs*. Try it: without checking the current price or using a calculator, ask yourself to put a dollar value on four gwei right now. You might be able to guess the rough order of magnitude, but "four gwei" is, at first blush, a somewhat meaningless quantity. Instead of using gwei/ether, use a familiar currency such as USD, EUR, or GBP (or, ideally, support all three and more). Even the tokens are generally thought of in terms of their own units or dollar amounts, typically not in terms of ether.

Aave gives a simple example of how this can be done well, abstracting away the gwei units entirely from the gas fees and revealing the relationship between token quantity and USD, as seen in Figure 3-1.

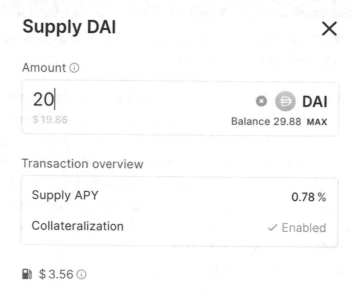

Figure 3-1. *Aave displays an estimated gas fee, priced in USD, at the bottom of its transaction UIs. Each token quantity is related to a common reference value (also USD)*

This problem is, of course, a specific form of a more general problem: the terminology that crypto has converged upon is often *not* what is useful to the user! Lots of DeFi protocols lean on properties of the protocol to provide the basic conceptual framework for the product, but the protocol is at a different level to the product, and it's not always desirable or necessary to do so. Abstract quantities such as APYs can often be better explained in terms of daily/weekly/monthly returns in dollars (see Figure 3-2). The "24-hour volume" can often be better explained in terms of today's fee accrual. Total Value Locked (TVL), sometimes used to indicate the popularity of a pool and to calculate the marginal return of the next dollar invested, can often be better explained in terms of the expected trend. And so on.

Figure 3-2. *The Beethoven platform displays a "potential weekly yield" value, which can be expanded into precise APR numbers*

What we're trying to do is figure out why a user wants to submit a transaction and give them the information that they need to make the various decisions they'll have to make. Should I submit a transaction? What parameters do I provide? What are the expected outcomes from this transaction? At what point will my returns exceed the gas fees? These kinds of questions are actually not about transactions at all! They're about how the user achieves their goals. And therefore, they are generally not best answered by referring to underlying properties of the protocol. Instead, your product should rely on the *user's domain* rather than *crypto's domain*.

Let's extract this insight out into a principle:

Matching Models

The design should speak the users' language. Use words, phrases, and concepts familiar to the user, rather than internal jargon. Follow real-world conventions, making information appear in a natural and logical order.

Matching Models is at the base of good design, because it encourages you to design tools that fit snugly with the user's existing conceptual scheme; it encourages you to minimize friction. If "gwei" or "ether" or "TVL" is entirely incidental to your use case, if these concepts are merely implementation details, then they don't need to be in your interface. This also gives us a sense of why designing a transaction interface is *specific* to your application. If you are doing something different from other services, your transaction UI should probably look different from those other services. Why? Because relying on community norms to indicate everything is going to obscure what makes your protocol unique, make the UI less useful, and *force one model on your users that doesn't align with the model they have when they try to solve the problem your application is solving.* Aave, again, does this well, communicating through a clear graph the various APR rates and how they change with respect to the utilization rate of the pool, as in Figure 3-3.

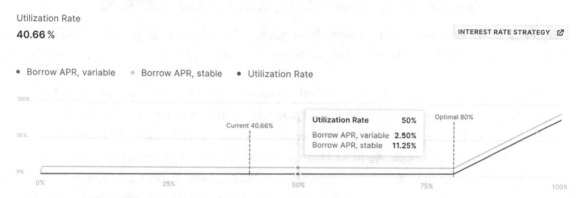

Figure 3-3. *Aave displays how the borrow APR rates change when the utilization rate changes. This sort of representation of complex data begins with a user-level question – "If a lot more people borrow money from this pool, how will it affect my borrowing rates?" – and answers it with a common visual device, a graph*

This sort of information visualization allows users to understand the nuances of your *specific* protocol, not just relying on existing knowledge of common crypto terms, but framing it in terms of the behavior of *this* protocol for *this* user. This is why it's incredibly important to understand both what your protocol does (and what it does differently) and what your users think, feel, and intend to do when interacting with it.

Dynamic Systems

Another important point to remember when designing transaction interfaces is that user decisions will have effects that may constrain future user actions. These are *dynamic systems*, systems that change over time. The Balancer UI in Figure 3-4 provides a helpful example of this sort of thinking in action.

Figure 3-4. *Balancer issues a helpful warning when the user is going to trade away too much of their ether to pay for the transaction fees*

While this is certainly imperfect – ideally, the system would abstract away the notion of gas fees entirely, since they're likely not present in the user's model – it nonetheless gives a sense of how a system needs to nudge users away from being in bad states and toward being in good states. We might frame this in terms of increasing optionality or just being a steward of a happy user experience. But the most important thing is that we inform the user as soon as we can tell they are likely to get stuck and give them advice as to how to avoid it.

Error Recognition

Error messages should be expressed in plain language (no error codes), precisely indicate the problem, and constructively suggest a solution. Errors should be obvious and clear. Warnings should be used to indicate when errors might occur in the future.

We'll revisit Error Recognition in the following parts of this section.

Transaction Intent

Another important constraint that Ethereum's transaction model forces upon us: transactions, at the network level, are opaque bytecode strings. We'll discover in Chapter 4 that they contain a rather predictable and elegant structure, but our users should never need to know about it. Because our transactions must at some point be passed off to the wallet, and the wallet is inevitably going to display the transaction in a less user model–specific manner, we should do everything we can to communicate the purpose, configuration, and consequences of the transaction long before we ask the user to change anything or submit it. Some Ethereum standards exist to try to mediate the relationship between the transaction in your UI and the transaction in the wallet software's UI, but it is not a panacea.[11]

There are things we can do in our UI to obey Matching Models and better communicate transaction intent. This starts with the page title, the call-to-action text, and any other forms of context signposting. Buttons should be labeled with the appropriate action: "Swap Tokens" is better than "Exchange," which is better in turn than "Send Transaction." "Transaction fee" or "Service fee" or even "Network fee" is better than "Gas fee," since most users don't – and don't need to – know what gas is. Explaining everything in natural language is helpful, avoiding jargon. We'll see more of this in the "Confirmation" section: give transactions natural language descriptions with contextual information ("Swapping 10 DAI to ETH"), and use these descriptions in confirmation modals and status updates.

Related: Signal outcomes early. What does this transaction achieve? Once the user has submitted it, and it is confirmed, what are its effects? Compound does this neatly, and almost imperceptibly, by indicating the resulting increase in a borrow limit when supplying funds to its pools with a simple arrow, as in Figure 3-5.

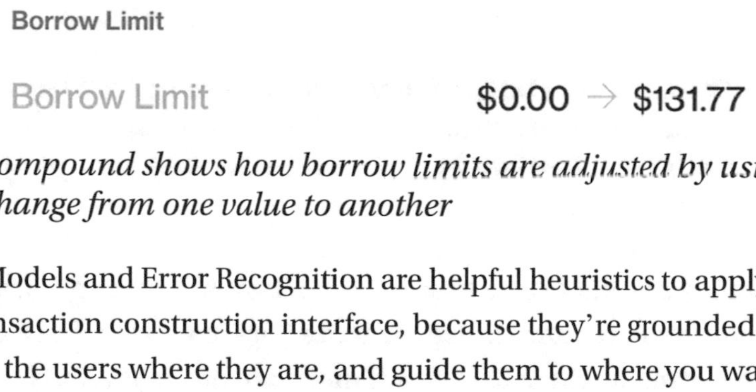

Borrow Limit

Borrow Limit $0.00 → $131.77

Figure 3-5. *Compound shows how borrow limits are adjusted by using an arrow to indicate a change from one value to another*

Matching Models and Error Recognition are helpful heuristics to apply to almost any form of transaction construction interface, because they're grounded in a simple principle: meet the users where they are, and guide them to where you want them to be. These clarificatory principles can also be used for marketing purposes as well as for improving the UX. ParaSwap displays a table with the prices and fees for competing pools, as seen in Figure 3-6.

---

[11] EIP-712, for instance, allows for structured data objects rather than raw text when signing messages (which is not the same thing as signing a transaction; https://eips.ethereum.org/EIPS/eip-712). Some wallets, including MetaMask, will inspect the smart contract ABI where possible and parse the transaction data, showing more structured data in the wallet's confirmation screen. Not every wallet does this, and no wallet does it perfectly. Even if they did, the data it would show would be the data that the protocol sees, which is generally *not* using the same conceptual model as the user.

EXCHANGE		PRICE (ETH/DAI)	YOU GET	FEES (i)
ParaSwapPool	BEST	1597.92 DAI	159.792 DAI	~ $1.51
ParaSwapPool3	-0.05%	1597.23 DAI	159.723 DAI	~ $1.53
ParaSwapPool10	-0.08%	1596.87 DAI	159.687 DAI	~ $1.53
ParaSwapPool7	-0.12%	1596.2 DAI	159.62 DAI	~ $1.53
DefiSwap	-0.18%	1594.41 DAI	159.441 DAI	~ $1.45
SushiSwap	-0.18%	1594.37 DAI	159.437 DAI	~ $1.45
UniswapV2	-0.2%	1593.37 DAI	159.337 DAI	~ $1.37
BalancerV2	-0.27%	1597.77 DAI	159.777 DAI	~ $1.93
UniswapV3	-0.36%	1600.39 DAI	160.039 DAI	~ $2.33

Figure 3-6. *ParaSwap shows not just what this transaction will do but also how it compares to a similar swap on other platforms. Thus, the UI can be both clarificatory and a helpful marketing tool – assuming that your platform is competitive!*

This sort of table is useful for the user, because it gives them a sense of the broader market and allows them to contextualize the trade they're making. But it's also useful for ParaSwap, because it allows them to show off their superior rates. And it's a natural fit for the Principle of Trust, because it signals transparency.

Let's have a brief think about how we might actually implement this in a frontend. The trick is to engineer a layer between the smart contract and the UI code, representing the transaction as a meaningful domain object with properties, behaviors, and metadata. This can be as simple as a JS object representing an individual transaction:

```
const swapTransaction = {
  metadata: {
    title: "Swap Tokens",
    titleInProgress: (data) => `Swapping ${data.fromToken} to ${data.toToken}`,
```

```
    callToAction: "Swap",
  },
  submit: (data) => provider.sendTransaction(data),
};
```

This allows us to isolate the transaction's behavior and metadata into one place, giving us a standardized interface. (By moving the submit logic here too, we can hide any default/app-level settings from the transaction UI code entirely.) The `titleInProgress` key is a function that takes our transaction data and returns a string; this shows how adding this abstraction can become quite powerful, allowing our metadata to be context sensitive. This can make the individual transaction UI simpler and will allow us to extend the transaction object to support some of the other types of UX improvements we'll discuss elsewhere in this chapter. It also allows us to move the transaction details outside of a specific frontend component, assisting separation of concerns and code cleanliness.

Regardless of how it's implemented, by trying always to explain transactions and their behaviors in natural language aligned with the user's model, you can strip away complexity from your UI, focus users toward interacting with your protocol rather than trying to understand it, and thus build an interface more effective and empathetic.

Control

But sometimes complexity is necessary. Sometimes, you require several inputs from users, or even several transactions, in order to provide value. At this point, we'll need to consider how the user provides these inputs. How should a user control the properties of the transaction they are to submit?

Progressive Expansion

One important constraint that is often overlooked, but falls out directly from Matching Models, is that *the right level of abstraction for the protocol is unlikely to be the right level of abstraction for the user*. Protocols think in terms of `uint256` values, account addresses, and arrays of bytes. These are syntactic properties, not semantic properties, of the input, so they are rarely, if ever, the model with which the user is thinking. Almost every product does this already, to some degree: token amounts are inputted in decimal form, rather than the e^18 raw values in which they're represented by the protocol; tokens are selected from lists rather than via contract addresses; helpful metadata and imagery is shown to indicate the meaning of what's being transacted. But many UIs don't go nearly far enough. As we saw in "Clarification," UIs can represent values in terms in which the user is already thinking. Putting a layer of abstraction between the user and the protocol is thus a liberating move conducive to good design, because it gives you the chance to align the UI with the user's model rather than the protocol's.

There is one obvious thing that you can do and that most product designers already do: provide different UIs for inputs of different types. Some numbers are bounded by ranges and can be inputted with a slider. Some numbers have a set of sensible defaults that are best expressed with a dropdown or radio select. Other numbers require explicit input boxes. Boolean values can be inputted with a toggle, etc.

But better designed input fields are inferior to no input fields at all; in many cases, you simply don't need to provide a configurable value. The frontend can calculate appropriate values or fall back to sensible defaults. One helpful approach here is to use *progressive expansion*: gradually showing more complexity as the user requests it and relying on such sensible defaults when the user doesn't. Matcha, for instance, offers an "Advanced Settings" panel on their standard swap interface that allows users to set slippage parameters, the exchange list they're trading from, and gas prices, as shown in Figure 3-7.

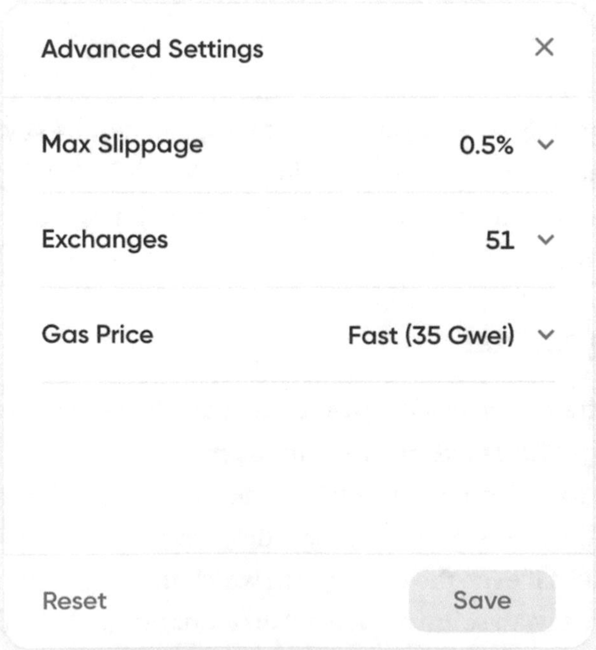

Figure 3-7. *Matcha has an "Advanced Settings" panel that reveals configurable values only if the user needs to change them*

Lots of trading UIs have some sort of "Advanced Settings" panel. But Matcha's goes deeper: the gas price setting also expands progressively, letting users select a custom gas price after clicking through, as shown in Figure 3-8.

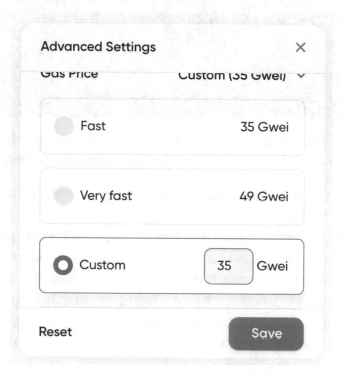

Figure 3-8. *Clicking "Gas Price" reveals a second level of configuration*

This is a great instance of progressive expansion, because it demonstrates that there can be multiple layers of configurability. Only some users will want to change the defaults at all, and only a subset of those users will want to change the gas price in gwei directly. Giving those users the flexibility to adjust these values, but adding a source of friction to do so, will help sort users into those with expertise and those who are happy to let the app make those decisions for them. SushiSwap takes this idea even further, allowing users to enable an "Expert Mode" toggle that not only reveals more granular configuration but also disables various security checks, as seen in Figure 3-9.

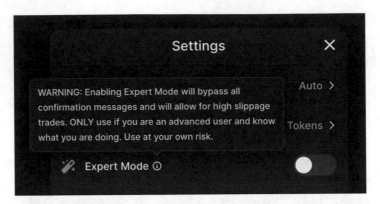

Figure 3-9. *SushiSwap allows advanced users to adjust the user flow mechanisms directly. A stellar example of progressive expansion (or, in this case, contraction)*

...and SpookySwap even displays an entirely new UI when their "Expert Mode" is enabled.

Some values are reasonably general and can be pulled out of the specific transaction context entirely: gas fees are a good example here, since every transaction that the user submits will require a gas fee setting. If you're not going to abstract away gas, and allow the user to configure their gas prices, then you might consider moving it outside of the context of any given transaction and instead let the user configure it globally across your app. Alchemix provides a "gas fee" dropdown that configures the gas price offered for subsequent transactions, regardless of what those transactions are (see Figure 3-10).

Figure 3-10. *Alchemix allows users to configure gas at the application level, rather than on a per-transaction basis*

This sort of technique works well for gas, but could be used for other transaction properties too. If your product deals with leverage, and your users are likely to use similar amounts of leverage on every trade, then you might want to move leverage out of the individual transaction UI and into the global UI. Similarly with slippage, most users may be happy setting a basic acceptable slippage percentage and tweaking occasionally. The benefit to this approach, of course, is that it reduces the number of configurable fields you need to include in your individual transaction UI, which reduces friction and can simplify the UI considerably. You might be able to get rid of a progressive expansion mechanism entirely if you can push the configurable values somewhere more general. (This approach, by the way, also works well for display configuration; see, for instance, in Figure 3-10 how Alchemix allows for base currency changes. This doesn't affect the transaction details, but it does affect the display.)

Transaction Sequencing

A slightly more challenging control problem concerns transaction sequencing: sometimes, multiple transactions are required to complete a specific user journey. Because Ethereum transactions are asynchronous, and we have to pass over responsibility for transaction submission to the wallet, this can present awkward sequencing issues and race conditions. What should happen if the first transaction fails? What about if the first succeeds, but the second is never submitted? What about if the first transaction succeeds, but is misconfigured in some subtle way that prevents the second from being successful? What about if the user leaves mid-journey and comes back? Managing the system state across multiple transactions is less than straightforward.

The first thing to check is whether it is possible to combine the steps into one smart contract call. If a user journey is supposed to represent an atomic set of changes, then by far the easiest way to implement the user journey is *to actually make them an atomic set of changes*. In previous projects, I have had some success from simply asking the protocol team to add a single wrapper function to the contract that calls out to the underlying steps, consolidating these separate calls into one interface.[12] Or, better yet, try implementing it yourself: add the wrapper function, write some unit tests, submit a PR, and see how you get on. At the very least, you'll learn a bit more about the protocol. ParaSwap, in Figure 3-11, shows how combining two stages (in this case, swapping and transferring) can extend the functionality of a basic exchange in a small but potentially important way.

---

[12] For more on smart contract function calls, and why this isn't always easy, see Chapter 4.

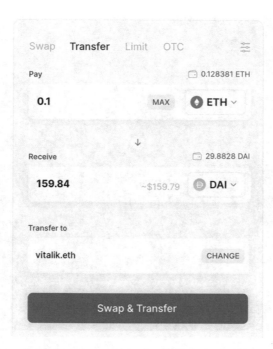

Figure 3-11. *ParaSwap has a swap-and-transfer dialog that combines two separate stages into one function call, which allows for an atomic update of both token quantities and owner*

There are, however, lots of scenarios when this won't be possible. The contracts in question may already be deployed. The protocol team may have frozen the feature set and may be mid-audit. You might not own the contract: it might be some third-party code you can't control. Or the protocol team might not be accommodating for some other reason.

In these cases, you'll need to design your product *around* the necessity for multicall logic. One important approach, which can be easy to forget, is just to force the user to go through each step sequentially. You can see a simple example of this in most token-related interfaces: users need to submit one transaction to approve the contract's spending of the tokens and another to actually perform the update. Check out the Uniswap interface, as shown in Figure 3-12. When a token is not approved, the "Swap" button is disabled. The user first needs to issue an allowance transaction.

Figure 3-12. *Uniswap (and basically everybody else) blocks the "main" token action until approvals are given*

If the approval has already been given, the "Allow" button isn't rendered, and the "Swap" button is enabled. This forces the user to execute a two-step process. This is, of course, hardly some great insight. But there are other contexts in which this two-stage process can be displayed more explicitly. You could, for instance, paginate the flow rather than update the dialog automatically. This allows you to focus the user on one specific task, exhibiting a meaningfully different UI for each stage, especially important when both steps allow for configuration. This also allows you to display a progress indicator. In these cases, you'll want to load the current user's state at the *page* level rather than the dialog level. Whether you do it via updating the UI dynamically or by blocking progress more explicitly via pagination, the point here is to block progress in the UI until you can be assured that the currently connected account is indeed in the state that it needs to be to continue.

We can extend the basic abstract transaction method that we discussed in the "Clarification" section to make these sorts of checks easier to reason about. A transaction object could support a `permissible()` function, which could take the proposed transaction data, query for more information, and return true if and only if the transaction is ready to be submitted:[13]

```
const swapTransaction = {
  // ...
  permissible: async (data, currentAccount) => {
    const userAllowance = await tokenContract.allowance(
      currentAccount.address,
      CONTRACT_ADDRESS
    );

    if (userAllowance.data.lt(data.amount)) {
      return {
        permissible: false,
        errors: [Errors.InsufficientTokenApproval]
      };
    }

    return { permissible: true, errors: [] }
  }
};
```

The UI could then, for instance, call `permissible()` with the transaction data to check whether the Swap button should be enabled and use its `errors` return value to display the Approve button.

Finally, some transactions are *optional*, in the sense that they will affect future transactions but aren't required. In these cases, you can nudge the user toward taking these optional steps by exposing them in the UI. Balancer suggests wrapping more stETH for its wstETH pool, as in Figure 3-13.

---

[13] Don't worry too much about the actual implementation here: we'll talk more about contract calls in future chapters. This code is meant as indicative, a way to demonstrate how various types of checks can be included in the transaction layer I'm suggesting.

Figure 3-13. *Balancer's wstETH pool points you toward wrapping more stETH. While not required, Balancer nudges the user effectively by noting that such an action is possible at this stage in the user journey*

Transaction sequencing is very use case specific, but it's likely that, at some point, you'll want to do something like this. Blocking the UI, paginating it, or even displaying the two actions in an ordered list can be a helpful way to indicate that the order matters. But you'll need to ensure that the user will be able to return to the same state if they close their browser, navigate away, or otherwise leave the journey midway through. Querying the blockchain for the user's current state on page load gives you the flexibility to adapt your UI accordingly.

Reversibility and Validation

One important constraint of Ethereum that has significant downstream effects on the products you build is that *transactions aren't reversible.*[14] Once the user has submitted a transaction, they've paid some gas fees. If the transaction is successful, they've modified the state. This makes it exceedingly important that you pay attention to possible violations of the Principle of Trust. If the user configures something incorrectly, they might end up submitting an invalid transaction or, worse, a perfectly valid transaction that doesn't express their intentions. Progressive expansion helps, since it forces the

---

[14] There are some proposed approaches to make transactions reversible, notably the ERC-20R proposal (https://mirror.xyz/kaili.eth/gB-rx89sNAT3CVuxWo6xVFS5ptNcllW7cVWVCfcFa6k), which rely on smart cryptography and decentralized jury systems to adjudicate competing claims. I suspect that they won't be accepted as core standards for cultural reasons. It's also not obvious to me that transaction reversibility should be implemented at the protocol level: it doesn't get us much more than a simpler escrow system, implemented at the application level in a smart contract, would.

user to decide whether they are sophisticated enough to configure. But it doesn't solve the problem, since you can't guarantee that they won't misjudge their abilities or make mistakes.

One potential solution to avoiding transaction errors – and something I've not seen implemented in DeFi products before – is to delay submitting a transaction by some period of time (say, 10 seconds) before it is submitted to the node. This could behave similarly to the "Undo" feature in Gmail, as shown in Figure 3-14.

Figure 3-14. *Gmail gives you the chance to "Undo" a sent email, within 10–15 seconds of the email being sent. A delayed send mechanism for transactions might be a natty bit of UX*

Such an undo feature won't work for every transaction. Some transactions are time sensitive: prices on a trade may change which can cause a revert due to slippage checks; new blocks might alter existing state. You can only be certain of the current state of the protocol at the moment you inspect it. But this is always a risk: data flows comparatively slowly through a decentralized network; some nodes only have a partial view of the mempool; indexing adds more delays. You will always need to handle cases where the transaction fails, for one reason or another. An "undo" or "cancel" feature gives your users an emergency exit, a chance to revoke the transaction quickly if they realize they've made a mistake. The biggest drawback, and the reason why, I suspect, this is rarely implemented, is that not every wallet – most notably MetaMask – supports the eth_signTransaction call. When not supported, the wallet will be responsible for submitting the transaction to the network, not the dapp, and this precludes a delayed send mechanism. But eth_signTransaction is a part of the core Ethereum JSON-RPC spec, and I expect that over time most wallets will support it.

Of course, the best way to reduce user regret is to not allow the user to regret their transaction in the first place. This allows us to bring Error Recognition back into the discussion. Error Recognition tells us that we should do our damndest to make sure that the user knows they are likely to cause errors, as early as we can. This centers around one core approach: always, always, *always* validate the user's inputs. Validation allows us to catch errors before they occur. Is a value obviously incorrect? Don't let the user proceed! Does a value look unusual/implausible? Warn the user!

Matcha offers a good model for warnings (Figure 3-15). If a user tries to issue a large trade on a low liquidity pool, the UI will warn the user that they are about to lose some money to slippage and force them to confirm again.

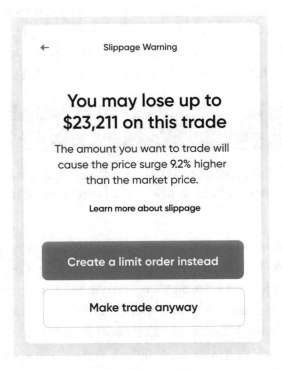

Figure 3-15. *Matcha adds an extra step to its trade modal when the expected slippage is large. Introducing this sort of friction is crucial; it gives users time to reflect about the consequences of the irreversible transaction they're about to submit*

But warnings needn't just take over the page, as in the Figure 3-15 case: user input should be validated just as it is in web2, by triggering error states on the inputs themselves. I won't include an image here, as it's such a common pattern, but I mention it here because the basic flow is still incredibly important. Inline validation states also allow the UI to render potential fixes. Has the user inputted a greater number of tokens than their account owns? Add a "MAX" button that sets the input to the correct token amount. The purpose of this sort of validation logic is to preempt a smart contract revert: smart contract errors are often underdescribed, overly technical, or just plain unhelpful. If you can copy the validation logic that the smart contract checks, as well as any other logic that might help nudge the user's input in the right direction, you can create much more enjoyable and tasteful experiences for your users using an idiom (i.e., input validation) that they already understand.

This validation logic can also be included in the transaction object, using the familiar pattern of normalize and validate:

```
const swapTransaction = {
  // ...

  normalize: (data) => ({
    ...data,
    amount: BigNumber.from(data.amount),
  }),

  validate: (data) => {
    let errors = [];
    let valid = true;

    if (!VALID_TOKENS.includes(data.token)) {
      valid = false;
      errors.push({
        field: 'token',
        message: `unknown token "${data.token}", valid tokens: ${VALID_
        TOKENS.join(', ')}`
      });
    }

    if (data.amount.lte(0)) {
      valid = false;
      errors.push({
        field: 'amount',
        message: 'amount must be more than 0',
        actions: [{
          label: 'Set to max',
          action: setInput(user.balances[data.fromToken])
        }]
      });
    }

    return { valid, errors };
  },
```

(Once again, the point of this code is not the implementation per se, it's that wrapping the transaction metadata and validation code in a transaction object can help isolate the relevant behavior and clean up the UI code.)[15] It is, incidentally, surprising how few crypto frontend codebases represent transactions in the way I've been describing: many simply call the smart contract directly with the input and allow the ABI/tools to do whatever syntax validation it can and let the smart contract itself pick up the slack. But this sort of information is several steps away from the user's input. A user has to submit a transaction before they find out whether the smart contract has failed, and this is true even if the tool (such as *ethers.js*) is running `eth_estimateGas` before proposing the transaction to the network. And this says nothing about the quality and user-friendliness of the average smart contract error. If you add another layer between the user's input and the smart contract, then you can do smart validation and suggest ways to fix the problems quickly and dynamically *at the point that the user is constructing the transaction*, not afterward.

This sort of validation behavior is expressive of another general principle that we can extract:

Status Visibility

The design should always keep users informed about what is going on, through appropriate feedback within a reasonable amount of time. When users know the current system status, they learn the outcome of their prior interactions and determine next steps. Predictable interactions create trust in the product as well as the brand.

Status Visibility is essential when we're working in an asynchronous environment, because we want to reveal the status of a transaction as soon as possible, in time for the user to course-correct. If we can match the input requirements of the smart contract in our own code, then we can hugely increase the user's confidence when submitting (and before paying gas fees). Whatever we can do to prevent failed transactions from occurring makes our lives easier as well as our users'.

---

[15] Another benefit to this sort of transaction object is that the various transaction behaviors can be isolated from the React render cycle. This means that our validation code can be unit tested, perhaps only requiring some basic dependency injection. In general, extracting business logic outside of React can be a useful way to increase test coverage without needing to worry about the underlying render logic and the awkwardness of tools like *react-test-renderer*.

Confirmation

We've shown how it's possible to clarify the properties of a transaction, its intent and its likely consequences, in a more user-friendly way. We've also described some approaches to improving the UX of transaction configuration. It's now time to look at the third stage in the transaction's story: once it has been submitted, how do we best indicate its status and its actual effects?

Transaction Status

As we've already mentioned, Ethereum transactions are executed asynchronously: they are submitted to the network and at some point in the future will be included in a block and validated by the committee of participating nodes. This means that we need to handle the asynchronous behavior in our UI.

Of course, the easiest way to handle asynchronous behavior is to *make it synchronous*! There's no reason why you can't disable your UI and put the frontend into a loading state until the transaction is successful. The SPA focus of a lot of crypto frontends can lead you to some dark and confusing places: often the cleanest thing to do is to get the user to wait for the transaction to be properly processed. This also allows you to combine on-chain asynchronous requests with on-chain transactions, if your use case demands it, as with Ramp in Figure 3-16.

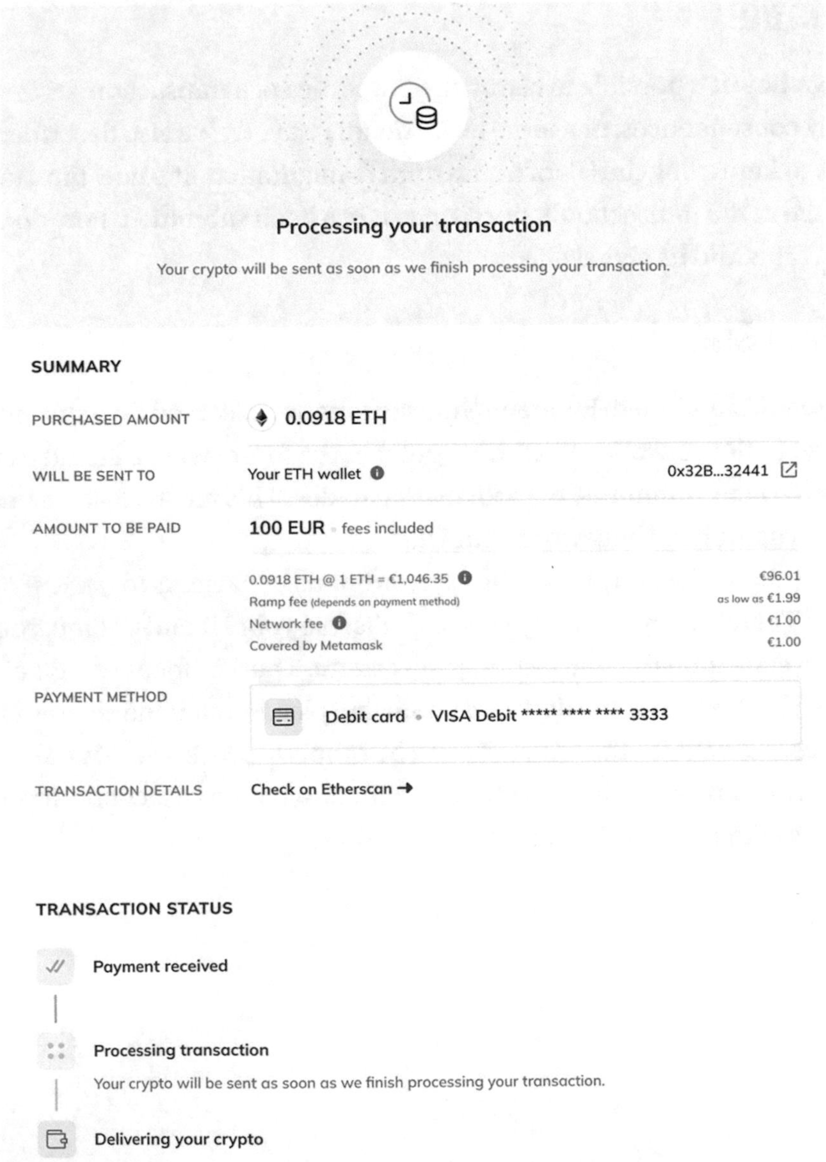

Processing your transaction

Your crypto will be sent as soon as we finish processing your transaction.

SUMMARY

PURCHASED AMOUNT	◆ **0.0918 ETH**
WILL BE SENT TO	Your ETH wallet ⓘ 0x32B...32441 ☐
AMOUNT TO BE PAID	**100 EUR** · fees included

0.0918 ETH @ 1 ETH = €1,046.35 ⓘ	€96.01
Ramp fee (depends on payment method)	as low as €1.99
Network fee ⓘ	€1.00
Covered by Metamask	€1.00

PAYMENT METHOD	🗒 Debit card · VISA Debit ***** **** **** 3333
TRANSACTION DETAILS	Check on Etherscan →

TRANSACTION STATUS

✓ Payment received

:: Processing transaction
Your crypto will be sent as soon as we finish processing your transaction.

▢ Delivering your crypto

Figure 3-16. *Ramp, a crypto on-ramp platform, handles both on- and off-chain asynchronous behaviors by leaving the UI in a pending state until it is confirmed. This is one tasty bit of UX design*

Where possible, just block the UI. It's generally not a big imposition to your users, is usually easier to implement, and, as Figure 3-16 demonstrates, can often leave you more room to display other important bits of information. There are very few instances where this isn't – at least directionally – the right approach. If, however, your use case demands that the user can continue to interact with the UI, then you'll need to handle the transaction status updates in another way. Many UIs provide transaction notifications in a snackbar-style interface. Figure 3-17 shows some examples from an old Blocknative UI library that helps generate these sorts of alerts.

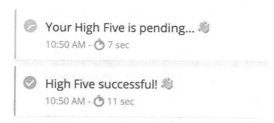

Figure 3-17. *The Blocknative assist library (`https://github.com/blocknative/assist`) provides a standard set of transaction notifications. It's an old library and hasn't been updated since 2019, but it gives a sense of what this sort of UI might look like*

Integrating these sorts of notifications is a good idea, because it gives your users a sense of progress as well as informs them of the actual current state of the transaction. You might also want to integrate other asynchronous mechanisms to update the user regarding the transaction status, such as email, text, or browser notifications, if possible and where appropriate. Respecting the user's time and allowing them to leave your frontend and come back later is a great way to engineer trust and create delightful experiences.

Once the transaction has been validated and we have a receipt, there's another constraint we need to bear in mind: blocks can be reorganized. This means that even inclusion in the last block is not a strict confirmation. Confirmation is a matter of *confidence*, not a binary state, and so we'll need to be able to wait for a sufficient number of blocks until we can be sure that we can confirm the results to the user. This is not the sort of thing that a user should have to care about, and so therefore the best thing to do is (usually) stipulate a level of confidence – five blocks? Ten blocks? – based on our use case, and communicate to the user. Blocks are validated every 12 seconds, so we can include a reasonably accurate progress bar or countdown timer. Even if we decide not to update the user via a progress bar, we should definitely not indicate that the transaction is successful until we meet our confidence threshold. *That a transaction has been accepted into a block is not its success state*: only once we are confident that the transaction won't be reversed by the next validator can we be sure that the transaction has successfully, and irreversibly, been added to the blockchain.

Once again, these considerations are expressive of the important heuristic of Status Visibility: the current status of a transaction isn't always obvious to the user. It's often hidden behind a few clicks in the user's wallet, and therefore transaction status should be immediately surfaced in the dapp itself.

Updating State

There is one final constraint that we should think about. The effects of transactions – that is, the updates to state – will take time to filter through the network (and any intermediaries, such as indexers), before our app is able to see them. This can cause some strange race conditions, where the transaction is marked as complete in our UI but the data itself isn't updated to reflect it. This can, at worst, be a violation of the Principle of Trust and becomes especially pernicious if there is some subsequent problem pulling the updated data from on-chain sources. If the indexer goes down, or the websocket connection is dropped at just the wrong time, we can display all the wrong information at just the moment the user needs it to be correct. At best, the UI updates can appear as if from nowhere, several render cycles after the transaction is marked successful. This might be good enough for a small demo, but if we're trying to create beautiful, tasteful products, we should aim for something better.

A simple way to minimize this sort of behavior is to add a delay between confirming the transaction and fetching the new state. If we wait, say, two seconds between registering the confirmed transaction and displaying the transaction success state, we give the intermediaries some leeway to fetch and update the state. This, unfortunately, won't fix every problem: we won't be updating our UI atomically, so there may still be funky rendering behavior, and we'll also still be vulnerable to flaky connections and unreliable indexers.

A more robust approach is to add a *transaction lock* and report our transaction as successful based not only on the transaction's status itself but on its changes to the state. The logic for locking and unlocking will vary depending on the effects that the transaction has: it's a lock based on the object-level properties of the state change, not the meta-level properties that the state change has occurred (e.g., the transaction being confirmed). So we'll need to decide for each transaction what sort of state update we consider to be successful. This might be listening out for specific contract events (see Chapter 4) or checking for specific changes in values.

We can add this logic quite neatly to the transaction object that we've been interweaving with the UI discussion:

```
const swapTransaction = {
  // ...
  unlock: async (data, user) => {
    const currentBalance = await tokenContract
      .balanceOf(user.address);
    return currentBalance.gte(data.amount);
  },
```

In this example, we check to see whether the user's balance of a token is greater than or equal to the amount we specified in the transaction data. This gives us a guarantee that the transaction actually occurred *and* that the data has reached our frontend. We can wait for the transaction's confirmation, *then* poll the unlock() function every 200ms or so using setTimeout() to ensure that the transaction has made it fully through the lifecycle and that our frontend reflects its changes.

This approach allows us to disable our UI, or indicate a refresh, until the lock is removed. This is much easier when you're controlling the user flow via a sequence of steps: in this case, you can simply prevent the next page from ever being seen until the data has been updated in the background. But even if your application is more dynamic, you can disable the relevant portions of the UI, or at the very least display a loading indicator, until the lock is removed.

This is, naturally, quite a bit more complex than just checking the transaction status, so you'll want to weigh up the benefits of this approach with the cost of writing it and the ongoing costs of maintaining it. But if the effects of a transaction are fairly legible, then it can help remove a class of race conditions and substantially improve the UX. In some use cases, it won't be practical or relevant. But it's much better to let the user know that something is happening and only return control to them when that something is done. That something is done not when the transaction is added to a block nor when it is confirmed: it is done when your local instance of the application is aware of the state changes.

Some Final Thoughts on UX

If you're well-read in the design thinking literature, the three principles that we extracted in this section – Matching Models, Error Recognition, and Status Visibility – may seem rather familiar. If you're especially well-read in the design thinking literature, you may know why: each one was taken – with a little rewording – from Jakob Nielsen's *10 Usability Heuristics for User Interface Design*, an important and helpful list of heuristics for good design.[16] Why is this pertinent? Firstly so that I can avoid plagiarism and also because it means that *very little of this is new*. The vast majority of good UX principles are timeless and apply just as readily to crypto applications as to web apps as to dishwashers as to bicycles as to governments. While crypto does present an interesting set of novel challenges, these characteristics shouldn't be used as an excuse for sloppy design. Many hundreds of thousands of very bright people have been building interfaces for augmenting intelligence and achieving goals for centuries, from the abaci of Mesopotamia to the iPhone of today. Products built on Ethereum are a *part* of this legacy, not *apart* from it.

I'll conclude this section by addressing a few common pieces of crypto UX advice and why I think they are erroneous.

Firstly, just because your application is built on crypto, *it doesn't mean that your application needs to educate people about crypto*. If a user needs to know that an application is running on Ethereum, then it's quite possible that the application is resting on a leaky set of abstractions, violating the Matching Models heuristic. In other words, Ethereum will truly be considered a UX success when it sits underneath a rich application ecosystem without ever infecting those applications with its own vocabulary. Sometimes, doing so is inevitable, but, in general, we shouldn't need to teach users new patterns or behaviors. Many, if not most, contemporary crypto applications are *re*implementations of existing applications on a decentralized substrate. This means that there are already well-known and intuitive ways of thinking about the problem. Where possible, we should rely on these existing memes and models.

Secondly, *your application doesn't need to be a SPA*. Or, at least, it certainly doesn't need to look like one: if you have a specific workflow, then you can force the user through that workflow page by page. Blocking the next steps until a transaction has been

---

[16]www.nngroup.com/articles/ten-usability-heuristics/

submitted is a common and reliable way to ensure the right sequence of user actions. And it also allows you to restore the user to their current state when they leave and come back. Not everything needs to be maximally dynamic.

Thirdly, and building on the first point, *you should aim wherever possible to distance your UI from the underlying smart contract*. Errors should be parsed and reformatted, displayed for them in their language and with an idiom common to your user's model and your product's brand. This has engineering benefits as well as UX benefits: it makes your application more robust to changes in the underlying contract, because you're creating layers of abstraction between them.

Lots of the UX problems we've talked about here come from constraints that you can't control: the wallet software, the asynchronous nature of the network, data availability, and the user's idiosyncratic inputs. But these constraints can often be worked around, and it's imperative in these cases to focus on product quality. Build around the constraints, and you'll have a more beautiful and tasteful product.

Your job, ultimately, is to be like the annoying venture capitalist in a coffee shop meeting. Constantly ask: How can I add value? If you can't, then nobody is going to use your product. But worse is when *you* know you add value, but nobody else can recognize it, because your interface is clunky and counterintuitive. Adhering to the principles outlined here, ignoring them when the trade-off is appropriate, and always revising and iterating your UI based on user feedback, usually won't lead you astray.[17]

Summary

We've covered a lot of ground in this chapter. Transactions are the language of the Ethereum protocol, and as such those of us building products on top of the platform have to think deeply and build tools around their idiosyncrasies. Signatures and gas fees demand extra steps and force integrations between software you control – your apps – and software you don't – the user's wallet interface. They generate new classes of runtime errors and exist within underdeveloped UI paradigms. Nonces solve an

---

[17] The Blocknative team has assembled a helpful checklist of usability issues that you can work against. It includes some parts of what we've discussed here and also covers other parts of the UX, such as wallet connections. `https://github.com/blocknative/dapp-usability-checklist/blob/master/README.md`

important problem in the system design, but they too are not without complications. It is these sorts of complications that give building on Ethereum its distinctive – and sometimes unpalatable – flavor.

Transaction UX is complicated, but can be made simpler by referring back to Jakob Nielsen's *10 Usability Heuristics for User Interface Design*. We should clarify the properties and intention of transactions in terms that the user has already, not crypto-specific terms that we think they should know (the Matching Models heuristic). We should gradually increase the specificity of our user's input through techniques such as progressive expansion, allowing our interface to make sensible assumptions and simplify the UI. We should validate inputs as much as possible ahead of time, predicting potential errors and nudging our user toward the correct behaviors (the Error Recognition heuristic). We should help guide our users through sequences of transactions by blocking the UI where appropriate. Similarly, we should help guide our users through the lifecycle of a transaction by revealing its status clearly and visibly (the Status Visibility heuristic). Crypto products don't need to educate their users about crypto – indeed, a successful product is one that solves the user's problem without needing to mention the underlying implementation details – and crypto products don't need to always behave like SPAs. Our job as designers is to let the user solve their problems, and our job as developers is to do so in a tasteful and robust manner.

In this chapter, we've made several opaque references to smart contracts. In the next chapter, we'll begin to make the opaque translucent, building up intuitions around how smart contracts work and exploring their various properties.

CHAPTER 4

Contracts

Smart contracts are the programs of Ethereum. But they're also APIs, and their design characteristics can affect the products we build significantly. In this chapter, we'll explore how smart contracts work, what their interfaces look like, what sorts of primitives they express, and what sorts of abstractions we can build upon those primitives. We'll also explore indexing, a powerful approach to separate data processing concerns from your products and the protocols they interface with.

Smart Contracts

Ethereum uses smart contracts to allow for a general form of programmable state changes. Smart contracts are uniform blocks of bytecode that get run on the EVM; functions are a useful fiction added by higher-level languages such as Solidity. Smart contracts are APIs that you use to read from and update the global state. ABIs allow you to describe these APIs, making the contract run as bytecode easier to integrate with. You can use helpful command-line tools and some ingenuity to reverse-engineer transaction calldata, which helps reveal the predictable structure behind the hexadecimal. ABIs reflect the interfaces of the smart contracts from which they're compiled, so they need to be designed with the products in mind and updated when the contract updates.

The Bitcoin whitepaper from 2008 was a remarkable innovation, because it managed to solve a trenchant issue in the design of electronic currencies. A digital currency where individuals sign transactions using digital signatures would generally suffer from the double-spend problem: How does the system prevent somebody from sending the same assets twice? Traditionally, digital currencies resolve this problem by introducing a trusted third party. But trusted third parties introduce their own trade-offs:

> *Completely non-reversible transactions are not really possible, since financial institutions cannot avoid mediating disputes. The cost of mediation increases transaction costs, limiting the minimum practical transaction*

size and cutting off the possibility for small casual transactions ... With the possibility of reversal, the need for trust spreads. Merchants must be wary of their customers, hassling them for more information than they would otherwise need. A certain percentage of fraud is accepted as unavoidable.[1]

In short, trusted third parties increase costs and reduce the privacy benefits to using digital signatures. Bitcoin removed the need for this trust by creating a mechanism for distributed, trustless consensus of a payment mechanism.

We can model these payments neatly. Consider a standard database table. Each row represents an object, each column represents an attribute, and each cell represents a value (Figure 4-1).

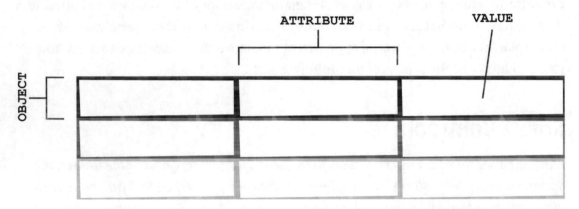

Figure 4-1. *Rows are objects, objects have attributes, and those (object, attribute) pairs have values*

So a single object (row) might have several attributes (columns) with corresponding values (cells). We can model Bitcoin accounts in the same way (Figure 4-2).

---

[1] From the Bitcoin whitepaper (https://web.archive.org/web/20140320135003/https://bitcoin.org/bitcoin.pdf); do read the whole thing, it's excellent.

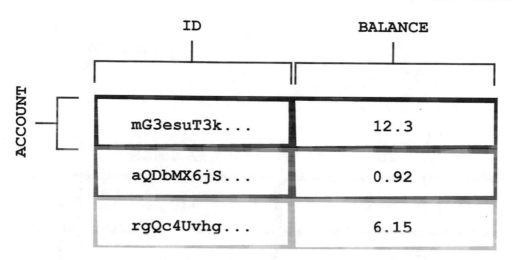

Figure 4-2. *Bitcoin accounts modeled in terms of objects, attributes, and values*

So a Bitcoin account (row) has two attributes: an id and a balance. A Bitcoin transaction moves an amount from one value on one row to another value on another row, as in Figure 4-3.[2]

---

[2] Bitcoin is actually implemented as an Unspent Transaction Output (UTXO); a Bitcoin transaction doesn't update an account in place, it destroys the first row and replaces it with the new value. This is an important part of the Bitcoin mechanism and is the most significant way in which this naïve account-based model doesn't fit to how Bitcoin actually works. But this isn't a book about Bitcoin; these paragraphs are used to motivate how and why Ethereum generalizes Bitcoin's functionality.

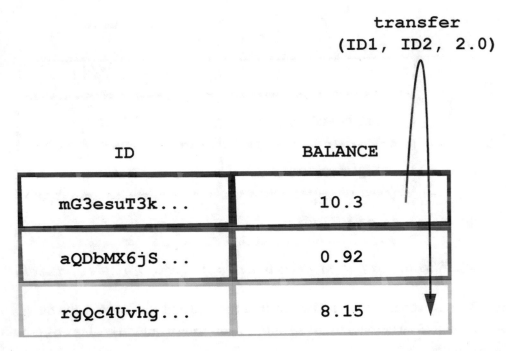

Figure 4-3. *Transferring an amount from one account to another can be modeled as moving it from one value on one row to another value on another row*

Our transfer function knows how to read our table and move an amount from one row to the other. What if we wanted to support multiple balances per account? We could add a second balance column. We'd then need to introduce a second transfer function which moved amounts from and to the second column. We might also want to introduce two other functions, to allow movement of amounts *between* the columns. Let's see what this looks like in Figure 4-4.

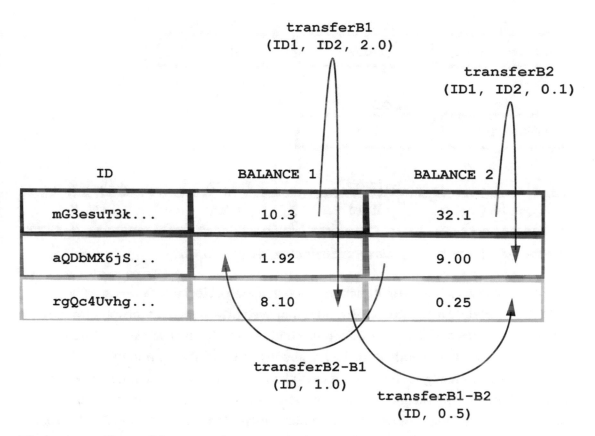

Figure 4-4. *If we add more columns, we need more functions to describe the movement of values between those columns (and between rows within a single column)*

This is already getting confusing, and if we wanted any more attributes than two, it would quickly get out of hand.

Instead of adding a bunch of columns (and the corresponding transfer functions), we could generalize the idea. Instead of attributes known *a priori*, we could say that rows can have any number of columns that they want, of whatever type they want. Each account then functions as its own database table, with its own, distinctive columns and rows, as in Figure 4-5.

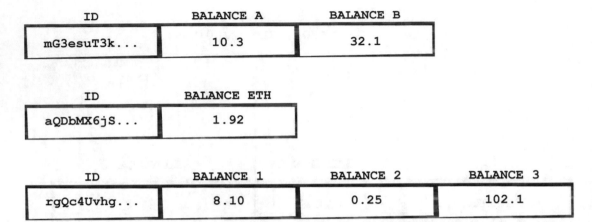

ID	BALANCE A	BALANCE B
mG3esuT3k...	10.3	32.1

ID	BALANCE ETH
aQDbMX6jS...	1.92

ID	BALANCE 1	BALANCE 2	BALANCE 3
rgQc4Uvhg...	8.10	0.25	102.1

Figure 4-5. *Each row has its own distinctive set of columns*

But this raises a bunch of implementation questions. How does a row specify that it holds certain attributes? (What does that even mean?) What's the logic for moving between columns of different types? Some computations won't even know which columns they want to update until they're already running: if a column name is generated dynamically, for instance, it won't know that it needs to change some value until after the user has begun the computation. So what would the semantics for a transfer look like if the column names are not known ahead of time? And, finally, what if the computation wanted to restrict which columns and rows can be updated based on who has permission? These sorts of issues are tricky to reason about when you're thinking in terms of a database table.

What you really need is a programming language: a way of declaring in code what data transformations you want to make and where. You could run an API that hosts blocks of code, and these blocks of code can then specify their own semantics for changes to the state.

What Ethereum gives us is a way of doing exactly this, but in a distributed and trustless manner. Our blocks of code are called *smart contracts*; these contracts can specify which attributes they care about, and, crucially, these contracts decide the rules through which the values of those attributes change. Smart contracts are therefore just computer programs, with some state, running on a computing platform hosted on the decentralized Ethereum network. This platform is called the *Ethereum virtual machine*.

This chapter explores smart contracts in a technical and detailed way. How do smart contracts work? How do they store state, and how do products read this state? And, above all, what does all this mean for the user?

What Does a Smart Contract Look Like?

As we've just discussed, smart contracts are programs. Programs are generally written in programming languages, with different languages designed to run at different levels of the stack, and for different sorts of programming. Ethereum is no exception: there are high-level languages and lower-level languages and the bytecode that sits underneath them. The most popular and well-known high-level smart contract programming language is called Solidity, and it's as close to an "official" high-level language as the Ethereum ecosystem is likely to get.

Contracts written in Solidity – or in any other high-level language, for that matter – get compiled down to bytecode. The bytecode is then executed on the EVM. This is essentially analogous to how hardware computers work: the bytecode refers to various operations that are executed on the abstract model – the instruction set – that the computer's hardware exposes. The CPU knows where to look for instructions (generally some a priori known portion of the computer's memory) and then reads the instructions sequentially. To make it easier to reason about, bytecode is mapped to a very slightly higher-level language called assembly. I'll use "bytecode" and "assembly" interchangeably here, but note that they are different.[3]

Note   The EVM is a stack machine, which means that working values are moved from temporary memory and permanent storage into a last-in, first-out list of values called a stack. It extends the standard sort of stack functions – arithmetic operations such as ADD, MUL, SUB, MOD, and friends; comparators such as LT, GT, and EQ; memory management functions such as MLOAD and MSTORE; and control flow operators such as JUMP and JUMPI – with various opcodes related to the Ethereum blockchain as a blockchain: ADDRESS, which returns the currently executing contract's address; GASPRICE, which returns the current gas price; BALANCE, which returns the ETH balance of a given account; and much more.

---

[3] Assembly code statements usually map 1:1 to the corresponding bytecode, and often assembly interpreters support comments, symbolic labels of various blocks of code, in-code constants such as strings, and other tools for making the code more legible, but as a general matter we can treat them as equivalents.

But the EVM is a virtual machine because contracts don't know in advance what underlying hardware the contracts will be run on. A validator node might be running on anything from a dedicated rig with custom chips to a Raspberry Pi. The EVM provides an abstraction layer between the code and the hardware, allowing the program to run anywhere that can support the EVM.

Writing a simple contract directly in bytecode is an informative exercise: you'll learn a lot in a short time how powerful the EVM can be, how it actually functions, and also how pleasurable writing code in modern languages is by comparison.[4] But for real-world programs, there are very few circumstances under which you will ever need to write directly in assembly. Higher-level languages are not only easier to write and read, they are also generally more performant and safer: the compiler knows a lot about how the EVM works and is able to add constraints to your code (such as strict typing and overflow/underflow checks) that make your code less error-prone and, in many cases, faster.

With that in mind, let's take a look at a simple contract written in Solidity:

```solidity
pragma solidity ^0.8.3;

contract HelloWorld {
    function greeting() public pure returns (string memory message) {
        message = "Hello, World!";
    }
}
```

There is quite a lot going on – Solidity, much like Swift, has a tendency to introduce new keywords in order to extend the language while maximizing backward compatibility – but the basic logic is simple. We specify a contract and give it a name. We then expose a public function called greeting. greeting takes no arguments and is marked pure – a way to tell Solidity that it doesn't access any storage – which allows the compiler to be stricter with the range of operations it will accept and optimize the code accordingly. greeting also returns a string which is held in memory. This string, called message, is set to "Hello, World!" and the value of the string is set into the function's return data.

When compiled to assembly, it looks like this:

---

[4] You'll also develop a renewed appreciation for the first generations of programmers, who wrote their software in assembly languages similar to the EVM's. For two great examples, see the source code to an early version of Microsoft's BASIC product (https://github.com/microsoft/GW-BASIC) or the Apollo 11 Guidance Computer source code by Margaret Hamilton's team at MIT (https://github.com/chrislgarry/Apollo-11).

```
PUSH1 80 PUSH1 40 MSTORE CALLVALUE DUP1 ISZERO PUSH2 0010 JUMPI PUSH1 00
DUP1 REVERT JUMPDEST POP PUSH2 017c DUP1 PUSH2 0020 PUSH1 00 CODECOPY PUSH1
00 RETURN INVALID PUSH1 80 PUSH1 40 MSTORE CALLVALUE DUP1 ISZERO ...
```

...and it goes on for another 1677 characters. I'll spare you the full bytecode here, but do run it through the compiler and take a look.[5] This assembly can then be transpiled into raw bytecode. For instance, the first few opcodes (up to and including the first CALLVALUE statement) become

```
60 80 60 40 52 34
```

It is this bytecode that the EVM executes. As you can see, writing in bytecode directly, or even the higher-level assembly, is far from straightforward and exposes the internals of the EVM to the programmer. Much of the assembly is not the program "proper": it has been amended by the compiler to handle bootstrapping and function execution. This bootstrapping logic may well vary between different compiler versions and different higher-level languages. What you write and what the compiler gives you are far from identical, functionally speaking.

For our current purposes, it is important to note that the entire smart contract's code is contained in this sequence of bytecode. A smart contract is simply its bytecode. And invoking the smart contract is the same thing as running the bytecode on the EVM – with the contract's state and the state of the broader blockchain harnessed around it – executing it fully for each function call.

Where is it executed? It's executed on the EVM. When a smart contract that writes to storage is executed, it needs to be validated by the rest of the network, so it is sent to the network to be executed and confirmed via the consensus mechanism (discussed in Chapter 1). When a smart contract that doesn't give rise to any state changes is executed, like ours, it can be run by whatever node receives the request. In both cases, the contract is run on the EVM hosted by a node.

A more abstract way to think of a smart contract, then, is a sequence of bytecode that performs a computation somewhere. The computation itself might be performed "over here," on a local node, or it might be performed "over there," on a set of validator nodes. This difference, and how it is implemented, is interesting and technical and outside the scope of this book. But it gives us a sense of what a smart contract is: it's a set of instructions for some computer to perform on our behalf.

---

[5] A good tool for playing with Solidity online is `www.evm.codes/playground`

The upshot of all this is that a smart contract is just a block of code, and that block of code is run whenever we call it. It might be structured into functions, as our example was. It might not be. We can call these functions, we may or may not pass some arguments to the functions, things may or may not happen, and we may or may not get a return value.

But what we can be sure of is that when we invoke a smart contract, we are running the contract in its entirety, and it is up to the contract to implement the conditional logic necessary to read our request and direct it within the assumed control flow of the contract. Functions are therefore a form of useful fiction, invisible to the EVM. We'll explore what this means in more detail – and how it affects building products – later in this chapter.

Contracts Are APIs

We began this chapter describing the most basic representation that a contract has: the bytecode that the EVM executes directly. We showed how higher-level languages such as Solidity wrap this bytecode in a different abstraction: one of functions and parameters and control structures. We also discussed how these programs are executed on a virtual machine, completely independent of the underlying hardware. This is a bottom-up inventory of the pieces of our contract.

These pieces, when assembled, give us something resembling the contracts as we thought of them during the introduction: as a way of expressing, in a Turing-complete language, transformations from one state to another. They also give us the framework for how we should think about contracts from the top-down: contracts are APIs.

An API, as you will know, is an Application Programming Interface: a protocol for communicating between two programs. It exposes an interface for applications to talk to one another through code. Our smart contract is an application responsible for managing state; our frontend is an application responsible for displaying and interacting with that state.

A large part of a product engineer's job is to understand the relationship between these two applications, to understand how to integrate their frontend, toolchain, analytics pipeline, or other off-chain applications with the underlying smart contract. And integrating with a smart contract is much the same as integrating with an API.

Of course, actually doing it has some complications, but the model in your head needn't be any more complex than that. A smart contract is an API. The API is an interface to some computation and some state. You call it when you want things and when you want things to happen.

So how do you call the API? Well, as we discussed in Chapter 2, you don't interact with the blockchain "directly." Your products will communicate with a node hosted on your behalf, and it is these nodes that provide the API. For this purpose, Ethereum nodes expose a JSON-RPC API that supports various standard methods.

It's worth reading the Ethereum docs[6] for the full list, but the two methods we'll be interested in here are eth_call, which is used for executing read transactions, and eth_sendRawTransaction, which is used for executing write transactions.

eth_call takes a simple JSON object as a payload. In its most basic form, it requires only one parameter:

```
{
  "to": "0x6B175474E89094C44Da98b954EedeAC495271d0F"
}
```

Issuing a generic read request to a contract is equivalent to saying "run the contract's bytecode." If the address is an EOA and not a contract, it's equivalent to saying "do nothing." Since at the EVM level there is no such thing as a function, running a contract runs the entire contract's code. Even when calling contracts written in a higher-level language such as Solidity, this is a valid request – Solidity will return 0x if a contract is invoked and no methods are defined – it's just not that useful.

We might wish to send some data along with our request so the contract can make some decisions about what we want to do:

```
{
"to": "0x6B175474E89094C44Da98b954EedeAC495271d0F",
"data": "0x0000000000000000000000000000000000000000000000000000000000000001
"
}
```

(Note that the calldata is hex-encoded and is a padded 32-byte word.) In this case, the contract can use the CALLDATALOAD opcode to bring the data value into the stack and begin operating with it. For instance, a basic contract written in bytecode might take the value from the calldata, add one to it, and return the resulting value:

```
PUSH1 0
CALLDATALOAD
```

---

[6]https://ethereum.org/en/developers/docs/apis/json-rpc

```
PUSH1 1
ADD
PUSH1 0
MSTORE
PUSH1 32
PUSH1 0
RETURN
```

A more complicated contract might use the calldata to point to various sections of the code, allowing the user to invoke a subset of the contract's functionality. This, of course, is exactly what the Solidity compiler does for us: it wraps our contract code with an efficient routing logic. Here's an example of a data field of a random transaction I pulled from Etherscan:

0x095ea7b3000000000000000000000000eafa962e6b2b49308bfbaca5d9955f46422dd9f70
00000000000000000000000000000000000000000000000007a120000000000000000000

This is basically incomprehensible: don't worry, we'll parse and explain it later! For now, all we need to understand is that this data field, like most transactions, is giving the contract bootstrap code instructions for which function to call, with which parameters.

As well as passing data, we can also send an amount of eth along with our contract call. This is what value is used for:

```
{
    "to": "0x6B175474E89094C44Da98b954EedeAC495271d0F",
    "value": "0x1"
}
```

In this case, the contract can use the CALLVALUE opcode to retrieve the value, send it elsewhere, or ignore it altogether. We won't linger on bytecode contracts for much longer, but it is useful to illustrate quite how simple the basic implementation of a contract is: it is a place where code is stored, and you can send it ether and data. We cover the various other properties of a transaction in Chapter 3 and explore the different semantics of transactions when these properties are used in combination.

One peculiarity you might have noticed earlier: eth_call supports keys that are related to write transactions. value is the amount of ether to be sent with the transaction, and value transfer requires a write to the blockchain. This exposes an interesting implementation detail of EVM clients.

`eth_call` can be used to simulate transactions, which allows the wallet and frontend to check that the transaction won't revert before any gas gets spent. The thing can be done via `eth_estimateGas`, which returns an estimated quantity of gas (we discuss this more in Chapter 3). `eth_call` is just a way of marking a transaction to the processing node as a read-only request. Nodes see that the transaction is marked read only and will prevent it from writing any state changes to the blockchain.

`eth_sendRawTransaction` is in some ways even simpler, because it takes a single parameter: the hex-encoded, signed bytecode string that describes the transaction. We won't worry about transaction signing here, but in order for a node to write to the blockchain, it needs a transaction cryptographically signed by the sender, to ensure its authenticity, as well as the gas required to process it.

Both of these methods are used by a node to read, verify, and calculate the desired state. Read transactions are executed locally by the node, the value returned to the sender. Write transactions are verified like read transactions, then broadcast to the network, as described in Chapter 2.

What node you use – what actual instance of the node software you connect to – is up to you. You can run your own node, participating in the network fully. But for most products, this is overkill. Running a node can be technically challenging: you are responsible for operating and scaling a complicated piece of software. Fortunately, there are several node-as-a-service providers that host a node for you, allowing you to read from and write to the blockchain with no operational overhead.

At the time of writing, the two most popular services are Alchemy[7] and Infura.[8] Both offer a similar product range, comparable speed and scalability, and a familiar use-based pricing model. Both also offer generous free plans, so it's easy to build and begin to serve customers without paying a penny. While Alchemy and Infura are the market leaders, there are other service providers that compete by providing adjacent APIs or support for different networks, such as QuickNode.[9] Even traditional cloud infrastructure providers such as Cloudflare, Amazon, and Google offer hosted Ethereum node services. Every provider implements the full Ethereum JSON-RPC specification.

---

[7] `www.alchemy.com`

[8] `http://infura.io`

[9] `www.quicknode.com`

Choosing between these providers is an important, but ultimately reversible, decision, so my advice is not to sweat it. I generally use Alchemy and have found their service excellent and their support superlative. But the core product is consumed in a simple way: many of the applications you build will only rely on basic EVM behavior, and therefore you can switch between node providers by changing a few lines of code.

Your node, then, whether hosted by a provider or run internally, is the gateway you use to connect to the various SCs (smart contracts) you interact with. It is the gateway to your API. You construct messages according to a standard set of conventions and submit them to the EVM via a node. The node executes the request and returns the response. (In practice, you don't even need to worry about that; later, we'll introduce frontend tooling that abstracts away the transaction construction process entirely.)

But before we move on to discussing how you construct these transactions, it's worth thinking about what the contracts-as-APIs model suggests and how far it applies. While the basic model seems correct, modern APIs have evolved to be functional and consumer focused, and the commonplace idea of an API has evolved far beyond. There are complications when integrating with smart contracts that are often not present with standard API integrations, and it's important not to think of smart contracts as much more than a list of functions.

Read functions of modern APIs have several desirable properties that contracts-as-APIs lack:

- Modern APIs are often **self-documenting and discoverable**. Parameter names, structured values, and what endpoints can be queried are often revealed by the API itself. Smart contracts don't have this sort of self-documenting behavior. Instead, product engineers rely on ABIs to describe the API, which we'll discuss in the next section.

- Modern APIs often provide **filtering, sorting, searching**, and other forms of data manipulation and querying. Smart contracts don't. When querying a smart contract, you'll usually get a raw form of the data and will have to filter and query it yourself. We'll discuss this in much more detail toward the end of this chapter.

- Modern APIs often provide **standardized error codes and messages**, using HTTP status codes, custom error objects, or a combination of both. Error handling when interacting with the EVM can be quite a bit more complicated. We discussed how it works – and, importantly, how it affects products – in the previous chapter.

- Modern APIs are often **versioned**, allowing the API developer to release backward-incompatible changes and allow clients to migrate over. Contracts at the bytecode level are immutable, but there are different methods used to version contracts which have various positives and negatives. Contract versioning is mostly a matter for protocol teams and therefore out of the scope of this book.

Modern APIs also provide support to clients making writes that smart contracts typically don't:

- Modern APIs often **return the results of state changes instantly**. Smart contracts generally don't. If an API is putting data into a centralized database, it can make certain guarantees about data durability at the moment it issues the write; SCs rely on a decentralized network to provide those guarantees, so estimating the duration and detecting when a transaction is successful can be more complicated.

- Modern APIs often provide **syntax and semantic input validation**. Smart contracts often don't, both because of gas costs – superfluous validation steps can be expensive – and because Solidity puts strict constraints on types, so a lot of the contract-level validation can be handled by the type checker.

Contracts are APIs, but these differences show that they are, in some ways, a primitive form of APIs, without the modern creature comforts of purpose-designed client libraries, rich and expressive self-documentation, complete input validation, and immediate feedback. Tooling has been developed to try to smooth over these rougher edges, and much of this book is concerned with how to smooth over them further. But computing is the science of the art of trade-offs, and this is no different: executing your code on a decentralized platform puts new and sometimes unfamiliar constraints on how to build products.

Commonly, the contracts-as-APIs model pushes a lot of work onto the frontend. Many crypto frontends are just UI wrappers around the contracts: they query the contracts directly and perform all filtering, sorting, etc., locally. This expands the remit of what product engineers need to care about. Often, a lot of business logic is held in the frontend. This logic is important and can be sophisticated: testing it properly is an important part of the job. Frontends also need to handle loading and confirmation states, data updates, and all the rest of the complexity associated with an external data store that can change underneath you. Toward the end of this chapter, we'll discuss how indexing can simplify some of these challenges, but be in no doubt: this can all get complicated. Most importantly, *you can rarely rely on the smart contract to give you what you need in the format in which you need it*. You should treat the protocol as a simple database table and generally consider yourself responsible for anything more advanced. We'll underline this point throughout this chapter.

From the perspective of a product, then, smart contracts should be treated as little more than a list of functions. This, however, raises a more specific question: If a smart contract should be treated as a list of functions, and the functions are useful fictions over a contract expressed in bytecode, how do we actually *call* them?

Application Binary Interfaces

So far, we've learned a lot about how smart contracts are implemented under the hood:

- Contracts are blocks of bytecode executed on the EVM.

- The EVM has no notion of a function; functions are a useful fiction.

- Nevertheless, products can treat smart contracts as lists of functions.

- These functions can be called through a JSON-RPC node, via `eth_call` (for reads) or `eth_sendRawTransaction` (for writes).

As we've seen already, contracts at the raw bytecode level are rather inscrutable. Even what constitutes a function call is a little unclear, since the very *concept* of a function is an abstraction provided to us by our higher-level language. This section is concerned with what this actually means in practice.

When you call a smart contract, the EVM executes whatever it finds at the contract's address. The EVM does not know about which function you wish to call, nor does it care. It's up to the contract's bytecode to handle an incoming request: decode the input, figure out what the user intends to do, disambiguate any values, and route these values through some sort of control flow. In other words, the contract itself implements its own function dispatch code.

Fortunately, as we've discussed, the compiler handles this for us when we write code in a higher-level language. Equally fortunately, most compilers have converged on a standardized way of doing it, which means that Solidity contracts can call Vyper functions, Vyper contracts can call Solidity functions, and that products off-chain can call functions written in either without needing to change the encoding to reflect the contract's higher-level language.

So, both Solidity and Vyper – and most other high-level smart contract languages – implement a standard set of representations for functions and parameters, allowing us to move from the scary and formless bytestring in the data field to something with some predictable structure.

This standard set of representations is an *encoding*, a set of rules that describes how to transform data into data that describes a function call and back again. This encoding is called an ABI, an *Application Binary Interface*. The rest of this section describes Ethereum ABIs in some detail. This stuff might seem overly formal, and deeply technical, and it is: but it's also one of the core pieces of infrastructure that links together products and smart contracts. Ignoring it and expecting to understand product engineering on Ethereum is equivalent to ignoring HTTP and expecting to understand websites; it's possible to get by, but implausible to understand, without it.

The best way to understand these encodings is to use them a few times, calling different functions with different values and observing how the changes in input affect the encoded output. But hidden behind the black box, illegible bytecode is a predictable and rather straightforward structure. In particular, this structure can be exposed visually, as in Figure 4-6.

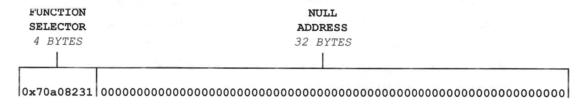

Figure 4-6. *We can break up the bytecode into different sections visually*

In the rest of this section, we will apply this visual pattern to show how the encoded bytecode expresses the function calls and real-world values to which we wish to refer.

Function and Argument Selectors

Remember the purpose of our encoding is to provide a standard way of selecting which function we'd like and specifying its arguments. So our encoding starts with the *function selector*.

In a standard smart contract *function call* transaction, the function selector is always the first four bytes of the ABI calldata and corresponds to the first four bytes of the hex-encoded hashed form of the canonical representation of the function signature. What does that mean? It sounds more complicated than it is. It boils down to this simple recipe:

1. **Write the canonical representation of the function signature.** This means the function's name and the types of its arguments, in order, in a specific, familiar form.[10] For example, let's say we have a balanceOf function, with a single argument of type address. We'd write it as balanceOf(address).

2. **Hash the function signature using the standard keccak hashing function.** balanceOf(address) hashes to 0x70a08231b98e-f4ca268c9cc3f6b4590e4bfec28280db06bb5d45e689f2a360be.

3. **Take the first four bytes.** Since a byte is eight bits, and therefore has 2^8 = 256 values, it can fit in two hex-encoded characters (since hex encoding has 16 possible values, instead of 2, and 16^2 = 256). So we want the first eight characters of the hex encoding, which gives us four bytes. (Remember that the 0x can be ignored; it's just an indicator that what is to follow is hex-encoded.) So our first four bytes are 0x70a08231.

4. **And that's it!** The call's data field will begin with 0x70a08231, which allows the dispatch code to identify the function balanceOf with a single address argument.

---

[10] "Canonical" here just means "standard." The ABI spec was developed into something resembling its current form during January 2015, before the network was launched in July of that year. By January 6, 2015, the spec used the first four bytes of the hashed function signature to encode the function selector (https://github.com/ethereum/wiki/wiki/Ethereum-Contract-ABI/e4a68831309765a13569a7bcba5359de0e38738e).

This is how we generate the function selector. (Another cool thing to notice: The argument types are included in the canonical representation. This means that higher-level languages like Solidity can support multiple dispatch on argument type; the ABI encodes the difference between balanceOf(address) and balanceOf(bool). The return type isn't included, so we can infer that Solidity doesn't support multiple dispatch on return type.)

We do the exact same thing that the dispatcher does, and then the dispatcher lines up the corresponding block of code to the function name we give it. That gets us our function. (In computer science lingo, the compiled contract contains a hash table from encoded function signatures to the location of the corresponding function implementation.) Since the dispatcher has done this process already, the dispatcher also now knows how many arguments there are and what types to expect for those arguments. The remaining calldata is the values for the arguments.

Sleuthing with Calldata

Let's dig into the calldata a little more and apply what we've learned to see how far we can reverse-engineer the scary data field earlier.

Each argument is padded to 32 bytes – so calldata length in bytes will always be a number divisible by 32, plus 4 for the signature – and there is a single 32-byte slot for each parameter. Some parameters are dynamically sized: in these cases – either an array, map, tuple, or a string/byte type – there is a 32-byte slot to encode the length and as many other slots needed to encode the individual values. Since the values are hex-encoded, 32 bytes is a 64-character string.[11]

Note   There are lots of excellent tools to help decoding and understanding hex values. I like the `cast` command-line tool from the Foundry project (`http://foundry.paradigm.xyz`) and especially the `checkthechain` tool (`https://github.com/fei-protocol/checkthechain`). Getting comfortable with tooling like this makes your life infinitely easier, and we'll see lots of examples of how.

---

[11] In binary, one byte is in the range 00000000 to 11111111. In hex encoding, one byte is in the range 0x00 to 0xFF. So a single byte is two characters long, and a 32-byte string is 64 characters long.

So our `balanceOf(address)` function needs a single 32-byte slot to encode a 20-byte address, plus the initial four bytes to encode the function signature. If we wanted to encode a call to get the balance of the null address, for instance, we can use the same bytecode as we saw in Figure 4-6:

```
0x70a082310000000000000000000000000000000000000000000000000000000000000000
```

We can apply the same visual approach to understanding the scary `data` value in the previous section. See Figure 4-7.

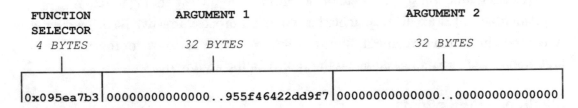

Figure 4-7. *Our 4-byte function selector is followed by two 32-byte arguments*

Our original `data` string:

```
0x095ea7b300000000000000000000000000eafa962e6b2b49308bfbaca5d9955f
46422dd9f7000000000000000000000000000000000000000000007a1200000000000000000000
```

Checking our visual representation tells us that our function selector is `0x095ea7b3`, and the argument list is

```
00000000000000000000000000eafa962e6b2b49308bfbaca5d9955f46422dd9f700000000
000000000000000000000000000000000007a1200000000000000000000.
```

The argument list is 64 bytes long, which suggests there are two 32-byte arguments. The first 32 bytes, our first argument:

```
00000000000000000000000000eafa962e6b2b49308bfbaca5d9955f46422dd9f7
```

We can use the `ctc` CLI tool to decode it to an integer representation:

```
$ ctc int 0x00000000000000000000000000eafa962e6b2b49308bfbaca5d9955
f46422dd9f7 1341492109310741895632184445170726783872781900279
```

A big number: We now know there aren't any dynamically sized arguments in our calldata. If there were, then we would need 1341492109310741895632184445170726783872781900279 32-byte slots! That would be a little excessive. So the argument list is definitely two arguments, not an array, or a string. It's also not a mapping: if it were a mapping, we'd expect to see a 0x0 value, since the storage layout rules work a little differently.[12] We have 64 bytes in our argument list, and the first argument isn't 1.

We have two arguments:

```
000000000000000000000000eafa962e6b2b49308bfbaca5d9955f46422dd9f7
```

and

```
000000000000000000000000000000000000000000000007a1200000000000000000
```

The first argument is probably an address. Why? Because the word is 20 bytes padded up to 32 bytes, and addresses are of length 20 bytes in hex. We can search the address in Etherscan to confirm. Our function selector therefore is of the form `someFunctionName(address,unknownType)`.

The second argument could be anything. If we try to decode it into an integer, we get another large number:

```
$ ctc int 0x000000000000000000000000000000000000000000000007a1200000000000000000
92233720368854775808000000
```

If we divide this number by 1e18 – ERC-20 tokens often have 18 decimal place precision – we get `92233.72036854775808000000`, which feels like a reasonable number of tokens to expect from some random transaction. But at this point, we're only doing guesswork.

Still, we've made some progress! Understood through this visual pattern, our bytecode string looks a little less scary. We still don't know what the function would be called in Solidity, because we only have the hashed function selector, and hashes aren't reversible. But we have an understanding of the *structure* and can infer a reasonable amount of information from just looking at this structure.

---

[12] Mappings store their data in the slot pointed to by the keccak256 hash of the mapping's index and the mapping's slot index. So if we wanted to get the value of a mapping stored at slot 0, at the string key foo, we'd need to calculate keccak("foo0") and then find the value at whatever slot that hex result gave us. Careful here, as certain keys also follow padding rules. See https://docs.soliditylang.org/en/v0.8.17/internals/layout_in_storage.html#mappings-and-dynamic-arrays for more. We'll look at how we can read mappings in more detail in Chapter 5 (section "Setting State Directly").

Finally, let's cross-reference what we know with the excellent 4byte directory. If we use the ctc tool ($ `ctc 4byte 0x095ea7b3`) to check our function signature, we see three[13] matching function signatures:

```
watch_tg_invmru_2f69f1b(address,address)
sign_szabo_bytecode(bytes16,uint128)
approve(address,uint256)
```

We can exclude the second signature easily: our first argument is an address of 20 bytes and so therefore isn't a `bytes16`. We can also probably exclude the first signature: the second argument likely isn't an `address`, because it's very unlikely that the first 19 characters of an address are zeroes! So we can, with some confidence, conclude that the matching function signature is the third option, `approve(address,uint256)`.

You won't need to do this sort of sleuthing very often, but understanding how it works is helpful. Moreover, this approach also extends to more complex cases. Suppose we have a contract that performs a calculation on an `initialValue` and a struct with two values, a `value` int and an `enabled` boolean. Our contract might look like this:

```solidity
pragma solidity ^0.8.16;

struct ToggledValue {
  uint value;
  bool enabled;
}

contract ToggledValueCalculator {
    function calculate(uint initialValue, ToggledValue calldata value)
    public pure returns (uint) {
        if (value.enabled) {
            return initialValue + value.value;
        }

        return initialValue;
    }
}
```

---

[13] As a useful exercise, consider why we often get more than one function signature for a given hash. Also consider what might happen if we defined two functions with the same function signature in the same contract.

We take the canonical form of uint (which is short for uint256), and we encode the struct as a tuple. Our function selector therefore looks like calculate(uint256,(uin t256,enabled)). With the initial value 0 and a ToggledValue of (404,true), we get

0x96ccb50300000000000000000000000000000000000000000000000000000000000000000000 0000000000000000000000000000000000000000000000000000000000000024000000000000 0000000000000000000000000000000000000000000000000000002000000000000000000000000 0000000000000000000000000000000000000034303400000000000000000000000000000000000 0000000000000000000000000001

which can be split up as in Figure 4-8.

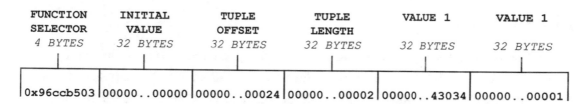

Figure 4-8. *The visual decoding is especially useful for larger bytecode strings*

Glancing at our visual encoding, we can see that our function selector is the first four bytes, 0x96ccb503. We then have the initial uint256 value:

0000000000000000000000000000000000000000000000000000000000000000

Then we have the offset for the tuple:

0000000000000000000000000000000000000000000000000000000000000024

Dynamic values, such as tuples and arrays, are encoded at the end of the function list. So instead of providing the tuple values themselves, we first provide the offset to *where in the calldata* the tuple begins. In our case, it's 36 bytes in: 4 bytes for the function name plus the 32 bytes for the initial value. 36 in hex is 0x24.

At that offset, we provide the *length* of the tuple:

0000000000000000000000000000000000000000000000000000000000000002

followed by the two values in sequence:

0000000000000000000000000000000000000000000000000000000000343034

117

and

001

Function and argument selectors look a lot more complicated than they actually are. Once parsed and broken down into function selector, plus argument list, and once the arrangement of dynamic values such as arrays and tuples are taken into account, the values can be read quite naturally. The trickiest bit is remembering that you're in hexadecimal!

We will, however, only get so far without knowledge of the underlying contract. That knowledge is what the ABI gives us.

ABI Schemas

Armed with our visual approach, and some sleuthing, the long strings of bytecode attached to transactions' calldatas look a little more familiar, even perhaps accessible. But in order to build a product against a set of contracts we know, we're still missing something important.

We know how to construct our calldata given we know the function. But contracts are APIs and can be thought of as a list of functions. An API without documentation would be an extremely hard thing to navigate; an ABI without a schema would be equally challenging.

It's especially difficult here because the mechanism that we use to generate the function selector – keccak256 hashing – isn't reversible. If you don't already know what the function signature looks like, it's impossible to get the human-readable function name from the encoded selector. The only thing you can do is have a list of function selectors and their corresponding signatures and map from selectors to signatures manually.

So each ABI offers a *schema*, a JSON file, an artifact that the compiler outputs alongside the bytecode for the contract, which describes the functions that the contract exposes. This is handy, because we can pull the schema into our frontend tooling and generate an API in our local language that allows us to call smart contract functions without ever considering the encoding step. As you build products on Ethereum, you'll see these ABI schemas everywhere: interacting with smart contracts would be nigh on impossible without them.

Because a contract is just a list of functions – and, as we've discovered, some dispatch code for switching between them – the ABI is also just a list of functions. For each function, the corresponding ABI describes the inputs and their types, the outputs and their types, and any events that the function might emit (we'll talk more about events in a bit). An example ABI for our `balanceOf(address)` function:

```
[{
  "inputs": [
    { "internalType": "address", "name": "account", "type": "address" }
  ],
  "name": "balanceOf",
  "outputs": [
    { "internalType": "uint256", "name": "", "type": "uint256" }
  ],
  "stateMutability": "view",
  "type": "function"
}]
```

This is incredibly helpful, because it gives us a description of the public interface for the API that we're building against. We have the name in English, the parameters in the `inputs` array, the values it outputs, and the function's *state mutability*, a Solidity keyword that describes whether the function reads from, writes to, or doesn't even touch the state.

What this ABI document gives us, then, is the list of functions we can call in our product. As I just mentioned, this list can be passed into our frontend tooling. *ethers.js*, for instance, has a `Contract` object that takes the ABI array as a parameter:

```
const contract = new ethers.Contract(contractAddress, abi);
```

The *ethers.js* system will read the ABI and generate functions on the contract object that we can call directly:

```
const result = await contract.balanceOf(accountAddress);
```

Importantly, it also marshals values into appropriate types. Values from smart contracts are often large numbers, far beyond what JS's native number handling can handle. So `balanceOf`-style calls will generally return an instance of `ethers.BigNumber`, an `ethers.js`-specific class that provides indefinitely large number representation and operation.[14]

Thanks to tooling like *ethers.js*, then, we can take an ABI and build against the contract, insulated from the underlying calldata entirely.

The Origins of ABIs

ABIs are important to validate, because changes to the contract's interface might change the ABI. Since the deployed contract is just bytecode, and we use the ABI to map our function calls onto this bytecode, if the bytecode changes and we don't update the ABI then our product could break at runtime.

This is especially important during development, when the underlying interface can change quite a bit as the functionality is refined. Product engineers should be in constant contact with protocol engineers, providing feedback on interfaces. There are lots of useful questions you can ask during contract development and review:

- Does the contract have the read functions you need?

- Do you need to pull a specific element from some map, and does the contract provide a getter for this map?

- What are the invariants for function arguments? Do they have minima/maxima that you need to validate in the frontend or design the UI around? What is the expected range for a return value?

- Under what conditions does the contract revert?

- Can the contract be paused in some way? In what other ways might the contract not work correctly at runtime?

---

[14] Be careful not to confuse `ethers.BigNumber` and one of the other JS big number libraries, such as *bignumber.js*. Many crypto frontends import both for various reasons. I've lost many hours of my life due to strange conversions between the two. TypeScript in-editor type hints help a little, but it's very easy to squint and miss the difference.

- Is there another interface in the application that has the same shape? Could we make sure that the method names and argument types are the same and in that way increase the amount of frontend code we can reuse?

- Does it emit events? Are the event arguments indexed? Are the event arguments you need indexed?

Being attentive during the smart contract development process can help shape the interface to the product's needs, and asking the preceding questions, regularly and forcefully, is a large part of making that happen. This extends also to the functionality of the contract itself. Could a parameter be validated more rigorously? Could an error message be more explicable or easier to parse? Will a particular user flow require several transactions, and, if so, can the contract expose a wrapper function to perform the flow in one? Your job as a product engineer is to worry not just about the technology but the humans using it, and this means pushing to ensure that the contract is easy to build against and produces minimal friction to the users.

It's also important to consider where you're getting the ABIs from. When using ABIs with a tool like *ethers.js*, as gestured to earlier, you'll need access to the ABI in your frontend code. Where is that coming from? If you're building against your protocol team's in-house codebase, you might be able to copy the ABI directly from the repository into your frontend. But what if your protocol team is shipping quickly and regularly? In that case, you might want to add an automated step to your build process to copy it across for you.

Some open source protocols may publish their ABIs in their GitHub repositories, but many don't. In those cases, you may need to clone the repository, install its dependencies, and figure out how to build it. Many legitimate protocols will also verify their contracts on Etherscan, which you can find on the contract's Etherscan page. Copying this ABI code into your repository can be the quickest way to begin building against the contract, but you'll need to check frequently to make sure the code doesn't change. Etherscan has an API which you can use to pull the latest ABI for a given contract, if one exists. You may also need to worry about whether the contract is a proxy contract, in which case you may wish to use the ABI of the underlying contract the proxy is proxying into.

In short, none of this is easy, and the tooling just isn't good enough yet.[15] One open source project idea is to package up many common contract ABIs into npm packages, to allow product engineers to add them as they would any other frontend dependency. This would provide an easy developer experience and ABI versioning. This sort of approach might be useful in larger teams internally, too. But I haven't seen many teams do this, and there currently isn't an open source repository of the sort that I am envisaging. The EIP-2678 standard, which provides a standard packaging format for smart contracts, has promise, but is not widely implemented, despite being over two years old.[16]

As of this writing, then, the "easiest" thing to do is to literally copy the files across into your repository. Many repos will have a `src/contracts` directory with various TypeScript and JSON files for each dependent contract, allowing the frontend to import the contract's address and ABI. But this can get messy quickly, especially when dealing with deployments with different addresses and/or ABIs over several chains. (Nor is this some five-sigma edge case; if developing against a forked local node with a new version of a contract, it's very likely that you'll have separate addresses for your updated local version and the current version on the mainnet.)

While the ABI gives you some guarantees, then, it has some limits. It only gives you guarantees about aspects of the contract's *interface*, not its runtime behavior. It also only gives you those guarantees if you are using the correct ABI. So it is important to get as much context from the protocol team, either by reading the contract yourself or by asking them directly or better still both. It's also important to ensure that you are building against an up-to-date ABI. If you lack context, ask for it. If a contract looks difficult to build against, message your teammates and ask them to change it. Provide feedback and suggestions. Make sure that product engineers are a part of the pull request review process and get good at reading and reasoning about Solidity. Be a fly on the wall of their meetings, and speak up if something is confusing or might make your life more difficult. Also, consider ways of making your ongoing development easier. How can you get updated ABIs and addresses of contracts into your repo with minimal fuss? Many protocol teams will host contract addresses and prebuilt ABIs in their GitHub repositories; could they publish it as an npm package?

---

[15] The `ctc` tool that we used earlier has an `abi` command, allowing you to pull the ABI from Etherscan from your terminal. Try running `$ ctc abi 0x1f9840a85d5aF5bf1D1762F925BDADdC4201F984 DOUBLEHYPHENjson` and see what you get.

[16] https://eips.ethereum.org/EIPS/eip-2678

That being said, there are times when the protocol team will be constrained in other ways. The audit cycle and the demand for correctness in smart contract code is much higher – it's a lot more expensive to push a fix to a smart contract than it is to a frontend – so there needs to be give and take. But in my experience, the voice of the product engineer, and therefore the voice of the user, is often drowned out by more immediate technical challenges. So, product engineers: be loud.

Contract State

There are several different places where Ethereum can store state. Some sources of state cost gas to read from and write to. Other sources of state are restricted to read-only or can only hold a limited amount of data. State is usually revealed through the contract's getter methods. In some cases, you may need to inspect the contract's storage directly. Contracts are severely memory and cost constrained. In many cases, then, you should handle filtering, sorting, and other operations at the product level rather than expect the contract to do it for you.

Ethereum is a state machine: it enables us to move the system from one state to another in an atomic way. We do this at the level of accounts: either smart contracts, with their own set of attributes and values, or EOAs, with their ether amount. Transactions, as we've discovered, then provide the mechanism for changing this state atomically. Given how central the notion of state is to Ethereum, it's worth spending a little bit of time on how smart contracts store state. In this section, we'll take a look at the different sorts of state available to contracts and consider the gas costs attached and the opcodes that do so.

Several Types of State

The majority of discussions of contract state draw attention to three main places where state can be stored. The first of these places is the **stack**. The EVM is a stack-based virtual machine: each contract gets a dedicated space of working memory called a stack, the parameters to its opcodes are stored in this working memory, and generally the results of its operations are written back there. The stack can hold 1024 items, where each item is 32 bytes long. The stack is last-in, first-out: so the last value pushed in will be read first.

Augmenting the stack, each contract is given an ephemeral block of **contract memory**. This block of memory is *addressable*: you can choose where you want to write and read from by specifying an address within the memory. Contract memory is a simple array of bytes, and reading and writing to contract memory is like reading and writing to a normal array. You specify an index and the value you wish to write; that value is written to memory at that index.

Ethereum's memory isn't limited per se; rather, it's limited by the total amount of gas you can fit into a given block. The MSTORE bytecode consumes three gas and, like the stack, stores 32-byte words. In theory, the total amount of gas you can use in a single transaction is the total amount of gas you can fit in a block (since, in theory, a block could contain one transaction only).

There is a hard gas limit on blocks (currently 30 million), so you could provide up to 30 million gas worth of memory, which is ~32MB.[17] But this would be rather a waste of money: the memory is ephemeral, so will be lost at the end of the transaction, and if you fill the transaction with millions of MSTORE codes, you won't have any other room to *do* anything with that data.

Finally, the third type of state is **contract storage**. This is permanent, addressable storage for your contract. It's where values go when you set them as contract-level variables in Solidity. Like everywhere else, storage is divided in 32-byte slots.

Storage is written using the SSTORE opcode, which takes the storage address as its first parameter and the value to write there as its second parameter. Storage is read using SLOAD, which takes the storage address as a parameter and puts the value on the stack.

Because it's permanent, it's also a lot more expensive. At the time of writing, an SSTORE opcode costs 100 gas at a minimum. If the value is new – that is, if the value before this transaction is 0 – the base cost is 20,000 gas. The gas cost is then increased by 2100 when the storage slot is *cold*: when it hasn't already been written to within the current transaction. Similar logic applies to SLOAD: a cold storage load costs 2100 gas, and a warm storage load costs 100.

---

[17] The cost of memory scales quadratically according to the formula $3a * (a^2 / 512)$, where a is the number of words allocated. So setting this equation to 30 million gets us $a = 123170$, or 3941440 bytes, or ~32MB.

This means that writing a value to a storage slot for the first time costs 22,100 gas, and reading from a storage slot for the first time this transaction costs 2100. On Ethereum, there are no ongoing fees for storage: once it's in storage, it's there for good. But it does mean that storing and reading lots of values can be expensive, and these are fees that your users are likely to have to pay.

Compilers can do some of the work in optimizing the gas requirements of the protocol code, but that optimization is imperfect. As a result, protocol engineers are wary of relying too much on storage. You can't just reach for more memory as you might in JavaScript.

There are four other forms of state on the EVM, lesser understood as such, but often just as useful.

The first is the **transaction logs**. As far as contracts are concerned, these logs are epiphenomenal: contracts cannot read from log storage, so logs (and the events that emit them) are simply side effects. We'll discuss logging in much greater detail later in this chapter.

But logging is reasonably cheap (up to 1875 gas), and logs can be queried off-chain. As such, they are a useful form of storage, especially for values the contract itself won't need to query later.

It's easy to forget, but the **calldata** in a transaction also encodes state. Indeed, that's the whole point of calldata; it's a way of getting state out of the user's system and into the smart contract's. Calldata can be loaded into the stack using CALLDATALOAD and into memory using CALLDATACOPY. Calldata is usually wrapped up in ABI semantics, but that doesn't mean it needs to be considered as separate from the contract's state.

If a piece of information is likely to stick around in the user's system, it might be worth considering passing it in as a part of the calldata (usually as a parameter to a function call), essentially outsourcing the storage requirement from the contract to the user. You might, for instance, not need to store a signature on the contract if the user's system can regenerate it; you can simply validate and discard it.

Finally, you can store state in the **contract runtime bytecode**. Contracts are created via a transaction. The transaction's bytecode is executed by the EVM, and the bytecode that that code returns is hosted as the contract; in Solidity, the contract's constructor is executed only when the contract is deployed. This means there are two types of contract bytecode: the *creation bytecode* and, the value it returns, the *runtime bytecode*.

Solidity contracts will embed the compiled runtime bytecode within the creation bytecode appropriately. But Solidity will also be smart about putting constants in the runtime bytecode, saving storage and memory space, as well as any arguments to the contract's constructor. Once the contract is deployed, you can't write to the runtime bytecode anymore – contracts are immutable – but it is worth poking around the bytecode of unfamiliar contracts to see what is stored there. This storage is limited: there is a 24KB limit on contract size, so the contract's runtime bytecode, plus any values, need to fit into this space.

Accessing State

Once we know where the state is going to go, we need to know how we can access it, especially from our products. So much of product engineering is about understanding the relationship between the state, the product that wishes to consume or alter it, and the limitations that need to be understood.

By far, the easiest way to access a piece of state through a node is to *call a smart contract function that returns it*. The smart contract can implement a getter function: a function that returns the value you're interested in. These functions can be inspected on Etherscan and invoked through the sort of tooling we've already discussed. Libraries like ethers.js can wrap a known contract, with a known ABI, giving you a simple function to call in your JavaScript. Sometimes, you might run into some weirdness with the types of inputs and outputs, but these confusions are usually cleared up by a careful reading of the smart contract code (or a productive conversation with its authors!).

If, however, the contract doesn't provide a getter, or the return value is hard to parse, consider *why*:

- It might be **a piece of state that is meaningless or incomplete** without some other computation; it might represent multiple values packed together or some other natty gas optimization.

- The contract can and may delete, change, update, transform, or otherwise alter the value. If the contract doesn't expect somebody to read it, **the contract has no obligation to not change** everything from out underneath you. No interface, no promise.

If using a contract's public API is an option, then you should always, always take it. And if you can be a part of *designing* this public API, you always, always should be. There are, however, a few conditions when you can't avoid reading from storage directly:

- You don't know the contract's ABI, and you're poking around the storage trying to ascertain what the contract does.

- The contract doesn't expose a reader method for the value you want.

- The contract does expose a method, but it is guarded – by some authentication mechanism – or otherwise difficult to access.

In these cases, you can use the RPC method eth_getStorageAt (or a local forked alternative such as hardhat_setStorageAt).

State and Product

The upshot of all this is that contract state is confusing, technical, and often hostile to building your products. Learning how and where Ethereum manages its state, even if you're only ever interacting with the public interface, is useful: knowledge of the underlying environment can be a valuable help when debugging and building tools.

In fact, this entire section came from notes that I took while building a tool to help seed testnet accounts with tokens and deposits. Our problem was that testing our frontend end to end was challenging, because various user flows required complicated test setup. An account might need certain tokens, deposits into various lending pools, or a specific NFT in order to test a certain scenario. Testing on the mainnet had all the problems you'd expect: it was expensive, slow, and cumbersome. Testing on a testnet wasn't possible either, since not every contract we needed had been deployed on our chosen testnet (and it was also slow and cumbersome). So we wanted to test locally, using a forked version of the mainnet, with pregenerated accounts that could be configured programmatically.

We wrote a tool so that we could specify, declaratively, an account and its relevant claims and deposits. This tool needed to work across many different contracts, some of which had permissions or other constraints that made doing it through a higher-level interface difficult. We used eth_getStorageAt and hardhat_setStorageAt to update the storage for our addresses directly, by "reaching in" to the state and adjusting it.

These sorts of skills are crucial for the product and platform engineer, as well as the protocol engineer, since the tooling in Ethereum is still so young and the set of technical problems that you'll face are still so varied.

There is another important consequence of these storage decisions and trade-offs: gas becomes a relevant constraint for both protocol and product.

Good protocol engineers are mindful of using storage, because using it too much pushes up the costs for anybody interacting with the protocol. This means that values are typically stored in a simple and often product-unfriendly way. Duplicating data costs gas, so values are stored on the contract in their canonical form. This can make querying the contract state directly inelegant. There is no `Object.keys` method available for Solidity mappings!

A lot of the computation typically associated with APIs, then – querying, filtering, sorting, transforming the raw data into something closer to what the frontend needs – is generally not conducted at the smart contract level. Unless you're doing indexing (see the "Indexing" section in this chapter for more), you'll need to do a lot of this work yourself in the frontend. Understanding where and how this state is stored is crucial to much of this work.

A final thought: Given these gas constraints and how they shape the smart contracts' public APIs, consider whether you can perform the more costly write work yourself. Google doesn't scrape the Web every time a user makes a search. That's because it needs to scrape the Web a lot less frequently than it is queried; so they do the costly work ahead of time and thereby speed up the queries. Similarly, by doing much of the writing ahead of time (either when needed or on some predefined cadence), you can save your users gas fees and reduce the friction in using your protocol. These decisions are *product* and *business* decisions as much as protocol decisions and give another reason why it's important for product engineers to be a part of the protocol's design phase. You might also make your protocol engineers happier in the process!

Ethereum's Event Model

Events are side effects of transactions. Events are an abstraction on top of a lower-level primitive, EVM logs. Logs can be filtered in various ways. Tools such as ethers.js *make handling events much easier. Events can be subscribed to as well as pulled on demand. The ease of subscribing to events needs to be balanced against the necessity for correct data, or else you may violate the Principle of Trust.*

Events are smart contract epiphenomena; they are side effects of smart contract execution. They cannot be read by smart contracts, either during the transaction in which they are emitted or later. As far as the contract is concerned, its event log is like an apartment block rubbish chute: you throw things down it and forget it ever existed.[18]

External observers to the blockchain, however, can read events. And this asymmetry of access is a superpower: it gives contracts a lightweight and cheap way to record data without worrying about the contract's history, and frontends a lightweight and cheap way to pull historical data from the blockchain.

In this section, we'll look into how events are implemented in contracts and, more importantly, how they power products built on top of those contracts.

Contract Logs

Logs are a cheap and general-purpose way for contracts to record information – cheap because the logging EVM opcodes are priced with in a reasonable range of values (approx. 375 to 1875 gas), and general purpose because logs are simple bytestrings; logs themselves contain little assumed structure.

The data field encodes whatever data the contract wishes to log: this is pulled from the contract's memory (see the section "Contract State" in this chapter for more on memory) and, like much else, is hex-encoded. The topics field is an array of up to four 32-byte words. Topics can be used for filtering – but we'll get on to that later.

Not all transactions will have logs. If you don't invoke a smart contract, there is nothing to log; the EVM doesn't create logs for ether transfers between accounts, for instance.[19] If you invoke a smart contract, that contract isn't required to call any of the logging opcodes. So it's up to the protocol team to decide whether the contracts will log events. As a result, you generally can't replace contract read calls with events entirely. But they can supplement direct reads, and many contracts will expose useful information in their logs. With these caveats in mind, let's see some examples of where we might find logs and what they look like.

---

[18] In fact, they're not even part of the blockchain proper: they aren't used for consensus, so participating nodes don't strictly need to know anything about them.

[19] Although it nearly did! See Vitalik's blog post "The roads not taken" for more (`https://vitalik.ca/general/2022/03/29/road.html`).

The first place where you'll notice these log outputs are in the transaction receipt. If we add to a call, we can see a transaction's receipt. We won't analyze the entire receipt in detail – we discussed receipts in the last chapter – instead, our focus will be on the key:

```
$ ctc tx 0xe981fe5c78d11d935a1dc35c579969e65e2dd6bb05ad321ea9670f8b1e203e
af --json --receipt
{
    ...
    "logs": [
        {
            "address": "0xfd3300a9a74b3250f1b2abc12b47611171910b07",
            "blockHash": "0x31ca8a95a453f99f903e1bce5f0cc2619a790e6c802d94e
            6495e30b35b44e8d3",
            "blockNumber": "0xdff643",
            "data": "0x00000000000000000000000000000000000000000000a696
            06d83098d8eea7e60800000000000000000000000000000000000000
            000000000000000093f16d65b5b8a0000000000000000000
            0000000000000000000000000000000ecaae6d5916c2350
            0000000000000000000000000000000000000000000005c6663
            dd81bf07a1f2d9",
            "logIndex": "0xe1",
            "removed": false,
            "topics": [
                "0x4dec04e750ca11537cabcd8a9eab06494de08d-
                a3735bc8871cd41250e190bc04"
            ],
            "transactionHash": "0xe981fe5c78d11d935a1dc35c579969e65e2
            dd6bb05ad321ea9670f8b1e203eaf",
            "transactionIndex": "0xef"
        },
        ...
    ],
    ...
}
```

Each log object gives us a full description of the log message, including the address that emitted it and the transaction in which it was emitted. Since a log is just some data, the key is generally the most important feature. And, as we've already said, it is general purpose. If a smart contract wishes to log a random string of bytes, it can.

We'll get the transaction receipt when we send a transaction to our provider, and, importantly, *once that transaction has been validated*:

```
const tx = {
  to: "0x8ba1f109551bD432803012645Ac136ddd64DBA72",
  value: utils.parseEther("1.0")
};

const transactionResponse = await signer.sendTransaction(tx);

const transactionReceipt = await provider.waitForTransaction(
  transactionResponse.hash
);

console.log(transactionReceipt.logs); // => []
```

(Our log output of the preceding function will be an empty array, since, as shown earlier, nonsmart contract calls don't output logs.) Managing the signer and provider can be fiddly, especially under the constraints of the React render cycle, so we can use the wagmi package to get the transaction receipt too:

```
const { config } = usePrepareSendTransaction({
  request: { to: '0x8ba1f109551bD432803012645Ac136ddd64DBA72', value:
  utils.parseEther("1.0") },
})

const { data: transactionResponse, sendTransaction } =
  useSendTransaction(config);

const { data: transactionReceipt } = useWaitForTransaction({
    hash: transactionResponse.hash,
});

useEffect(() => {
  console.log(transactionReceipt)
```

```
}, [transactionReceipt]);

return sendTransaction()}>Send;
```

We can also query the logs of an account directly:

```
const logs = await provider.getLogs({
  address: "0xdAC17F958D2ee523a2206206994597C13D831ec7",
});
```

Under the hood, the provider sends the node an RPC call, which the node then executes. But logs can add up quickly, and querying all possible logs from a busy address can overload the node and/or make the response value too large to send reliably over the network and parse. On a busy node, or when querying a busy contract, therefore, you will almost certainly run into problems getting the entire log output through getLogs.

To stop their nodes grinding to a halt, Alchemy puts some restrictions on read calls to logs. See what happens when we try to query a busy contract from block 0:

```
const logs = await provider.getLogs({
  address: "0xdAC17F958D2ee523a2206206994597C13D831ec7",
  fromBlock: 0,
})
// => Error: processing response error (body="{\"jsonrpc\":\"2.0\",\"id\"
:42,\"error\":{\"code\":-32602,\"message\":\"Log response size exceeded.
You can make eth_getLogs requests with up to a 2K block range and no limit
on the response size, or you can request any block range with a cap of 10K
logs in the response. Based on your parameters and the response size limit,
this block range should work: [0x0, 0x599bff]\"}}", error={"code":-32602},
requestBody="{\"method\":\"eth_getLogs\",\"params\":[{\"fromBlock\":\"0x0\
",\"address\":\"0xdac17f958d2ee523a2206206994597c13d831ec7\"}],\"id\":42,\
"jsonrpc\":\"2.0\"}", requestMethod="POST", url="...", code=SERVER_ERROR,
version=web/5.7.1)
```

Other nodes may drop the request entirely or only return a partial response. It's therefore advisable to query the most minimal possible subset of logs for a contract (or group of contracts). If, for some reason, you need everything, you can paginate the blocks into 2000 block chunks. But there are usually smarter strategies. We'll discuss how to filter in the section "Log Filters," a few pages later, and the implications of all this for frontends in the subsequent "Events and Product" section. For now, however, we'll take a look at the event abstraction, which sits on top of basic contract logs.

Events

In the section "Contracts Are APIs," we discussed how functions are a useful fiction on top of the smart contract primitive: an abstraction given to us from the Solidity compiler, rather than from the EVM itself. Events are much the same. As we've just seen, the EVM exposes logs. The EVM doesn't have the notion of an event; that's given to us by the ABI spec (and by whatever higher-level compiler and tooling that implements it).

So what does the ABI spec say about events? It's an elegant abstraction on top of the existing building blocks we already have:

- **Event selectors**, which encode through a keccak256 hash the name of a function and the types of its parameters

- **Contract logs**, which allow a contract to output data and up to four 32-byte words called topics

Events use these two features to encode and record events in a retrievable way. How does this work? Very similarly to functions. Events allow us to make sense of a transaction's logs, in the same way that functions allow us to make sense of a contract's bytecode. They give structure and names and semantics to transaction logs.

Firstly, let's look at how an event is declared in Solidity:

```
event Transfer(address indexed from, address indexed to, uint256 amount);
```

When compiled, the ABI spec will include this event in the following form:

```
{
    "anonymous": false,
    "inputs": [
        {
            "indexed": true,
            "internalType": "address",
            "name": "from",
            "type": "address"
        },
```

```
        {
            "indexed": true,
            "internalType": "address",
            "name": "to",
            "type": "address"
        },
        {
            "indexed": false,
            "internalType": "uint256",
            "name": "amount",
            "type": "uint256"
        }
    ],
    "name": "Transfer",
    "type": "event"
},
```

A quick glance at our Solidity code, and its corresponding ABI fragment, reveals a few interesting properties:

- Events can be **anonymous** or not.

- Events have **names**.

- Events have **typed inputs**.

- Those inputs can be **indexed** or not.

So events are named and typed, just like our functions. Some of the parameters are *indexed* – we'll talk about that more in a moment – and some of the events are marked *anonymous*. Our events can be emitted by the contract code:

```
emit Transfer(address(0), address(1), 2);
```

Note   The `emit` statement isn't quite state-modifying, since the contract's state itself won't change – events are epiphenomena! – but the total blockchain state will change, since the log needs to be tied to a validated transaction. So you can't emit events in read-only functions.

Since events are just an abstraction over logs, we can find our event in the output of the transaction receipt:

```
"logs": [
    {
        ...
        "data": "0x0000000000000000000000000000000000000000000000000000000000
        000000002",
        "topics": [
            "0xddf252ad1be2c89b69c2b068fc378daa952ba7f163c4a11628f55a4d
            f523b3ef",
            "0x0000000000000000000000000000000000000000000000000000000000000
            00000",
            "0x0000000000000000000000000000000000000000000000000000000000000
            00001",
        ],
    },
],
```

The first entry in the array is our *event selector*. We calculate it in exactly the same way as we calculate our function selectors. Take the canonical form of the event name, in our case:

```
Transfer(address,address,uint256)
```

And run it through keccak256:

```
$ ctc keccak "Transfer(address,address,uint256)"
0xddf252ad1be2c89b69c2b068fc378daa952ba7f163c4a11628f55a4df523b3ef
```

which matches our topics[0]!

The subsequent entries in the topics array are the *indexed* parameters. We can see two 32-byte words, representing from and to (the values we've emitted in our contract). We can only use four topics in total, so we can only provide three parameters. Finally, the string contains the remaining nonindexed parameters. In our case, there's just one: the integer 1, corresponding to the parameter amount.

And what about the `anonymous` marker? Events can be marked anonymous in the event declaration:

```
event Transfer(address indexed from, address indexed to, address amount)
anonymous;
```

This affects the output in one noticeable way:

```
"logs": [
    {
        ...
        "topics": ["0x0000000000000000000000000000000000000000000000
        000000000000000", "0x0000000000000000000000000000000000000000000
        0000000000000000000001",
```

The event signature is gone – `anonymous` simply removes the event signature from the topics output, freeing up an extra topic entry. Anonymous events can therefore have *four* parameters, rather than three – but lose the ability to filter by event name in the process.

So, to sum up, events are an abstraction over the log functionality in the same sort of way that functions are an abstraction over the contract bytecode functionality. It's an elegant abstraction, because it combines existing features and slots into the ABI spec without introducing too much extra complexity. But it's also a clever abstraction, because it allows products to use another piece of functionality that we'll talk about next: filtering over log topics.

Log Filters

We have discussed earlier how `getLogs` can return an overwhelming amount of data and how node software will generally limit the number of logs you can retrieve in one call. The best strategy is to request only a subset of the logs you need. Now we know how logs work and how they are wrapped up into events by Solidity and the ABI, we can discuss how we might filter our events and restrict the return data to a more manageable size.

It is, in fact, possible to query every event emitted by every block; each of the arguments to `getLogs` is optional – but your node provider might have something to say if you were to try. It is best to avoid such conversations with an angry DevOps engineer, and "I'm sorry I crashed your server" cards are hard to find in a Hallmark store. With these concerns in mind, no doubt, the Ethereum spec helpfully provides filtering mechanisms by contract, block, and topic.

We've actually already seen one example of filtering, filtering by contract address:

```
const logs = await provider.getLogs({
  address: "0xdAC17F958D2ee523a2206206994597C13D831ec7",
});
```

This call will return *some* subset of the most recent events from the USDT contract. What subset? It's kind of hard to tell. USDT is a popular token, with many events emitted. Let's scope down the events we're interested in and get a better idea of what's happening.

One way to scope our events down is by block. If we know the *block hash* – the 32-byte hash that represents the current block – we can query directly for a specific block:

```
const logs = await provider.getLogs({
  blockHash:
    "0xf2712eff4e94fee78b52dfb46b797c08394f69be1bea45e40245b12544003b59",
  address: "0xdAC17F958D2ee523a2206206994597C13D831ec7",
});
```

This returns 12 log events for this contract, at this block.[20] If we don't know the block hash, or we want to query several blocks at once, we can use a range of block numbers:

```
const logs = await provider.getLogs({
  fromBlock: 15725066,
  toBlock: 15725067,
  address: "0xdAC17F958D2ee523a2206206994597C13D831ec7",
});
```

---

[20] If you check the `topic[0]` value of any of these, you'll see `0xddf252ad` – the very same event selector that we used earlier. So each of these 12 events is `Transfer(address,address,uint256)` events! It does, however, also mean that we can't filter for anonymous events.

Finally, we can filter by topic. Since our value encodes the event selector, we can filter by event directly. For instance, let's find the token approvals for USDT. First, we need the canonical event name, which we can find by inspecting the contract ABI:

```json
{
  "anonymous": false,
  "inputs": [
    {
      "indexed": true,
      "name": "owner",
      "type": "address"
    },
    {
      "indexed": true,
      "name": "spender",
      "type": "address"
    },
    {
      "indexed": false,
      "name": "value",
      "type": "uint256"
    }
  ],
  "name": "Approval",
  "type": "event"
}
```

This gives us the event name Approval(address owner, address spender, uint256 value), which simplifies to the canonical name Approval(address,address,s pender), which hashes to 0x8c5...925. We can then provide this hash to the array:

```
const logs = await provider.getLogs({
  address: "0xdAC17F958D2ee523a2206206994597C13D831ec7",
  topics: [
    "0x8c5be1e5ebec7d5bd14f71427d1e84f3dd0314c0f7b2291e5b200ac8c7c3b925",
  ],
});
```

This may or may not return results. If you run it every 12 seconds or so, you will eventually see one or several matching events. If you check the block number, you'll notice that it is the most recent block. So, by default, the getLogs function returns the matching events from the current block.

We can add multiple topic filters too. Let's get all the Approval events, from the USDT token, since block 0, by vitalik.eth's address:

```
const logs = await provider.getLogs({
  fromBlock: 0,
  address: "0xdAC17F958D2ee523a2206206994597C13D831ec7",
  topics: [
"0x8c5be1e5ebec7d5bd14f71427d1e84f3dd0314c0f7b2291e5b200ac8c7c3b925",
"0x000000000000000000000000d8da6bf26964af9d7eed9e03e53415d37aa96045",
  ],
});
```

An empty array – at the time of writing, Vitalik hasn't approved any USDT tokens on his address. How about DAI?

```
const logs = await provider.getLogs({
  fromBlock: 0,
  address: "0x6B175474E89094C44Da98b954EedeAC495271d0F",
  topics: [
    "0x8c5be1e5ebec7d5bd14f71427d1e84f3dd0314c0f7b2291e5b200ac8c7c3b925",
    "0x000000000000000000000000d8da6bf26964af9d7eed9e03e53415d37aa96045",
  ],
});
```

Two logs: So `vitalik.eth` has approved some of his DAI, to two contracts.
The second contract address is `0x68b...c45`, which we can see in the `topics[2]` place
(which is the `spender` indexed parameter, padded to 32 bytes). We can inspect the full
transaction receipt for more:

```
{
  blockNumber: 14955435,
  blockHash: '0x483b7a34a508161cbd18aa3eccc2899d295042e3b08060fbb68ba
  2c025746089',
  transactionIndex: 144,
  removed: false,
  address: '0x6B175474E89094C44Da98b954EedeAC495271d0F',
  data: '0xffffffffffffffffffffffffffffffffffffffffffffffffffffffffffffffff',
  topics: [
    '0x8c5be1e5ebec7d5bd14f71427d1e84f3dd0314c0f7b2291e5b200ac8c7c3b925',
    '0x000000000000000000000000d8da6bf26964af9d7eed9e03e53415d37aa96045',
    '0x00000000000000000000000068b3465833fb72a70ecdf485e0e4c7bd8665fc45'
  ],
  transactionHash: '0x6e1a6db2dfb8f96cbcc5520f3c06aaa9aeaa1ba4457aa305985aa
  d2557ff82d2',
  logIndex: 218
}
```

Putting the `0x68b...c45` address into Etherscan, we discover that it is the *Uniswap
v3 router*, a contract responsible for managing swaps.

What if we wanted to find out who had approved DAI to this contract, regardless of
their address? We can pass `null` to the topic in our filter:

```
const logs = await provider.getLogs({
  blockHash: "0x483b7a34a508161cbd18aa3eccc2899d295042e3b08060fbb68ba
  2c025746089",
  address: "0x6B175474E89094C44Da98b954EedeAC495271d0F",
  topics: [
    "0x8c5be1e5ebec7d5bd14f71427d1e84f3dd0314c0f7b2291e5b200ac8c7c3b925",
    null,
    "0x00000000000000000000000068b3465833fb72a70ecdf485e0e4c7bd8665fc45",
  ],
});
```

At this block, then, only one account approved DAI to Uniswap: `vitalik.eth`.

Filters are powerful, because they allow us to strip away what we don't need from a large stream of logs and select only what we do need.[21] But we can only filter by the event parameters that are indexed. So, if you're going to be filtering against the Ethereum logs directly, you'll need to make sure that the smart contracts index the params you need.

Events and Product

Events now look much clearer. Logs provide a cheap way for transactions to record ephemeral data. Events give us a simple abstraction over these logs, allowing us to add semantics around a list of four 32-byte topics. And event filters let us use this abstraction to pick only those events that our use case needs.

But this is quite a low-level description of the event model. Ideally, we don't want to have to think about topic hashes or filtering at all. When writing our product code, it would be nice to rely on the ABI to give us the data that we need. It's also worth dwelling, for a short while, on some of the more fiddly issues that are likely to face a product engineer building a real-world application against the logstream.

ABIs Contain Events, Too

If you've made it this far, you can likely guess how we'll solve the first problem. We can rely on our tools! *ethers.js*, especially, gives us a solid implementation of the ABI spec that generates contract filters from a provided ABI. Pull the ABI for the DAI contract (0x6B175474E89094C44Da98b954EedeAC495271d0F) using `ctc`:

```
$ ctc abi 0x6B175474E89094C44Da98b954EedeAC495271d0F --json
[
...
  },
  {
    anonymous: false,
    inputs: [
```

---

[21] There's also a nice side effect of how filtering is implemented – the probability of false positives in the Bloom filter data structure – that makes queries with more filters faster than queries with fewer. The `logsBloom` property of a transaction receipt allows us to check very quickly whether a specific piece of indexed data is not included in the data (although it can't always tell us whether it *is* included; in other words, Bloom filters may return false positives but will never return false negatives).

```
    {
      indexed: true,
      internalType: "address",
      name: "src",
      type: "address",
    },
    {
      indexed: true,
      internalType: "address",
      name: "guy",
      type: "address",
    },
    {
      indexed: false,
      internalType: "uint256",
      name: "wad",
      type: "uint256",
    },
  ],
  name: "Approval",
  type: "event",
},
{
...
```

(I've truncated the output except for the Approval event ABI.) We can store it in an abi variable for testing and pass it into our Contract instance.[22] We can rewrite the last filter thus:

```
const contract = new ethers.Contract(
    "0x6B175474E89094C44Da98b954EedeAC495271d0F",
    abi,
    provider
);
```

---

[22] In fact, if you only know you are going to integrate against this one event, you only need to pass the relevant part of the ABI.

```
const logs = await contract.queryFilter(
  contract.filters.Approval(
    null,
    "0x68b3465833fb72a70ecdf485e0e4c7bd8665fc45"
  ),
  "0x483b7a34a508161cbd18aa3eccc2899d295042e3b08060fbb68ba2c025746089"
);
```

If you check the output, you'll also see something a little more richer than when we were filtering manually:

```
[
  {
    blockNumber: 14955435,
    blockHash: '0x483b7a34a508161cbd18aa3eccc2899d295042e3b08060fbb68ba
    2c025746089',
    transactionIndex: 144,
    removed: false,
    address: '0x6B175474E89094C44Da98b954EedeAC495271d0F',
    data: '0xffffffffffffffffffffffffffffffffffffffffffffffffffffffffffffff
    ffffff',
    topics: [
      '0x8c5be1e5ebec7d5bd14f71427d1e84f3dd0314c0f7b2291e5b200ac8c7c3b925',
      '0x0000000000000000000000000d8da6bf26964af9d7eed9e03e53415d37aa96045',
      '0x00000000000000000000000068b3465833fb72a70ecdf485e0e4c7bd8665fc45'
    ],
    transactionHash: '0x6e1a6db2dfb8f96cbcc5520f3c06aaa9aeaa1ba4457aa30598
    5aad2557ff82d2',
    logIndex: 218,
    removeListener: [Function (anonymous)],
    getBlock: [Function (anonymous)],
    getTransaction: [Function (anonymous)],
    getTransactionReceipt: [Function (anonymous)],
    event: 'Approval',
    eventSignature: 'Approval(address,address,uint256)',
    decode: [Function (anonymous)],
```

```
    args: [
      '0xd8dA6BF26964aF9D7eEd9e03E53415D37aA96045',
      '0x68b3465833fb72A70ecDF485E0e4C7bD8665Fc45',
      [BigNumber],
      src: '0xd8dA6BF26964aF9D7eEd9e03E53415D37aA96045',
      guy: '0x68b3465833fb72A70ecDF485E0e4C7bD8665Fc45',
      wad: [BigNumber]
    ]
  }
]
```

Now we're querying via our Contract instance and its ABI, we can add some more structure to the event data. Importantly, we know the *names* and *types* of the parameters, which allow *ethers.js* to cast the numbers into BigNumber instances and add an args object with named properties.

This is much neater:

- We don't need to manually figure out the event's canonical name or calculate its hash.

- We don't need to zero-pad addresses in our filters.

- We don't need to remember the order of the parameters when reading the output.

- We don't need to parse the data field separately: it's added to the args array, and the distinction between indexed and nonindexed parameters collapses.

- We don't need to manually convert the parameters to JS-appropriate types.

Where possible, then, rely on your tools! It's much better to let somebody else do your work for you. This is one of many examples where tools like *ethers.js* can remove a bunch of headaches, and many other tools understand the ABI spec and are only too eager to lean on it to make your life easier.

Listening to Events

So far, we've only been looking at examples where events are very much in the past: we are, in other words, querying for historical event data. But nothing stops the blockchain, and new events are always being produced by new blocks. If we're using the event log to update our application's state dynamically, we will need to be able to listen out for new events and respond to them with some immediacy.

This is what the eth_subscribe JSON-RPC method is for and its corresponding implementation in *ethers.js*: Contract.prototype.on. These functions give us a mechanism to wait for events rather than polling for them. Node providers typically use websockets to implement this "push" behavior:

```
contract.on("Approval", (owner, spender, value) => {
  console.log("Approval", owner, spender, value.toString());
});
```

Since you can't use filters here, you'll need to manually filter events based on the arguments:

```
contract.on("Approval", (owner, spender, value) => {
  if (owner !== "0xd8da6bf26964af9d7eed9e03e53415d37aa96045") return;

  console.log("vitalik.eth DAI Approval", owner, spender,
  value.toString());
});
```

If we're querying within a React component, we'll need to remember to wrap the whole thing in a useEffect to persist the listener between rerenders. Or we could use wagmi's useContractEvent, which does much the same thing.

This is all fine, as far as it goes. But there are lots of little idiosyncrasies that can make things challenging when you start using it in real-world contexts. Consider, for instance, how can we calculate the total amount of DAI that account A has transferred to others?

We know we'll need some basics:

- The DAI contract address and ABI

- The contract's Transfer event selector

- The account's address (let's use vitalik.eth again)

Okay. Let's construct a filter and query the contract's event log, then sum the wad amount:

```
const logs = await contract.queryFilter(
  contract.filters.Transfer("0xd8da6bf26964af9d7eed9e03e53415d37aa96045")
);

const sum = logs.reduce(
  (acc, log) => acc.add(log.args.wad),
  ethers.BigNumber.from(0)
);
```

Our sum is now a BigNumber object with the total amount of DAI that vitalik.eth has transferred out. But if Vitalik is feeling especially generous today, he might start transferring shortly *after* you've run queryFilter, and your app will be out of date. You *could* poll for the changes, but this is exactly what eth_subscribe is supposed to be used for.

(This might seem like a toy example, but what if, instead of an EOA, we want to calculate the total DAI received for a busy DEX contract? We'll need to paginate the historical queries to not hit our per-query limit as well as be subscribed to new events.)

Now we need some notion of local *state*, and some mechanism to update it. Let's assume we're writing a React component, so we can rely on React's useState function. We can then trigger an effect on initial render to calculate the historical sum and another to listen out for new events.

We'll wrap it in a custom hook too, giving us some reusability and a cleaner component:

```
function useDAITransfersSum(fromAddress) {
  const [sum, setSum] = useState(ethers.BigNumber.from(0));

  useEffect(() => {
    (async () => {
      const logs = await contract.queryFilter(
        contract.filters.Transfer(fromAddress)
      );

      const historicalSum = logs.reduce(
        (acc, log) => acc.add(log.args.wad),
        sum
      );
```

```
      setSum(historicalSum);
    })();
  }, [fromAddress]);

  useEffect(() => {
    contract.on("Transfer", (owner, _dest, value) => {
      if (owner !== fromAddress) return;
      setSum((sum) => sum.add(value));
    });

    return () => {
      contract.removeAllListeners("Transfer");
    };
  }, [fromAddress]);

  return sum;
}
```

We can then use it in our component:

```
const vitalikSum = useDAITransfersSum(
  "0xd8da6bf26964af9d7eed9e03e53415d37aa96045"
);
```

```
return <p>vitalik.eth has sent {vitalikSum.toString()} DAI^18</p>;
```

Okay, not exactly straightforward, but that works reasonably well: our component will rerender any time we get a new event. If we aren't using React, we can use another state management library, or even a simple let variable, which we can overwrite when a new event comes in. Events can change when blocks are reorganized, and if you're caching some state locally, you'll need to invalidate that cache when reorders occur (we talk more about block reorganizations in Chapter 2).

React's rerendering logic can be extremely fiddly when doing this sort of thing. Always check that your dependencies array is set correctly and that your effects aren't run more than they need to be. Some versions of React trigger two initial renders when strict mode is enabled too, so you might need to track or disable it to avoid unnecessary rerenders messing with your sums.

Whether the problem is React rerendering when you don't expect it, a dropped connection between you and your node provider, a logs query behaving unreliably (or becoming too big for a given node to handle), a block reorg, a shark biting the transatlantic cable, or anything else, I have found it extremely challenging to keep local state and blockchain state in sync using `queryFilter` and live updates, especially over a nonnegligible period of time. One of the worst things you can do to the UX of your app is show subtly incorrect information: it's hard for you to debug, it's unlikely the user will notice, and your janky frontend very well may lead to a loss of user funds. In short, dynamic event handling can lead you, in a pernicious and difficult-to-detect manner, into a violation of the *Principle of Trust*. You should do a hard refresh of your entire local state on a semiregular basis and, where possible, show live information at the point that the user confirms a write interaction.

In general, this sort of code – combining live and historical events, handling block reorgs, refreshing state – is quite boring to write, can be repetitive, and is necessary surprisingly often, so I highly recommend pulling it out into a reusable set of functions/hooks for your application. Nor is it always easy to write it at a maximum level of generality, so it's quite hard to find third-party versions ready to plug and play. As you build more frontends, you'll develop a sense of what level of abstraction is the right one for you and what sort of code you need to reuse. As with much else, it's mostly about developing a taste for it over time.

Indexing

Indexing puts a layer of abstraction between your application and the protocol and allows you to front-load work that you would otherwise have to do at runtime. There are several approaches to indexing, which need to be considered and evaluated. DIY approaches give you flexibility and improved developer experience, but are bottlenecked by hosting, operational costs, and worries over data freshness. The Graph trades off lots to achieve its decentralization. Centralized Indexing Services are a goldilocks solution, if you don't prioritize decentralization. Decentralized indexing is rarely worth the trade-offs.

Each section of this chapter has shown that getting information out of a smart contract can sometimes be straightforward, but can also be difficult.

Contracts are severely memory constrained, so writing to memory costs gas, so there are hard limits on the memory a transaction can use. There are also soft limits: your users will have to pay for writes, and there's some level of gas fees at which they will simply refuse to pay.

There are also security considerations. The smaller the surface area of a contract, the more secure it is: the more write and read calls you use, the more code there is to debug, test, and verify. It almost always isn't worth the protocol team's time, energy, or audit budget to write filtering and search functions in the contract itself.

As a result, frontends have to pick up the slack. We've already seen some ways they can do so: calling read functions directly and filtering locally, pulling information from the event log, and inspecting the contract state directly. But these methods are complicated and low level. These methods place processing and memory requirements on the frontend – which, in our examples, and very commonly in live applications – means the user's browser.

There are also issues associated with the decentralized nature of the network. Other users may be using the smart contract at the same time; the data may change between an initial load of the page and the user's actions. Even if the contract state is sandboxed per user, the contract may rely on other smart contracts or other network-wide properties to do its work. Every 12 seconds, a new block will be mined, and each block presents an opportunity for your frontend's data to go stale. Blocks get reorganized, websocket connections get dropped, and small errors in the data can compound.

So querying the blockchain directly and relying only on your local state is often problematic. It can lead to failed transactions and frustrated users – or, indeed, something much worse: a violation of the *Principle of Trust*.

One approach that addresses these problems is to add a layer between you and the node: an *index*. An index can simplify your frontend logic by moving the read functions into a single place. This allows the index to be responsible for reading the live data and transforming it in various ways: filtering it down into subsets of the data, sorting it according to your application's needs, and appending it with other pieces of information from other smart contracts (or even other off-chain data sources). It also allows your frontend to rely on a single source of truth, avoiding some of the complications of a decentralized network. In short, it allows you to concentrate much of the complexity inherent to Ethereum's data layer in one place away from your application code, as in Figure 4-9.

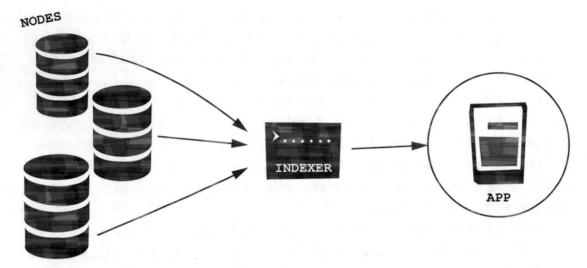

Figure 4-9. *Nodes feed data into an indexer, which sits between the node and your app*

Indexing is a powerful tool for product engineers, and it can take many forms, each with their own trade-offs. This sort of decision is also not one to take lightly: it can be very difficult to strip out something that your frontend relies on as much as the index. However, it's also not the most important decision you need to make. Like all technical decisions, the ultimate consideration is whether this piece of technology will make a better product that solves your users' problems, as opposed to its alternatives. This section will therefore describe and evaluate some of these different options.

How are we evaluating these approaches? We'll evaluate each against a rubric of trade-offs. It's important to view these explicitly as trade-offs, as optimizing for one is likely to come at the cost of another:

- **Speed and data freshness**: How long does it take to index the data your system needs? Does the solution update frequently enough? Is the data fresh? How fresh does the data need to be? And how quick do your frontend queries run?

- **Developer experience**: Is it easy to use your indexed data in your frontend? Is it easy to update the indexing parameters? How quickly can you add a new data source? Is there good tooling? Is your indexing code version controlled? Can you debug problems with the indexer with minimal extra tooling surface area?

- **Operational complexity**: What are the operational costs of running the indexer? Do you have to set up extra processes to develop, verify, and fund the indexing operations?

- **Cost**: How much does it cost to run your solution? How does the cost change when usage increases or decreases? Does the solution require sitting within certain usage bounds to be worth it? Does cost even matter to you? (Hint: On various margins, it might not.)

- **Decentralization**: How decentralized is your indexing solution? Is there a single point of failure? Is it possible to censor or otherwise restrict the data? Is it possible to switch between different hosts?

With this rubric in hand, we'll take a look at three approaches to indexing.

A Simple DIY Index

Technical decisions start at home: it's important when designing a system that you understand the problem space properly, and this means your local problem space. What are your specific constraints? What are you trying to achieve within those constraints? We've already identified the core problem of crypto data: getting information quickly, reliably, and in the format we need it for display. How does this core problem apply to you?

Because the problem is going to be described within your own specific constraints, the solution is likely to be too. This makes exploring a homemade solution a useful exercise, even if it isn't what you will in fact end up doing. I have benefited too many times to count from opening a blank editor screen and typing out, in near-pseudocode, how I'd like to integrate with a system before building it (or deciding to use a prebuilt solution).

So what would building your own index look like? And what can we learn from the process?

The simplest place to start is using the tools we already have to pull the data we want. We don't need to consider how we'll get this data to our frontend yet: we first need to consider what data we want and how we get it. We do, however, need to think about what we want our frontend to do, so we can compile the correct data.

For our purposes, the actual use case doesn't matter much, but we'll narrow one down so we can develop a better sense of what we'll need. Let's build a pool explorer for Curve pools: a simple, read-only interface to show recent transactions and some aggregate data. This suggests a few constraints:

- We will want to support **multiple pools** (even if we only test against one).

- For each pool, we need to **pull its recent swaps**. (How recent? Let's stipulate swaps within the last hour.)

- We're showing **aggregates**, so we'll also need to pull historical data per pool. What aggregates will we want to calculate? Lifetime transaction volume and 24-hour transaction volume seem useful. So we'll need to pull all swap events to calculate these aggregates.

- We might also want to think about **how fresh we need our data to be**. Given our use case, we can maybe put up with a ~2-minute time delay. That gives us an upper bound on our processing time.

Of course, this is an entirely contrived example. But these sorts of questions are useful to ask, since the answers within a noncontrived example are going to require introspection about what your users need and want and what is useful to meeting that need. Notice that none of the preceding points are really technical questions! They're all about how the use case bounds the technical.

We'll draw the data from the smart contracts exclusively, although some indexers might pull from multiple data sources (such as a third-party pricing API or some internal data source). We'll choose the 3pool (DAI/USDC/USDT) pool, because it has lots of transaction volume and so will give us a rich dataset to work with. It will also give us a sense whether we can meet our ~2-minute time delay.

Let's start by taking a look at the pool on Etherscan.[23] If you open the "Code" tab, you'll notice that it's written in Vyper, not Solidity. No problem: we have ABIs to solve that problem for us. Remember, functions are just a useful fiction.

---

[23] https://etherscan.io/address/0xbebc44782c7db0a1a60cb6fe97d0b483032ff1c7

I'm going to import the ethers package into an empty repository by running
npm install ethers. I'll also create an index.js file where we'll write the indexer
code.[24] We'll also use Alchemy, so let's set up a provider:

```
const provider = new ethers.providers.AlchemyProvider(
  "mainnet",
  "[[ALCHEMY KEY]]"
);
```

We'll set up an array of pools that our indexer can support. We'll only support one
for the time being, so let's add it in directly. We'll get the ABI using the usual methods:
although, for this specific contract, we'll need to remove the gas keys from each ABI
fragment.[25] We'll also pull the block number of the block from when the pool was deployed,
so we don't have to make some unnecessary requests. (We can get this block number by
finding the last transaction on the contract's Etherscan page or by running $ ctc
address 0xbebc44782c7db0a1a60cb6fe97d0b483032ff1c7 -v. In our case, it's 10809473.)

```
const pools = [
  {
    title: '3pool (DAI/USDC/USDT)',
    address: '0xbebc44782c7db0a1a60cb6fe97d0b483032ff1c7',
    deployedAtBlock: 10809473,
    abi: [...],
  }
];
```

We can now loop through our pools, mapping the current pools array to an array of
promises. This allows us to build the index for each pool in parallel (something we can
do, since pools are independent). We'll get the current block and an instance of ethers.
Contract for this pool:

```
const promises = pools.map(async (pool) => {
```

---

[24] In practice, I highly recommend you use TypeScript for everything: static typing, while not a
panacea, provides in-editor help, and a static type system helps eliminate certain classes of bugs.
This is especially important when the runtime language is fickle and finickerty, like JavaScript.
But let's not relitigate *that* question any further!

[25] Older versions of the Vyper compiler produced these values; *ethers.js* interprets them as
amounts of gas to send, and it usually results in request errors.

```
const currentBlock = await provider.getBlockNumber();

const contract = new ethers.Contract(
  pool.address,
  pool.abi,
  provider
);
```

It might be useful to know which tokens each pool supports, so we can fetch them from the contract's coins property. coins, according to the ABI, takes a single integer argument, which looks like an array index. If the index doesn't exist, the read call will revert. So we'll keep looping through the integers until we get an error. (Incidentally, this is exactly the sort of reason that indexing is useful. We want to get the entire contents of an array, but the contract doesn't have a direct getter for it; a perfect indexing use case.)

```
// Get the pool's tokens

console.log(`Fetching tokens for ${pool.name}`);

const tokenAddresses = [];
while (true) {
  try {
    const tokenAddress = await contract.coins(tokenAddresses.length);
    tokenAddresses.push(tokenAddress);
  } catch (e) {
    break;
  }
}
```

Now we'll want to get our events. Let's look at the ABI again. If we search for type: "event", we should find a fragment like the following:

```
{
  anonymous: false,
  inputs: [
    {
      indexed: true,
      name: "buyer",
```

```
      type: "address",
    },
    {
      indexed: false,
      name: "sold_id",
      type: "int128",
    },
    {
      indexed: false,
      name: "tokens_sold",
      type: "uint256",
    },
    {
      indexed: false,
      name: "bought_id",
      type: "int128",
    },
    {
      indexed: false,
      name: "tokens_bought",
      type: "uint256",
    },
  ],
  name: "TokenExchange",
  type: "event",
}
```

Exactly what we need! We have a buyer, which is the buyer's address. We have a bought_id and a sold_id, which seem to be the index to the array, giving us the tokens bought and sold. And we have the respective quantities. If you check Etherscan, you'll notice there's a lot of these events. They come in very frequently; it's a popular pool.

We'll therefore need to paginate the events. Let's loop through and collect every event in 100,000 block chunks:[26]

```
// Get every TokenExchange event, paginated into 100000 block chunks

const chunkSize = 100000;
const rawEvents = [];

let fromBlock = pool.deployedAtBlock;

while (true) {
  const toBlock = fromBlock + chunkSize;

  console.log(
    `Fetching events for ${pool.title} from block ${fromBlock} to ${toBlock}`
  );

  const eventsChunk = await contract.queryFilter(
    contract.filters.TokenExchange(),
    fromBlock,
    toBlock
  );

  rawEvents.push(...eventsChunk);

  if (currentBlock <= toBlock) {
    break;
  }

  fromBlock = toBlock + 1;
}
```

---

[26] Why 100,000? We have a ~200,000 event limit before Alchemy complains. There are ~7200 blocks per day. So this gives us the events for approximately two weeks. This feels like a reasonable amount of time: large enough to minimize the number of requests made, small enough to give us headroom and allow for particularly busy days/blocks; feel free to play around with different values and see when it breaks. At the time of writing, there are roughly 5m blocks to process – the number of blocks between the current block and the block of the contract's deployment – so it will take roughly 50 chunks to get our events. Assuming ~1 second per chunk, it'll take ~50 seconds to pull the events. Remember, also, that this number will keep going up as time passes: each fortnight it will increase by a second. At some point soon, we'll need to add some caching!

We'll then loop through the events, extracting their args and matching up the token IDs to the list we compiled before. We'll also grab the transaction hash and the block number:

```
const events = rawEvents.map(({ blockNumber, transactionHash, args }) => ({
  blockNumber,
  transactionHash,
  buyer: args.buyer,
  boughtToken: tokenAddresses[args.bought_id.toNumber()],
  boughtAmount: args.tokens_bought,
  soldToken: tokenAddresses[args.sold_id.toNumber()],
  soldAmount: args.tokens_sold,
}));
```

Then we can return a simple object, combining together our per-pool info and closing out our async function:

```
console.log(`Found ${events.length} events and ${tokenAddresses.length}
tokens for ${pool.title}`);

return {
  pool,
  tokenAddresses,
  events,
};
});
```

Our promises object then needs to be resolved:

```
const index = await Promise.all(promises);
```

And that's essentially it! A rough and ready and horribly unoptimized indexer that will consolidate our pool and its TokenExchange events into a single object. There are some obvious optimizations we could make:

- Could we **hard-code the token addresses**? Yes, the `coins` array is set in the contract's initializer, so the array won't ever change. We could pull it manually and hard-code it, removing that query entirely. (A good example of why being able to read these contracts' source code is useful.)

- Performing **delta updates**: Caching values locally, so we don't have to fetch them anew every time. We could store a `latestBlock` variable and only get events that occur after it. This might work, except we'll then have to worry about block reorgs. So it's generally a good idea to do a "hard refresh" once every few hours regardless.

- Try **parallelizing the event fetcher**: Moving it into a callback and running it through `Promise.all` (though we might run into problems here by hammering our Alchemy node).

But I'll leave these as an exercise for the more enthusiastic reader. Even after introducing these optimizations, however, it's still likely to be quite slow. And here's the rub: you will never be able to index extremely quickly unless you're running your own node. You will always have to pay the roundtrip latency to the node provider. You will also lose out on any potential node-level optimizations you might be able to do for your use case. But for simple, nontime-sensitive tasks, perhaps that's not a problem.

Once we have our indexer, we then need to decide how to get it to our frontend. The simplest way is to write it to a file somewhere on our web server or maybe a file host such as Amazon S3 (or, if you are so inclined, IPFS; although the next chapter will argue against all that malarkey). Pulling it into our frontend is then just a matter of issuing an HTTP request.

A more advanced approach could write the indexed data, in either a processed or rawer form, to a database. Querying then looks like writing some SQL on a backend service, wrapped round an API for the frontend to access. To do this with minimal overhead, you could even use a hosted Postgres API service, such as Supabase.[27]

---

[27] `http://supabase.com`

The indexer then needs to be run at some interval, either by a cronjob on a server somewhere or by some sort of serverless platform such as AWS Lambda or Google Cloud Functions.

Given all this, then, how does the roll-your-own approach fare on our trade-off rubric?

- **Speed and data freshness**: As we've seen, the bottleneck here is likely to be the node provider. You will also need to ensure that any processing you do takes into account block reorgs, network latency, etc. – so it's important to not *overly* cache the data. It is unlikely that without superlative in-house resources you *will* pay a performance hit when rolling your own. For many use cases, this is totally acceptable.

- **Developer experience**: DX is where the roll-your-own approach shines, since you can decide how you want to integrate and precisely how you structure the task. You will have to write more code, but the code you write will be yours and tailored to your use case. It can also be integrated directly into the mental model you have of your system, using the same domain concepts, hosting infrastructure, etc., which is not a benefit to be discounted! But, again, you'll have to write a lot more code.

- **Operational complexity**: The largest trade-off here is operational complexity. You are responsible for running, monitoring, and scaling each part of the indexer. If an indexer fails, you need to know about it quickly, and your indexing code needs to be resilient to failure. This will be made more straightforward if you have an existing monitoring infrastructure to plug into, but it will require thoughtful coding and regular reassessment.

- **Cost**: If you run your own node, your server costs are likely to stack up quite significantly. Running an Ethereum mainnet archive node requires a lot of SSD space and RAM – the total blockchain size is ~1TB right now – and this doesn't include equivalent nodes for other chains, if required. On the plus side, you won't have to pay query fees.

- **Decentralization**: There are ways of adding some decentralization to this approach, notably, and as discussed earlier, hosting the data on a decentralized platform. But this brings with it more operational complexity. And you will still need to run your indexer somewhere. If decentralization is your priority, then you'll be better off letting a decentralized indexing service handle it for you.

Rolling your own can be a smart move, if your use case is simple or esoteric and you are comfortable taking on the operational overhead. But most of these issues are issues that have been solved by others already, and so there will be a lot of reinventing the wheel. Writing your own indexer is a good learning exercise, but eschewing Not-Invented-Here syndrome is the first step toward a happy life.

Decentralized Indexing: The Graph

The Graph is perhaps the most popular and well-known indexing platform. The Graph is an indexing protocol that serves *subgraphs* – isolated APIs for specific pieces of blockchain data. Product/platform engineers list the smart contracts they'd like to index and the logic by which they'd like to index those contracts. This behavior is bundled into a *subgraph*, the result of which is then served via a GraphQL endpoint to a frontend. Frontends then use standard GraphQL libraries, such as Apollo, to pull the data into their frontends.

This basic model is extremely sensible. We can break it down into three key components:

- **Source**: Where does the data come from? Subgraphs specify the relevant smart contracts in a manifest file, and the subgraph also provides mapping code to process incoming data and store it inside the index.

- **Indexer**: Who actually performs the indexing work? Network participants run an instance of the Graph Node, which connects to the network and provides indexing services.

- **Interface**: How is the indexed data made available to the frontend? Subgraphs provide a GraphQL schema, and the Indexer then hosts this schema as a GraphQL endpoint. The Graph's gateway then routes requests to an appropriate indexer.

It is also, by design, highly decentralized. And this commitment to decentralization adds much more complexity into the Indexer and Interface components.

The actual indexing is processed by an indexing node, which is incentivized to do so correctly through a complicated system of GRT (the protocol's native token) staking rewards and querying fees:

- GRT holders attest to the quality and usefulness of a specific indexer by staking GRT against that indexer. These participants are called **Delegators**, as these GRT holders delegate to specific indexers to signal confidence in their behavior as an indexer. Does the indexing process run quickly? Is the data fresh? Are the fees reasonable? Delegators let the network know the answers to these questions.

- Other GRT holders provide a similar signal to subgraphs: **Curators**. These holders provide a mechanism for indexers to decide which subgraphs to index and which subgraphs to ignore: Which subgraphs are popular, provide sufficient information to build against, are optimized at the subgraph mapping level, and are up to date with the relevant contracts? Curators let the network know the answers to these questions.

Once the network is incentivized to index the most useful subgraphs on the most reliable indexing nodes, the mechanism then attends to the querying layer:

- Queries are billed in GRT, with the query fee set by the indexer.[28] This fee is paid to the indexer, delegators, curators, and the network at large.

- Queries are routed to the appropriate Indexer through the graph's **Gateway**, which is an HTTP endpoint hosted by The Graph's core team that matches requests to indexers willing to serve the query. There is also some operational logic here: the Gateway will route based on data availability and query budget, so there's no guarantee that your particular combination of budget and subgraph will be met by an available indexer. This introduces a market mechanism into querying as well as indexing.

---

[28] The actual fees per query vary depending on dynamic logic decided by the indexer, expressed in a custom query-pricing language called Agora (`https://github.com/graphprotocol/agora/tree/master/docs`).

In order to fend off early-stage challengers, and to allow the protocol to grow and iterate into something useful, The Graph have provided a **Hosted Service**, which strips out much of the operational complexity associated with staking, curating, and indexing. However, staying true to their decentralized vision, The Graph are in the process of deprecating the Hosted Service, and it is likely that by the time this book is published the Hosted Service will be either deprecated fully or closed to new subgraphs.

Once the Hosted Service is fully deprecated, the indexing, delegation, and curation operations will be fully decentralized. It will be impossible to prevent a subgraph from being indexed without shutting down the entire network. But querying will still be routed through the Gateway. The Graph will need to decentralize the Gateway in order to achieve its vision of a fully decentralized indexing platform. They have yet to provide plans for doing so.

Let's apply our rubric:

- **Speed and data freshness**: Generally, The Graph's indexers manage to index within a block, so you can expect your data to be ~10 seconds old. Regarding querying latency, the most up-to-date numbers I could find reported a ~300ms query time for the decentralized network.[29] Checking this against their query playground gave similar results. For many use cases, this is fine; for use cases where speed is important, the decentralized nature of the network may cause problems.

- **Developer experience**: If you don't need to write your own subgraph – that is, if you're integrating with contracts that already have subgraphs – then the developer experience can be quite straightforward. There are lots of existing frontend tools for querying GraphQL endpoints. If you need to write a subgraph, however, it can get quite awkward quite quickly. Subgraphs are written in a variant of TypeScript which is compiled down to WebAssembly, which can limit the dependencies you can use. The Graph's subgraph API is in some places incomplete. They provide a CLI tool for building and deploying these subgraphs.

---

[29] https://twitter.com/RezBrandon/status/1578034869363695619

- **Operational complexity**: The Graph introduces a huge amount of operational complexity, some of which will be simplified with progress in their tooling, some of which is inherent. You will need to purchase from or bridge GRT onto Polygon, the layer 2 network which hosts their billing mechanism.

- **Cost**: The Graph's costs are somewhat difficult to calculate ahead of time. Different indexers have different query pricing, and you may need to spend some GRT ahead of time incentivizing indexers to index your subgraph. You will also have to factor in any forex risk; the GRT token is a tradable token with some speculative trading activity. The Graph's documentation offers an approximate cost of $15 per month for 30,000 queries, though it's unlikely this includes any of the hidden costs just mentioned.[30]

- **Decentralization**: If this is your priority, then this is where The Graph will shine. The network is remarkably decentralized already, and they are progressing further with each release. The Gateway is still centralized, but they have plans to move to a decentralized model.

As you'll see from the preceding description, the decision to pursue full decentralization introduces a staggering amount of complexity to the network and the process by which you query it. The Graph is a remarkable piece of software and protocol engineering, carefully balancing incentives against one another and providing a genuinely useful service within challenging social and technical constraints. But this all comes at a cost. The Graph's core team – and wider community – has worked hard to simplify certain aspects, building tooling and dashboards. And it's clear that the team cares about developer experience and reducing the operational complexities.[31] But a lot of the complexity is inherent in the system design.

So, after all this, the question you need to answer: Is decentralization worth it?

---

[30] https://thegraph.com/docs/en/network/benefits/#lower-and-more-flexible-cost-structure
[31] https://twitter.com/RezBrandon/status/1578035416376430592

Centralized Indexing Services

If we take the basic model of Source, Indexer, and Interface and strip out the requirement for decentralization, we end up with a Centralized Indexing Service, the third approach that we'll discuss here. Centralized Indexing Services trade off decentralization for every other criteria in our rubric. They optimize for speed, developer experience, minimizing operational complexity, and reducing cost. This makes them substantially simpler to integrate initially and run over time.

There are plenty of such services already on the market. In fact, while I was writing this chapter, no fewer than three new venture-funded projects were announced.

Each of these platforms provides similar sorts of services: direct indexing services, webhooks, REST APIs, GraphQL endpoints, and SQL querying over indexed data. They support a range of layer 2 networks and have varying commitments to indexing speed and data availability:

- **Moralis** (`https://moralis.io`): A mature provider with a rich set of APIs

- **Goldsky** (`https://goldsky.com`): Well funded with a very compelling website and full The Graph subgraph compatibility; still in private beta (at the time of writing)

- **NXYZ** (`https://n.xyz`): Equally well funded, earlier stage, still in private beta (at the time of writing)

- **0xfast** (`www.0xfast.com`): A very early-stage project aimed at streaming lower-level data to consumers as quickly as possible

Even the node hosting services are getting in on the action: Alchemy, for instance, provides an NFT API that indexes and returns NFT metadata and a Notify service that sends webhooks based on certain on-chain triggers.

I think it's fair to assume that the feature sets of most of these services will converge quite quickly. It is a hot market, and competition will be fierce. So choosing a centralized indexing service will come down to, mostly, cost and developer experience and broader considerations such as longevity (Is it well funded? Does the team look competent? Does the team look like they care?), customer support, and brand.

One last time, then, our rubric is as follows:

- **Speed and data freshness**: Different providers will have different guarantees. But the ability to index data quickly, and serve queries to users quickly, is their core competency. Since they do not have to manage a decentralized network, these providers will be able to implement optimizations quickly, structure their indexing servers appropriately, scale effectively, and maybe distribute indexes across multiple geographies to minimize query latency.

- **Developer experience**: This is the trade-off to consider the most. How sensible is the API? How readable is its documentation? Does it integrate with existing tools you might be using – SQL queries, GraphQL – or does it require more frontend code to query? Do they provide a CLI tool for creating indexes, and can the indexing code be checked into your version control system? Do they provide libraries for React and any backend technologies you might be building with, and how frequently are those libraries updated? How much cognitive overhead will using this tool add to a developer on your team?

- **Operational complexity**: Centralized services minimize operational complexity as a matter of design; it's their job to run the nodes, serve the queries, manage billing through traditional SaaS subscription plans, etc. You can expect a centralized service to present very few operational complexities.

- **Cost**: I also expect prices to converge as the product offerings converge. All of the services listed earlier offer – or suggest they will offer – a monthly payment plan that caps usage, similar to most other paid-for developer services. Each has – or will have – a generous free plan and reasonably priced monthly plans for products that exceed the usage parameters.

- **Decentralization**: These services are not, by design, decentralized. If the service goes down, your application will break. If the service is blacklisted, or censored, or banned, your application may lose its access.

Centralized Indexing Services sit at the sweet spot for most web3 indexing use cases. They provide fast and reliable access to data, a rich set of APIs, one or several interfaces to this data, and simple payment plans. Unless you have strong ideological objections to using a centralized service, or your indexing requirements are so esoteric that integrating with them will be as difficult as rolling your own, your life is going to be considerably simpler if you use one of these services over a decentralized or roll-your-own alternative.

Final Considerations

The discussions earlier in this chapter illustrate, I think, how important it is to do some sort of indexing when building a product of any significant complexity. Some use cases won't require it: a very simple frontend wrapper around a very simple smart contract can make do with querying a node directly. But the moment your frontend logic becomes more complicated – in particular, the moment you need to do any sort of aggregation or filtering and searching over the raw data exposed by the SC – the complexities begin to pile up. Abstracting this complexity away into an indexing layer is very often the best thing you can do for your code and your sanity.

It also seems quite obvious to me that outsourcing your indexing requirements to a third party is generally the best approach. Rolling your own is sometimes important: if you need the data in its raw format, if you need to process it in an idiosyncratic way, you may run up against their limits quickly. Decentralization is sometimes important: it is a matter of principle for some developers, and it is a matter of legal necessity for others. But my hunch, and my experience, has taught me that these sorts of use cases are few and far between.

Evaluate the trade-off rubric earlier against your own use cases, and consider what matters most to you. It is also worth inspecting the network requests of frontends that seem to do a good job at the things you care about. Is there a dapp you admire, with fresh data, fast loading times, helpful contextual information? Open up the Network tab in your web inspector. See what it's sending and where. Count how often it polls the backend for changes. Get a sense of what sources it draws on and how it might combine them in application code.

On the margin, however, you should weight decentralization lower than other requirements. Different approaches will have varying levels of decentralization and, with it, varying levels of censorship resistance and trustlessness. I will make the case elsewhere in this book (especially in Chapters 6 and 7) that decentralization is less important than the community typically thinks. This seems especially true when considering indexing. There is an aspect of vendor lock-in, but a lot of the centralized services provide standard interfaces such as GraphQL, which will make switching over relatively straightforward. If you need to trade away decentralization for speed, operational complexity, developer experience, and cost, my advice is that you should generally do so.

Summary

In this chapter, we've described smart contracts in detail, modeling them as APIs and exploring how, with a bit of ingenuity and some good tooling, we can make sense of their interface without knowing much about the code. We've talked about ABIs, and they are the description of the API. We've talked about the limitations of smart contracts and how this pushes more responsibility onto the product. We've looked at the different types of state available to smart contracts and how they might affect our products. We've looked at EVM logs and the event abstraction. And we've looked at indexing, evaluating three approaches against a rubric of trade-offs. Finally, we've raised the question: Is decentralization worth it?

We'll come back to this question in more detail in Chapter 6. In the next chapter, however, we'll build upon the intuitions we've been developing over the previous few chapters and explore the testing, hosting, and deployment parameters for Ethereum products. In particular, we'll get a sense of ways in which decentralization makes the product infrastructure layer more difficult. We'll also see some creative ways around these difficulties.

CHAPTER 5

Infrastructure

In previous chapters, we've focused mainly on the *content* of your application: the smart contracts that serve as your API, the sorts of UX considerations you should think about, and the decentralized network that sits underneath it all. As we turn to the final few chapters of this book, we'll start to think more holistically about the relationship between crypto and products.

In this chapter, our last truly technical chapter, we'll look at some important parts of the infrastructure – meant in a broad sense – that your product will rely on. Infrastructure, to me, means more than the servers hosting your website. It means the processes that underpin your product quality, which allow your product to live, grow, and thrive.

To that end, we'll first look at testing, both automated and manual, and how this might be done. Second, we'll look at hosting itself and sketch out some ideas around the trade-offs between decentralization and ease of development and maintenance inherent in hosting your application. And finally we'll think a bit about fragility, sources of disorder, and how these concepts might affect the way you think about your products.

Testing

Unit tests provide focused testing for your application's business logic. The majority of your tests should be unit tests. Unit testing is easy in JavaScript, and mocking out the boundaries between your on-chain API and your frontend code makes it easier. You should also perform lots of manual end-to-end tests, because these tests provide robustness guarantees and expose you to the UX. You can use tools such as anvil *to run a local fork of the mainnet. These manual tests need test setup. Creating files for test scenarios allows you to produce replicable, deterministic initial conditions for your manual testing.*

© Jamie Rumbelow 2023
J. Rumbelow, *Building With Ethereum*, https://doi.org/10.1007/978-1-4842-9045-3_5

If there's one thing that separates excellent products from the merely good, it is a rigorous approach to testing. Testing gives us reliability and empathy: reliability, because we can use automated testing techniques to reach code paths that are forgettable, infrequently triggered, or otherwise awkward to do manually; empathy, because testing forces you to consider the application from the outside view. Unit tests force you to specify and validate the requirements of individual blocks of code. Integration tests force you to specify and validate the requirements of the local system. And end-to-end tests force you to specify and validate the requirements of the user.

Unit and Integration Testing

I'm a firm believer of the view that the vast majority of your tests should be unit tests. There are many, many benefits to writing unit tests as a core part of your development flow. It forces your code to be built up from small, composable units. It gives you strong guarantees about the essential logic of your product. It helps guide design: if testing a small unit is difficult, then it's likely that your unit of code is too tightly coupled to other bits of your code, or that you've not done enough conceptual work figuring out what it is actually supposed to do. Most importantly, thinking about your code in terms of small, isolated units allows you to make bounded progress toward a product goal.

It's also very easy to write good, small, composable units of code in Type/JavaScript, even when you're working within a React application. JavaScript is an excellent language for this sort of testing, because it gives us lightweight functions and simple data representation structures such as maps/objects and arrays. Testing in JavaScript is *cheap*.

What, then, should we write unit tests *for*? There's a simple version of the answer: our *business logic*. But "business logic" is one of those terms that people use to mean whatever they want it to mean. More practically, there are two key areas that we should focus our unit tests on:

- **Logic that transforms data**, such as parsing the result of a smart contract call and formatting it, preparing input values for inclusion in a transaction

- **Logic that changes the program's behavior**, including user input validation, complicated UI state calculations (e.g., "if the user is on this page and is connected but hasn't submitted, display X")

This is especially true if we're writing a backend service or some sort of tooling. But it's also true for our frontend code! Much frontend logic gets hidden within components and is only tested incidentally. In fact, the vast majority of the actual code that you write on the frontend falls into one of these two camps. But so much of the time, it rarely gets tested; we can do better than that.

In JavaScript, functions are cheap, so extract out the logic that would otherwise sit in useMemo calls into separate functions. These functions are pure – they don't need to trigger side effects – so they're the perfect candidates for extraction and unit testing. If all your components do is set up state and pass off responsibility to a set of small, discrete functions, you'll have a lot more confidence in the logic implicit within them, because you'll be making that logic explicit and tested.[1]

This gives us a program: move our logic for data transformation and program control flow out of the context of React components and into pure functions. For instance, consider a function that validates user input against some requirements within a component:

```
const [amount, setAmount] = useState("0");

const validation = useMemo(() => {
  const amountBn = ethers.utils.parseEther(amount);

  const checks = [
    {
      condition: amountBn.gt(0),
      error: "Amount must be greater than 0",
    },
    {
      condition: amountBn.lte(currentEtherBalance),
      error: "Amount must be less than your current balance",
    },
  ];
```

---

[1] A previous version of this chapter had an example of how to turn a gnarly React component into a series of small, tested functions. I've cut it for space reasons, and because much of what I was writing about ended up being more about React than Ethereum, but feel free to email me at jamie@jamierumbelow.net if you want to see how this can happen in practice. Instead, I'll show a small, isolated example.

```
const errors = checks.map((check) => !check.condition && check.error)
  .filter(Boolean);

return {
  isValid: !errors.length,
  errors,
};
}, [amount, currentEtherBalance]);
```

This is the sort of code that a million frontend engineers write every day. Set up some React state and check it against a set of criteria, returning both the computer-readable status – to, for example, disable submit on the form and change the border coloring to indicate an error – and the human-readable error message. What's important to note about the validation logic here is that *it is independent of the source of the data*. It can therefore be extracted out into a separate function *outside* the component:

```
const validate = (values, context) => {
  const amountBn = ethers.utils.parseEther(values.amount);

  const checks = [
    {
      condition: amountBn.gt(0),
      error: "Amount must be greater than 0",
    },
    {
      condition: amountBn.lte(currentEtherBalance),
      error: "Amount must be less than your current balance",
    },
  ];

  const errors = checks.map((check) => !check.condition && check.error)
    .filter(Boolean);

  return {
    isValid: !errors.length,
    errors,
  };
};
```

...and then tested using standard jest tests:

```
describe("validate", () => {
  describe("failures", () => {
    it("should return an error if amount is 0", () => {
      const { isValid, error } = validate({ amount: 0 }, {
      currentEtherBalance: 1 });
      expect(isValid).toBe(false);
      expect(error).toEqual("Amount must be greater than 0");
    });

    it("should return an error if amount is greater than current
    balance", () => {
      const { isValid, error } = validate({ amount: 2 }, {
      currentEtherBalance: 1 });
      expect(isValid).toEqual(false);
      expect(error).toEqual("Amount must be less than your current
      balance");
    });
  });

  describe("success", () => {
    it("should be valid if amount is less than current balance", () => {
      const { isValid, error } = validate({ amount: 1 }, {
      currentEtherBalance: 2 });
      expect(isValid).toEqual(true);
      expect(error).toEqual(null);
    });
  });
})
```

...and then integrated back into the component:

```
const validation = useMemo(
  () => validate({ amount }, { currentEtherBalance }),
  [amount, currentEtherBalance]
);
```

This approach also gives us a clearer sense of where there exists overlap between similar functionality in different components, allowing us to generalize our validator:

```
const validate = (checks) => (values, context) => {
  const errors = checks(values, context)
    .map((check) => !check.condition && check.error)
    .filter(Boolean);

  return {
    isValid: !errors.length,
    errors,
  };
};
```

...and then specify our checks for whatever component we want:

```
const validateComponentName = validate(({ amount }, {
currentEtherBalance }) => {
  const amountBn = ethers.utils.parseEther(amount);

  return [
    {
      condition: amountBn.gt(0),
      error: "Amount must be greater than 0",
    },
    {
      condition: amountBn.lte(currentEtherBalance),
      error: "Amount must be less than your current balance",
    },
  ];
});
```

Our tests should still be valid when run against our new `validateComponentName` function.

Notice that none of the preceding examples needs to know about React state or about any live values from the blockchain. The `useMemo` call in our component will refresh whenever those values change. Our logic gets broken apart into small, discrete functions that can be tested independently and recomposed in our component. We get robust, tested business logic and a component layout that is extremely easy to reason about.

Once we've separated our business logic into units and tested them with unit tests, we're left with what Tony Kay calls "a loose bag of working parts."[2] This is already a good position to be in; we can do a lot with a loose bag of working parts! But we'll want to ensure that these parts gel together nicely. We will therefore build upon our unit testing to also test the boundaries between the different components of our application. This is called *integration testing* and allows us to get closer to testing the entire system without having to test against a real backend.

Integration testing over Ethereum products is perfectly doable. If we can abstract the representation of transactions and on-chain data away from our UI – taking the sort of approach I suggested in Chapter 3 – then we have a well-defined boundary between the blockchain and our product. This enables us to mock out the node and test not only that the rest of the application works as intended but that it calls out to our data layer appropriately.

Mocking out our Ethereum requests can be reasonably straightforward: again, on the assumption that we have an abstraction layer between our blockchain calls and our UI code. We can do this for read requests by moving these requests into individual functions:

```
export const getBalance = (token, account) =>
  new ethers.contracts.Contract(
    token,
    ERC20ABI
  ).balanceOf(account);

export const getTotalAcrossPools = async () => {
  const poolOne = new ethers.contract.Contract(
    POOL_1_ADDR, PoolABI
  );

  const poolTwo = new ethers.contract.Contract(
    POOL_2_ADDR, PoolABI
  );
```

---

[2] From his 2017 Clojure/West talk, "Testing Made Simple" (www.youtube.com/watch?v=OdpOM39g-LM).

```
  const [poolOneTotal, poolTwoTotal] = await Promise.all([
    poolOne.total(),
    poolTwo.total(),
  ]);

  return poolOneTotal.add(poolTwoTotal);
}
```

These functions then form the boundary between the on-chain stuff and product stuff within our application. They can then be mocked using the standard jest mocking tools:

```
import { getBalance } from './data';
import { utils } from "ethers";

jest.mock('getBalance');

describe('some business logic', () => {
  it('should call getBalance and return the balance minus 1 eth',
  async () => {
    const account = '0x123...xyz';
    const value = utils.parseEther('2');

    getBalance.mockResolvedValue(value);

    const result = await callSomeBusinessLogic(account);

    expect(getBalance).toHaveBeenCalledWith(account);

    expect(result.toString()).toBe(
      value.sub(utils.parseEther('1')).toString();
    );
  });
});
```

We will probably want to use our provider, and we may wish to use some user-provided values. In this case, we can wrap our data requests in a lightweight dependency container:

```
export const data = (provider, currentAccountAddress) => ({
  getBalance: (token) =>
    new ethers.contracts.Contract(token, ERC20ABI)
      .connect(provider)
      .balanceOf(currentAccountAddress),
})
```

which can then be given to a React context in our application:

```
const DataProvider = ({ children }) => {
  const [data, setData] = useState({});

  const provider = useProvider();
  const account = useAccount();

  useEffect(() => {
    setData(data(provider, account.address))
  }, [provider, account.address]);

  return (
    <DataContext.Provider value={data}>
      {children}
    </DataContext.Provider>
  );
}
```

The broad strategy, then, is to apply the same techniques to integration testing as we do to unit testing, by making the testable unit something that spans multiple levels of the stack trace. This sort of approach can be extended further to support transaction objects, as in Chapter 3. It allows us to isolate the on-chain calls somewhere outside of the React environment, injecting in state-dependent runtime values where necessary. And the React context can be called within custom hooks to simplify the call sites. It's a simple solution that scales reasonably well and avoids overengineering.

There are more sophisticated approaches to mocking the data layer that involve mocking out the `window.ethereum` object or providing a mocked provider object to give to *ethers.js*. Tools such as *web3-mock* and *mockthereum* make this easier.[3] But these approaches give us few benefits over this simple abstractive approach and increase the number of dependencies and moving parts in a way that I find inelegant.

End-to-End Testing

Once we are happy that our business logic is behaving properly and that it integrates well with the other units of code in our frontend, we still need to ensure that the full user journey behaves properly. Why? Three reasons:

1. **Unit and integration testing doesn't ever verify that the smart contract does what our frontend expects it to do**: These tests, by definition, isolate our code from the smart contract layer. The contract could return values of a different type from what we expect, or the implementation could have some strange side effects that aren't captured by our integration tests.

2. **There are lots of background facts that might matter**: The contract could emit events or could rely on third-party contracts being in such and such a state. We need to be able to test how our product handles network failures and how our product handles transactions that take time to complete.

3. **We want a good sense that the user's experience is appropriate**: Remember that testing is not just about correctness, it's also about UX, and the only way we can check some of these fuzzier requirements is to get more shots on goal, to actually use our application as a user would.

So we'll want to do plenty of end-to-end testing, too: testing that gets us as close to running the real-world application as possible. Some crypto teams are happy testing on the mainnet during development. This is a strange kind of masochism. It is slow, expensive, can be insecure, and most importantly won't always be possible. A mainnet test

---

[3] https://github.com/DePayFi/web3-mock and https://github.com/httptoolkit/mockthereum

right before deploy, where appropriate, can provide you with the final jolt of confidence necessary to launch. But during development and QA, testing on the mainnet is likely to frustrate you – and therefore disincentivize you to test as much as you should.

If we are going to test our product end to end, then we need to test that the frontend integrates well with the backend and that the backend behaves as we expect. Because our backend is powered by Ethereum, it is an unstable target: the blockchain is an ever-changing set of state transitions.

To perform these tests, we need a version of the Ethereum blockchain that we can test against reliably.

Test Networks

One of the most powerful Ethereum testing tools you will ever learn is how to run a local fork of the mainnet. Running a local fork allows you to run contracts, submit transactions and view their receipts, control how blocks get validated (i.e., at what pace), call every function that exists on the mainnet, and *modify the current state of the blockchain according to your whims*. In short, it gives you the ability to simulate and alter the blockchain locally for essentially zero cost.

There are two important tools that allow for local forking which I will discuss here: the grand old stalwart of smart contract testing, *hardhat*, and the impressive new up-and-comer, *anvil*.[4] I use anvil almost exclusively, so the commands here will be anvil's, although the underlying approaches are extremely similar.

We can run anvil by running the `anvil` command directly, no command-line flags required. This gives us an empty state and some test accounts with some ether:

```
$ anvil
```

---

[4] http://hardhat.org/ and https://book.getfoundry.sh/reference/anvil/; the latter is part of the *foundry* package, which we've discussed already. There are others too, such as Ganache (https://trufflesuite.com/ganache/).

```
0.1.0 (6d94a10 2022-11-04T00:17:06.152829Z)
https://github.com/foundry-rs/foundry

Available Accounts
==================

(0) 0xf39fd6e51aad88f6f4ce6ab8827279cfffb92266 (10000 ETH)
(1) 0x70997970c51812dc3a010c7d01b50e0d17dc79c8 (10000 ETH)

...

Private Keys
==================

(0) 0xac0974bec39a17e36ba4a6b4d238ff944bacb478cbed5efcae784d7bf4f2ff80
(1) 0x59c6995e998f97a5a0044966f0945389dc9e86dae88c7a8412f4603b6b78690d

...

Listening on 127.0.0.1:8545
```

We now have an instance of the Ethereum blockchain running locally. We can point our MetaMask at the 127.0.0.1:8545, import one of the private keys, and check the account's balance – you'll see it has 10,000 ETH (if forking made it so…). We can also point our frontend at this same URL and run queries and submit transactions.

Where this becomes especially useful, however, is when we add the --fork-url option:

```
$ anvil --fork-url [[NODE_URL]]
```

This option instructs anvil to query our node for the current state and set our fork's current state to whatever the most recent block is on the mainnet. It then proxies through to this URL whenever we request data that isn't available on the local chain. If you fork the mainnet and switch your MetaMask to the local network, then check one of your actual accounts, you'll see it has the same balances as you see when you're checking Etherscan on the mainnet.

When forking the mainnet, anvil will still generate the test accounts, which allows you to interact with already deployed contracts using fake ether, locally. If you break something, or trigger an error, or make a bad trade, it won't matter; you can just reset your fork and try again.

If you are building a frontend against an existing set of contracts, this is very powerful. You can test your frontend in an end-to-end fashion to your heart's content. It's a little more awkward to test against contracts that aren't already deployed; to do this, you'll need to run a setup script to deploy the contract first. We'll see an example of this later.

Some protocol teams deploy their contracts to a public testnet, either for internal testing or for public beta testing. In Chapter 2, I mentioned in passing that there aren't many benefits to using a public testnet. The network's performance can be slow, and your degree of control over contract state is small. There are also some security worries: anything deployed to a public testnet is, by definition, public, and your protocol team might not be eager to show off their work-in-progress bytecode to the hostile environment of a public testnet. I'd like to reiterate that here: public testnets will offer you nothing that a local fork cannot and in many cases will hold you back. You won't be able to change the running smart contract state as you can with a local fork – and we'll see an example of how powerful this capability can be shortly.

One potential benefit to using a public testnet is its public *accessibility*: people who can't access your local computer can query the blockchain anyway. But you needn't lose this public accessibility if running a local fork. Tools such as the excellent *ngrok* allow you to publish a local instance to a public URL, to which your frontends can then connect. If you run anvil with its defaults, it'll spin up a local node on port 8545. Leaving that instance running, you can open another terminal window and run ngrok on that port:

```
$ ngrok http 8545
Session Status              online
Account                     Jamie Rumbelow (Plan: Pro)
Version                     3.1.0
Region                      Europe (eu)
Latency                     66.806375ms
Web Interface               http://127.0.0.1:4040
Forwarding                  https://22cc02fcedc6.eu.ngrok.io -> http://
                            localhost:8545
```

ngrok opens a tunnel between their public servers and your local server, running, in this case, on port 8545. The forwarding URL seen in the preceding output – https://4735935aeab6.eu.ngrok.io – will route any requests to your local fork.

You can then add this URL as a custom network in MetaMask and point your frontend to the same place. Similarly, other testers can add the same URL as a custom network in their wallet software, which allows all of you to test on the same fork, sharing the same state. As long as your terminal remains open and your computer remains connected to the Internet, you should be able to continue to test over a period of time.

There are, however, some gotchas to this approach:

- **Your ngrok session and your local fork are both ephemeral.** It's very easy to close your laptop accidentally and kick everybody off the network, or close the terminal, or for some other reason lose your connection.

- **Configuring both the frontend's URL and adding new custom networks can be complicated**, and the latter requires reasonable familiarity with wallet software. Each time you restart the ngrok instance, you'll get a new URL.[5]

- **Your local node will diverge from the mainnet quickly**; if you're developing with other contracts that you don't control, you'll either need to reset the fork regularly (which has its downsides; more later) or spoof the data using the anvil helper methods (which has its downsides; more later).

Fortunately, these gotchas can be worked around, more or less. You might, for instance, run an instance of anvil on a web server, giving it a permanent process and a permanent URL. (You'll want to secure that server, of course, which might get challenging.)

Note   There are times when using a local fork can trip you up. If you're testing against contracts that rely on oracles to read off-chain data, and the current values of those oracles need to update when you make state changes, then you'll need to make sure that you run off-chain versions of those oracles. This can be extremely complicated. Do what you can to minimize the necessity: write tight, focused unit tests of the relevant frontend functionality and make sure the protocol is similarly

---

[5] ngrok's pro plans support reserved forwarding URLs, so you can specify a permanent URL ahead of time, which can help reduce this complexity.

tested; deploy an isomorphic contract to the same address locally, allowing you to override the values directly; factor in the expected difference between the current, invalid oracle value and the expected one. Defer to your protocol team on the best approach here. Unfortunately, this is much too complex a topic to cover in a book like this one.

So, using a local fork for the bulk of your end-to-end testing comes with many benefits, foremost of which is that you can control the state in a very fine-grained way. Let's look into what "updating the state" means. Tools such as hardhat and anvil support a range of helper RPC methods that allow you to modify the network state and behavior at runtime. You trigger these in the same way that you'd call `eth_call`, `eth_sendRawTransaction`, `eth_getBalance`, or any other RPC method. The forking tools supplement these RPC methods with custom helper functions.

The full list can be found on the tools' websites.[6] There are three helpers, in particular, that we'll focus on here: `anvil_impersonateAccount`, `anvil_setStorageAt`, and `anvil_reset`.

Account Impersonation

Account impersonation is a formidable tool. It lets you pretend to be another account, allowing you to bypass the normal signature checks that public blockchains require. This means you can submit transactions as this other user: move funds, gain admin access to contracts, make trades on their behalf.

We can impersonate an account in JavaScript with *ethers.js* using the provider request:

```
const addressToImpersonate = "0xd8da6bf26964af9d7eed9e03e53415d37aa96045";

await provider.send("anvil_impersonateAccount", [
  addressToImpersonate
]);
```

---

[6] https://hardhat.org/hardhat-network/docs/reference#json-rpc-methods-support and https://book.getfoundry.sh/reference/anvil/#custom-methods; although anvil aliases the hardhat_ methods so they should be interchangeable.

We can then fetch an ethers.js signer that allows us to sign on our impersonated account:

```
const signer = provider.getSigner(addressToImpersonate);
```

The transactions we sign won't actually be valid – they'll fail the normal cryptographic checks – but, since we've instructed our local fork to ignore these checks for this account, we'll be able to issue transactions using it. We can, for instance, send the total amount of eth from our impersonated address to one of our test addresses:

```
const addressToSendTo = "0xf39fd6e51aad88f6f4ce6ab8827279cfffb92266";

const vitaliksEth = await provider.getBalance(addressToImpersonate);

const tx = await signer.sendTransaction({
  to: addressToSendTo,
  value: vitaliksEth,
});
```

At the time of writing, vitalik.eth (0xd8d...045) has ~900 ether on the mainnet, so we should expect the ether balance of our test account (0xf39...266) to go up correspondingly. This might not seem especially useful, especially considering anvil already grants our test account 10,000 ether. But the same approach works for ERC-20 tokens too:

```
const daiContract = new ethers.Contract(
  "0x6B175474E89094C44Da98b954EedeAC495271d0F",
  ["function transfer(address recipient, uint256 amount) returns (bool)"],
  signer
);

const vitaliksDai = await daiContract.balanceOf(addressToImpersonate);

await daiContract.transfer(
  addressToSendTo,
  vitaliksDai
);
```

So we can fill our account with whatever tokens we want, without having to meddle around in the internal state of the contract.[7] It's a fast and elegant way to help set up some of your test environment locally.

While this is cool, it's important to remember that account impersonation happens *at the level of the node,* not at the level of your frontend or your wallet. You can't call `anvil_impersonateAccount` and then expect your frontend to use the account you're impersonating (at least not without some messy runtime code contortions). This makes it suitable for setup scripts and for experimenting locally, but not for running automated tests with tools like Selenium.

Once we're done messing around, we can tell anvil to stop impersonating the account:

```
await provider.send("anvil_stopImpersonatingAccount", [
  addressToImpersonate,
]);
```

Once run, calling methods with our impersonated signer should fail. We can create a helper method allowing us to wrap a callback with address impersonation:

```
const impersonate = async (address, callback) => {
  await provider.send("anvil_impersonateAccount", [address]);

  const signer = provider.getSigner(address);
  await callback(signer);

  await provider.send("anvil_stopImpersonatingAccount", [address]);
};
```

This helper method will make impersonating accounts less repetitive and ensure that our signer is reset after use.

---

[7] You should, of course, find an account with enough tokens to meet your need at the block you've forked from, and impersonate that, rather than just hoping that Vitalik has enough. Etherscan's token pages have a list of the largest holders, sorted in descending order.

Setting State Directly

In some cases, impersonating an account will give us too coarse-grained access over a contract's state. The underlying assumption is that some user somewhere *can* change some state, which relies on the contract actually giving that control. In other words, the contract needs to expose a method that gives this control. But for reasons we've already discussed, a lot of contracts don't: Solidity doesn't generate setters for variables by default, and values are therefore treated as private/protected until a protocol engineer explicitly adds a setter.

In these cases, if we want to modify the state of a contract, we'll need to do so directly. This is possible because the state of a contract is public, and high-level languages organize this state in a predictable way.

Let's jump into the bowels of the EVM for a moment and see what we can pull out.

We'll look at the DAI contract (0x6b175474e89094c44da98b954eedeac495271d0f) because it's simple, and we'll play with the `balanceOf` mapping, because it gives us a chance to look at how mappings work. Make sure we have a fresh `anvil` instance running and `ctc` installed to follow along.[8]

In order to read from a mapping, we need two pieces of information: the mapping's storage slot and the key that we'd like to read.

A quick glance at the contract shows that the `balanceOf` mapping takes up the third storage slot. Why? The first storage slot is taken by

```
mapping (address => uint) public wards;
```

There is then a list of constants:

```
string  public constant name     = "Dai Stablecoin";
string  public constant symbol   = "DAI";
string  public constant version  = "1";
uint8   public constant decimals = 18;
```

Solidity pulls out constants and stores them in the contract bytecode directly, not in the contract's permanent storage. So we can discard them when calculating the storage slot. Next is a `totalSupply` variable:

---

[8] The following code examples intermix `ctc` and `cast` calls. You can do all of this with one or the other, but I like to mix them: `cast` will automatically query the local chain if it detects it is running, and I find the `ctc` interface a little awkward. So we'll get the best of both worlds and pass the results of one into the other.

```
uint256 public totalSupply;
```

We can check that we're on track by using cast to read the value of totalSupply, by passing the slot index (it's the second slot, so the index is 1):

```
$ cast storage 0x6b1...d0f 1
0x00000000000000000000000000000000000000001271db3db4ea25616291855a
```

We get the 32-byte hex value of the storage slot at index 1. We can push this into ctc to read it as an integer:

```
$ ctc int $(cast storage 0x6b1...d0f 1)
5708374130948074453945386330
```

If we compare this with the totalSupply value in the "Read Contract" section of Etherscan, we see they are the same. Cool!

So we know that slot 1 is the slot for totalSupply. The next line of code in the contract is our balanceOf mapping:

```
mapping (address => uint) public balanceOf;
```

This allows us to conclude that the balanceOf mapping is stored at slot 2. Finding the correct slot index can be a little tricky. Since Solidity contracts can inherit from other contracts, you sometimes need to trace the contracts back through the inheritance chain, counting as you go. I haven't been able to find a tool to make this easier, although you can get quite far from just reading the contract carefully, iterating through the various slot numbers, and seeing what looks to be plausible values.

We also need to decide on the key of the mapping that we want to query. The key is typed address, so we'll use an Ethereum address we think is likely to have some DAI. Lots of accounts have DAI; let's use Vitalik's again (0xd8dA6BF26964aF9D7eEd9e03E53415D37aA96045).

In order to turn this key into a pointer to our value in the mapping, we need to perform a few steps. First, we need to pad our address and our mapping's storage slot index to 32-byte hex strings:

```
$ ctc encode address 0xd8d...045
0x000000000000000000000000d8da6bf26964af9d7eed9e03e53415d37aa96045
```

```
$ ctc encode int 2
0x0000000000000000000000000000000000000000000000000000000000000002
```

We can then concatenate them into a hex string, giving us

0x000000000000000000000000d8dA6BF26964aF9D7eEd9e0
3E53415D37aA9604500000000000000000000000000000000000000000000000
0000000000000000002

We then need to run this through the keccak256 hashing function:

```
$ ctc keccak 0x000...002
0x85efa08969febcb72bd7c79e3795763c6a77762d27bd830f8777227bf55e86a3
```

If the hash contains leading zeroes, we'll strip them out. This hashed 32-byte hex string is the key where our value will reside! We can then query this value on the contract using cast:

```
$ cast storage 0x6b1...d0f 0x85e...6a3
0x00000000000000000000000000000000000000000000000075a22d004033dca95036
```

And convert it back to an integer:

```
$ ctc int 0x000...036
555508493698012633714742
```

If we then divide this by 1e18 (the number of decimals used by the DAI contract), we get 555508.49369801 – the amount of DAI that vitalik.eth holds! We can check the account's Etherscan page to verify.

This process is a little arduous, but we can do it relatively simply in JavaScript using *ethers.js*:

```
const getStorageMappingKey = (
  storageLocation,
  key,
  types = ["address", "uint"]
) =>
  "0x" +
  ethers.utils
    .keccak256(
      ethers.utils.defaultAbiCoder.encode(
        types, [key, storageLocation]
      )
```

```
)
    .replace(/^0x0*/, "");
```

With this function, we can then query the chain directly using the eth_getStorageAt
RPC method:

```
const key = getStorageMappingKey(
  2,
  ACCOUNT_ADDR
);

const accountBalance = await provider.send(
  "eth_getStorageAt",
  [
    TOKEN_ADDR,
    key
  ]
);
```

The same logic applies to setting these values. We can simply replace the eth_
getStorageAt call with anvil_setStorageAt and provide a 32-byte padded value. Let's
set Vitalik's DAI balance on our local fork to zero:

```
await provider.send("anvil_setStorageAt", [
  token.address,
  key,
  utils.hexZeroPad("0x0", 32),
]);
```

If we now run our cast storage call again:

```
$ cast storage 0x6b175474e89094c44da98b954eedeac495271d0f
0x85efa08969febcb72bd7c79e3795763c6a77762d27bd830f8777227bf55e86a3
0x0000000000000000000000000000000000000000000000000000000000000000
```

We get a zero! We've vanished vitalik.eth's DAI balance by removing it from the
contract entirely.

So, using anvil_setStorageAt, we are able to write the values of contract storage
running on our local chain directly. It's rare that you'll need to do this during test setup,
and it's complicated enough that you'll want to avoid it where possible. It's also a bit of

CHAPTER 5   INFRASTRUCTURE

a code smell, since it is messing with the inner data representation of the contract. Your job is not to test the contract, and you should always be wary of making changes behind the public interface, since this makes your tests vulnerable to code changes that you can't control. But contracts are generally immutable, and the risk of running into such troubles is much less than if you were, for instance, writing directly into the database behind a web2 API. In some cases, you have no other option than to reach directly into the contract and modify its state; in those cases, this can be an incredibly powerful tool.

Test Scenarios

When building complicated frontends with several user journeys and several branches within those user journeys, fiddling with the state in an unsystematic way won't cut it. Many of these journeys will require several commands to set up the state correctly before each test run. You might need a token, deploy a new contract, fill your account with some of those tokens, and make a deposit: whatever is required to get your account in the beginning state to test a specific user flow. Some of these things may be on the mainnet already (e.g., the token), so will be inherited by our fork. But if the protocol is new, or if the changes we're testing are yet to be deployed, or if we're testing some edge-case regression, we might not have a contract, or a pool with the right amount of liquidity, or a user with the right amount of liquidity, already deployed and ready to use from the mainnet.

And even if we *can* rely on existing on-chain data, we still want a clean slate before each test run. On-chain data is likely to change, and we want to be able to test the scenario in the closest state possible to what it will look like when our product goes live. In other words, we want our tests to be as *replicable* and *deterministic* as possible. We're unlikely to get our tests to be *fully* replicable and deterministic; there are just too many moving pieces when dealing with live contracts on the mainnet. This is one of the reasons why fully automated end-to-end testing is very difficult.

But we can get some of the way. What we need is a method to represent *different test scenarios* based on *a well-known set of initial conditions*. We can then use this account within this basic environment to test multiple user journeys several times over, giving us more confidence and exposing us to the user's experience. What we want, in short, are *fixtures*.

The notion of a fixture will be a familiar one: fixtures are used in lots of testing platforms in web2 technologies. We use fixtures to specify our test setup and ensure that any preconditions our system might have are met. We can extend the notion of a fixture into web3 end-to-end testing, using the tools we've already discussed such as *ethers.js* and the `anvil_` helper RPC methods.

I like to put my fixtures in a *test/scenarios* folder within my application's repository. This keeps the test code close to the application code, part of the same Git commit history. I then write my test scenarios as individual files, each representing a user story to be tested. Because we're writing most of our application code in JavaScript, we can write our test scenarios in JavaScript too.

Each test needs to set up the on-chain state to reflect the state that the user will be in when they begin the user journey you are going to test. Let's come up with a test example. We're going to test a user story for a simple escrow contract:

```
contract Escrow {
    address public admin;
    address payable public receiver;
    uint public amount;

    constructor(address _admin,
                address payable _receiver) {
        admin = _admin;
        receiver = _receiver;
    }

    function deposit() external payable {
        amount = msg.value;
    }

    function withdraw() external {
        require(msg.sender == admin, "only admin");
        require(amount != 0, "amount is 0");

        uint _amount = amount;
        amount = 0;
        receiver.transfer(_amount);
    }
}
```

We've not seen much Solidity, but this contract is relatively straightforward. Our depositor deploys the contract, giving it an admin (who is allowed to issue the withdrawal) and a receiver (who will receive the funds). Anybody can then move funds into the contract by sending it ether. At some point in the future, the admin can call `withdraw()` and the funds will be sent to the `receiver` account.

There are a few different user journeys here that we might want to test:

1. A failure case, **when a non-admin tries to withdraw**

2. Another failure case, **when an admin tries to withdraw before anything has been deposited**

3. A success case, **when an admin withdraws a positive amount**

In every one of these cases, we'll need to deploy the contract and set the admin and receiver. In cases 2 and 3, we'll want to test the admin's behavior. In case 3, we'll want to deposit some funds into the contract.

This describes the setup in technical detail, though often these user stories will be based on actual user goals and worded in nontechnical terms:

(1) As a non-admin, I want to try to withdraw funds from the contract, so that I can see that I'm not allowed to do so.

(2) As an admin, I want to try to withdraw funds from the contract before any have been deposited, so that I can see that I'm not allowed to do so.

(3) As an admin, I want to withdraw funds from the contract after they have been deposited, so that I can see that I'm allowed to do so.

The task of our testing scenario infrastructure is to convert those user stories into initial conditions from within which we can follow these stories. Since it's the most complex, we'll go for (3), the success case. What do we need to set up? Well, we need the contract. We'll need to be an admin, so we'll need to set the admin to one of our test accounts. And we'll need to deposit some funds. Only then can the user actually go into our frontend and use the application to achieve the goal laid out in scenario (3).

Let's create a test scenario file: *test/scenarios/003-admin-can-withdraw.js*. We can store our addresses, etc., in some constants at the top of the file; in more sophisticated setups, these could be imported from the `process.env`.

```
const ADMIN_ADDR = "0xf39fd6e51aad88f6f4ce6ab8827279cfffb92266";
```

```
const RECEIVER_ADDR = "0x70997970c51812dc3a010c7d01b50e0d17dc79c8";
```

Since our admin account is one of our test accounts with plenty of ether, we'll just use that to do the deploys:

```
const SETUP_ADDR = ADMIN_ADDR;
```

Firstly, we'll want an ethers.js provider pointing toward our local fork. We'll also fetch a signer for our test account:

```
const provider = new ethers.providers.JsonRpcProvider("http://
localhost:8545");

const signer = provider.getSigner(SETUP_ADDR);
```

We can tell anvil to reset to the current mainnet block:[9]

```
await provider.send("anvil_reset");
```

In some cases, this can make our test setup more brittle: if we're relying on other contracts to be in a certain state, then updating the current block could well break it. But this seems to me to be a bad antipattern: we should make our background assumptions explicit and, wherever possible, use our test scenario to set them up correctly.

Note   Every time you reset your fork, you'll need to reset your account in MetaMask too, to ensure that your nonce is reset. Subsequent transactions will increase the nonce, but resetting the fork won't trigger a reset in MetaMask automatically. If you don't reset MetaMask, your test transactions will be posted with a higher nonce than the network expects, and any transactions will get stuck in your local mempool until the nonce reaches the pending transaction's nonce. This is an awkward and somewhat unavoidable complication of resetting your local state in this way.

---

[9] At the time of writing, anvil_reset wasn't implemented (though hardhat_reset is in the more mature hardhat tool). I expect it to be so in time for this book's publication. If it isn't, you'll need to manually restart the anvil process before each test run.

We can now deploy our contract. Let's assume that we've compiled the contract using the forge tool and stored it in *src/contracts/Escrow.json*:

```
const Escrow = require("../src/contracts/Escrow.json");

const escrowContractFactory = new ethers.ContractFactory(
  Escrow.abi,
  Escrow.bytecode,
  signer
);

const escrowContract = await escrowContractFactory.deploy(
  ADMIN_ADDR,
  RECEIVER_ADDR
);
```

In the call to deploy(), we passed through the two constructor parameters: our admin address and our receiver address. Our escrowContract object is now an instance of ethers.contract.Contract, set to the newly deployed address and with the correct ABI.

Let's send some ether to the contract:

```
await signer.sendTransaction({
    to: escrowContract.address,
    value: ethers.utils.parseEther("1.0"),
});
```

Finally, let's output the various addresses we used in JSON format:

```
console.log(
  JSON.stringify({
    success: true,
    admin: ADMIN_ADDR,
    receiver: RECEIVER_ADDR,
    contract: escrowContract.address,
  }, null, 2)
);
```

Make sure we have an anvil instance running on localhost:8545. If we now run our script, we should see the output:

```
{
  "success": true,
  "admin": "0xf39...266",
  "receiver": "0x709...9c8",
  "contract": "0x2c7...ad2"
}
```

(You may see a different contract address, since contract deployment calculates addresses based on the deployer address and current nonce.)

I've added a success boolean, included the various addresses, and chosen to output in JSON so that, if we ever need to, we can parse it programmatically. We might, for instance, want to run this script via an npm script, pull the contract address, and update our frontend's environment variables with the newly deployed address automatically.

For today, though, we'll run it manually, grabbing the contract address from the output and putting it into our frontend. Since we're using anvil, we can also check the contract's balance using cast (cast will notice that we're running an anvil instance locally and default to it):

```
$ cast balance 0x2c7...ad2
1000000000000000000
```

Perfect – it worked! We can also check to see whether our contract address has bytecode:

```
$ cast code 0x2c7...ad2
0x60806040523480...
```

Splendid. If we update our frontend, we can load it in our browser, import our test account into MetaMask – 0xf39...266; you can find the private key in anvil's initial output – connect to this account in the frontend, and run through our test scenario.

Each time we want to run our scenario again, all we need to do is restart anvil, rerun the test scenario script, and reset our MetaMask account from the advanced settings panel. We'll have a reliable, deterministic setup that allows us to test various user journeys of whatever complexity we need.

If we find ourselves being repetitive, we can move some of the test setup into some helper functions and reuse it across scenarios. As you build your test infrastructure, you'll spot all kinds of opportunities to improve the flow. Take them – the beauty of this setup is that it is extremely flexible and compellingly simple. If we need to impersonate accounts, fill them with tokens, set contract state, call functions, or even perform calculations, we can do so. The aim is always to get our local fork into such a state as to make it easy for us to test and retest in the browser.

So, we have a basic infrastructure for testing our contracts end to end. If the contract interactions are particularly gruesome, you can ask for help from the protocol team; they're likely to use similar sorts of scripts for their own purposes.

End-to-end testing can be fiddly, but it is often rewarding. As I said at the beginning of this section, I think most of your testing should be unit tests. Some people wrap this up in a rule – the 70/20/10 rule: 70% of your tests should be unit tests, 20% should be integration tests, and 10% should be end-to-end tests – but given the increasing demands of these types of tests, it's likely this rule will emerge seminaturally out of your behavior anyway. It's a bit like Moore's Law in that regard: a normative goal that falls out of the natural behavior of participants.

Regardless of how the numbers actually shake up, the most important thing is that *you do write tests*, and *you do perform manual tests*. I would like to be able to advocate for fully automated end-to-end testing, and the test scenario approach I've presented here gets us incrementally toward that goal. But today's wallet software simply isn't designed for this use case, and it will take some serious effort from wallet developers to make it so. So, for the meantime, we can automate the test setup, handle the test execution manually, and institute a deep cultural commitment to testing rigorously. And start lobbying wallet developers to give their wallets a programmable interface.

Hosting

Once you've built your product, you need to host it somewhere. There are several approaches to decentralized hosting. IPFS gives you an important degree of decentralization, but actually achieving that decentralization can come with costs. The Malkovich deployment allows you to pass over hosting responsibilities to multiple people, giving some of the benefits of decentralization, at the cost of some security concerns and a natural limit to your application. Competitive frontends do something similar, but improve upon the Malkovich deployment with a smart system of incentives. All three decentralized approaches make it challenging to run server-side code. Finally, remember that there's nothing special about hosting web3 frontends: you can just do it as you normally would. Decentralized hosting is rarely worth the trade-offs.

You've built your product. It's gorgeous, follows sensible UX patterns, and is powered by an underlying smart contract API. Taken all together, it adds meaningful value to the user by solving some important problems. It's been tested, with rigor, lots of small unit tests, and a large suite of manual testing scenarios. You're happy, nervous, and ready to deploy.

Doing so is another important infrastructure decision that you'll need to make. It can be as easy as hosting anything else – running a server, using a cloud platform, or via a hosted platform such as Heroku, Vercel, or GitHub pages. Or, if you require a decentralized frontend, you'll need to think a little more deeply about how to do it properly.

In the last chapter, we used a rubric of trade-offs to evaluate different indexing approaches. Let's do the same thing with hosting. Our rubric is as follows:

- **User experience**: How easy is it to find your frontend? Can the user load your app by clicking through from a Google search? Is any special browser extension required? And is there an obvious way to integrate help, support, and monitoring to create a tight UX feedback loop?

- **Developer experience**: Can you deploy easily? Can you easily monitor various metrics of application performance? Is deploying automatable? Can you implement continuous deployment methodologies with this hosting strategy? How configurable is your hosting platform?

- **Operational complexity**: How difficult is it to keep the application running over time? What are the ongoing costs? And how easy is it to expand the remit of what your hosting platform needs to do?

- **Decentralization**: How decentralized is your hosting solution? Are there single sources of failure? Can the application be shut down?

We'll sketch out three decentralized options and compare them against the centralized alternative. As with our discussion on indexing in Chapter 4, these are just sketches: this isn't a book about decentralized hosting. But I hope that this section gives you a sense for the sort of technical choices you will need to make.

Decentralized Hosting on IPFS

IPFS is a peer-to-peer network that stores files in a decentralized way: files are addressed by hashing their content, and the network distributes parts of files across participating nodes. A user then requests the file, either by running a node directly or via an HTTP-hosted gateway, which then fetches the various parts of the file, assembles them, and serves them to the user. This is, of course, a very high-level description of how it works.[10]

IPFS gets your frontend as decentralized as it is likely to ever be: the file is distributed in many parts across many nodes, it is immutable by design – due to its content-addressing mechanism – and your files can be accessible from whichever node hosts it.

There are, however, three great problems with the current IPFS system as it pertains to those of us building real products for real users.

First, your users are unlikely to be running an IPFS-enabled browser or their own node. In order to serve files to them, you'll need to use an IPFS gateway. These gateways are centralized providers that route requests through to the network and serve the underlying file content.[11] Not the end of the world, but bad if you're longing for maximum decentralization and can come with some UX complications. (Among other things, if you use a public gateway, your users will be routed through an unfamiliar and hash-laden URL.)

Second, IPFS runs no *application server*: it can only host static files. This means that you are not able to run any server-side code. This can severely limit the amount of off-chain work that you can do for your users and may limit the user experience you wish to provide.

Third, and most importantly, IPFS is not really a storage protocol. The great misconception of IPFS is that it is a big, immutable, global hard drive: once you store a file there, it is always accessible. This isn't true in any meaningful way. IPFS is better thought of as a content routing and distribution protocol, one that understands how to get files across the network but not which files to store. It's a peer-to-peer CDN (content delivery network). *Which files to store* is a matter for each node to decide. Moreover, the IPFS system has a pretty aggressive garbage collection system which removes unused files. So you need to incentivize nodes to "pin" your content to the network, keeping it both available and hosted in multiple places across the system.

---

[10] How it actually works is fascinating and is another great example of the crypto space solving meaningful technological problems by assembling smart cryptography and networking primitives in a clever way. See `https://docs.ipfs.tech/concepts/how-ipfs-works/` for more.

[11] Protocol Labs, the core team of IPFS, offers a gateway at `https://ipfs.io`; Cloudflare has their own; Google Cloud allows you to provision a private gateway; there's a full list of public gateways at `https://ipfs.github.io/public-gateway-checker/`.

Pinning can be done by relying on a protocol such as Filecoin,[12] which uses crypto-incentives to keep files pinned, or through a centralized pinning service such as Fleek or Pinata.[13] These providers pin files by running their own nodes and serve them from their own file servers (often hosting the files on Amazon S3). In order to pin easily, you'll want to use a centralized service such as Fleek, which offers a familiar UI and CLI tooling, as well as an integration with GitHub that makes deployment straightforward.[14] Otherwise, deployment means using incentive systems such as Filecoin or hosting your own IPFS nodes and running deployment scripts to keep the file pinned and served.

In light of all this, then, let's evaluate this approach against our rubric:

- **User experience**: Most users don't have a browser with IPFS support; IPFS gateway URLs are messy and unbranded (although services like Pinata or Cloudflare's IPFS gateway service allow you to serve files from a custom domain over regular HTTP). The static file restriction means that your UX is limited to what you can build in the frontend and compute on-chain.

- **Developer experience**: Services like Fleek make the experience feel like normal; otherwise, the developer experience can be quite troublesome. You'll need to manage a gateway, and nodes, and find/manage/write deployment flows that build your application, host it somewhere, and pin it to an IPFS node that you'll also need to find or run yourself.

- **Operational complexity**: The ongoing maintenance complexities are significant, unless, again, you're using a centralized pinning service to handle it for you. It's equivalent to running your own file server – or managing a system to incentivize others to do so on your behalf, which has its own operational complexities – and then distributing the file via IPFS.

---

[12] https://filecoin.io/

[13] https://fleek.co/hosting/ and www.pinata.cloud/dedicated-gateways

[14] Uniswap's frontend, for instance, is released via a GitHub Actions workflow and then pinned via Pinata. The app.uniswap.org domain itself routes via the Cloudflare IPFS gateway. See https://github.com/Uniswap/interface/blob/e0767b1cb7a9ff7e93b58c63bc705432142f2fb4/.github/workflows/release.yaml for an example of how deploys work at the time of writing.

- **Decentralization**: IPFS is strongly decentralized, in the sense that the protocol's rules allow file access from any node that hosts it, and nodes can be hosted globally. Gateways provide points of centralization, as does the pinning mechanism. You can use systems like Filecoin to work around some, but not all, of these constraints. Or you can use hosted services like Fleek, which make your system less decentralized.

So it looks as though IPFS is going to introduce a lot of complexity for any serious level of decentralization.

It's tempting to think, as with our discussion of decentralized indexing in the previous chapter, that an improvement in tools will fix these problems. But some of them are inherent to the structure of IPFS: in order to keep a file pinned, there needs to be a pinning mechanism. Services like Fleek show us what these tools, when well designed, can look like – but this comes at the cost of relying on Fleek to continue to run their service and to do so honestly. We are also restricted in what we can host, and we end up relying on a centralized server to perform any server-side code execution that our product needs. Perhaps these are appropriate trade-offs. You will need to decide for your own case whether you think they are.

The Malkovich Deployment

In the 1999 cult comedy film *Being John Malkovich*, the fictionalized John Malkovich goes through a portal into his own head. He steps into a room full of clones of himself, each of whom walks around and only says the word "Malkovich." It's a preposterous concept, but I think captures quite nicely an approach to deploying that gives some of the protections of a decentralized host, without some of the preceding trade-offs.

We'll call this approach "the Malkovich deployment," and it consists of two important steps:

1. Open source your frontend, or otherwise package it up in such a way as to make it easy for others to run.

2. Encourage others to run it on their own host, behind their own domain names.

Step 1 is reasonably straightforward. You'll need to parameterize your frontend properly: remove any secret API keys; move the node URLs into environment variables/a *.env* file; make sure that any links are generated using a configurable base URL; etc. You'll need to write plenty of documentation and devise a path to provide updates (such as making it updatable and restartable via a `git pull`). And you should simplify the setup process as much as you can: write a script to install dependencies; enumerate any underlying software (such as `node` or `nginx`) and the appropriate versions; perhaps even include a Docker container so that the execution environment can remain stable and predictable.

Step 2 is a matter of marketing. You could pay individuals some money to run instances of your frontend on their own servers. You could encourage a strong community norm of participation and incentivize hosts with status. You could encourage some tasteful advertising to pay for hosting costs. Or you could run several different hosts, on several different hosting platforms, yourself – or all of the above. The goal is to get as many instances as you can deployed in as many different places by as many different people.

There are, of course, plenty of problems with the Malkovich deployment, the biggest of which is that you're trusting others to not maliciously modify your frontend. This includes obvious attacks such as embedding malware, as well as more subtle changes that might be harder to detect, such as changing the contract address or a transaction's properties. This can be a surmountable problem, though, by including various user-facing integrity mechanisms, as well as some kind of community policing/moderation.

Another problem is that it only works if you're able to execute step 2 effectively: in order to get the decentralization benefits, you need a critical mass of users to participate. A third problem is that deploys become extremely difficult: you need to coordinate between many different individual hosts and deployments, some of which will be more difficult to contact, or more reluctant to update, than others.

How does the Malkovich deployment fare on our rubric?

- **User experience**: The Malkovich deployment will only cause UX problems if none of the frontends are easy to locate. This can be averted by publishing a list of community-approved frontends, posting about frontends regularly in various fora, linking to them from other sources (such as community blogs and Twitter), and/ or hosting a server picker that redirects a user to a random frontend when visiting a URL. Otherwise, it's just a website that users visit.

- **Developer experience**: Deployment, monitoring, and configurability are necessarily curtailed by the structure of the Malkovich deployment. If you need to do anything complicated to host your application or anticipate frequent updates, it's a nonstarter.

- **Operational complexity**: Most of the operational complexities are pushed onto the hosts, who, by definition, are not you, so in this respect it is not especially complex. But there may be ongoing work needed to source willing hosts, finagle them for updates, verify integrity and protect against malicious behavior, and publicize the existence of hosts. These are operational costs that can be kept down but may flare up, depending on your use case.

- **Decentralization**: Malkovich deployments give you quite a few of the benefits of a decentralized host: there will be multiple instances of the application running, on multiple hosting platforms, behind multiple domains. It will require a serious coordinated effort – or a huge stroke of bad luck – to take it down, so you can be confident that there will be some version of your site running as long as you (or your community) are there to incentivize it.

Not bad, if decentralization is what we're going for, and our site is simple. If our product becomes more complex – if, for instance, we need to run some server-side code – we'll need to start thinking very carefully about the developer experience and security considerations. We may be able to use integrity checks for our frontend, but once the application code is hiding, opaquely, behind an HTTP request, we're going to struggle executing the Malkovich deployment safely except from within a strong trusted circle of known hosts.

I don't know of any Ethereum products that use the Malkovich deployment. It was an idea that we devised, evaluated, and rejected at my last company. But, within certain parameters, it might be a smart and straightforward way to get some decentralization benefits without having to contort yourself around the nightmarish development processes of hosting on IPFS.

Competitive Frontends

We can extend the Malkovich deployment a little further and explore what might happen if we were to build a market dynamic into frontend hosting. We'll call this approach "competitive frontends," and it has some very desirable properties.

How does the competitive frontend approach work? You build some parameters into your protocol code that allows the contracts to track which frontend has routed a specific transaction to the protocol. You then incentivize the creation and hosting of those frontends by paying an account associated to that frontend based on their usage. This can be done on- or off-chain, with a token native to your protocol or something else such as ether or DAI.

You can combine it with the Malkovich deployment, packaging up the frontend as in Step 1 and encouraging other users to host it. You can abandon the idea of building a frontend entirely and allow others to do the work for you (although, if you do, you might have wasted some time reading large parts of this book!). Or you can meet somewhere in the middle, offering an SDK and some standard UI patterns that frontends can, but need not, use to speed up their development time and create some consistency.

The central benefit of the competitive frontend approach, as opposed to the Malkovich deployment, is that it gives a direct and simple incentive to play fairly, keep the frontend running well, and market the frontend to a user base. Competitive frontend hosts make more money when they increase the volume of transactions that go through their platform. You might, however, still want to do regular checks and only *promote* specific frontends that meet your stringent safety criteria.

There's another important benefit too: the frontends are competing with one another for eyeballs and mouse clicks, which can encourage them to experiment and iterate with different user experiences and target different user bases. This allows there to be innovation at the frontend level driven by supply and demand, unconstrained by the specific vision of the core team.

Let's see how it stacks against our rubric:

- **User experience**: Competitive frontends have the same basic UX constraint as the Malkovich deployment. Users will need to figure out what frontends are available, and which to use, although the incentives here are better aligned: it's in frontends' hosts' interest to get more people using their sites, so they are likely to do a lot of the promotional work for you.

- **Developer experience**: Deployment, monitoring, and configurability are similarly curtailed by the structure of the competitive frontend approach as it is by the Malkovich deployment. If you're providing a frontend to host, that is, if you allow hosts to build their own frontends, then your development requirements drop close to zero. You will need to integrate some tracking into your on-chain code, and this may or may not be aligned with the protocol team's plans: have this conversation early.

- **Operational complexity**: Similarly, most of the operational complexities are pushed onto the hosts. You may want to do some ongoing work and provide a first-party approval/trusted list of frontends, which may take up some hours every month. But, as with the developer experience point, it is much simpler when it is somebody else's responsibility.

- **Decentralization**: Competitive frontends give you all the same decentralization benefits of the Malkovich deployment, with one additional benefit: your frontend hosts are incentivized to better and improve their frontends, so you gain some of the idea-generative and quality-pursuing benefits of competitive decentralization, as well as the censorship resistance and network-wide reliability. A big win.

The Liquity protocol uses the competitive frontend approach with great success. Their website hosts a list of known frontends,[15] and their contracts include a frontend tag that can identify the source of the requests. The frontend is then paid a pro-rata share of their LQTY incentive token, multiplied by a kickback rate that the frontend can choose. This seems to work rather well: their approved frontend list, at the time of writing, offers 19 different options for using the platform, so the incentives seem to be encouraging individuals to host their own frontends and encouraging product teams such as DeFi Saver and Instadapp to integrate Liquity support in their apps. Liquity's core team, in fact, don't even run a frontend of their own.

So, of the decentralized hosting approaches, competitive frontends seem to be the strongest way to get your application hosted by a wide range of people. And, since they're incentivized directly to make the system better, stronger, faster, and more

---

[15] www.liquity.org/frontend#frontends

reliable, then you can expect your frontend ecosystem to remain strong. In exchange, you knowingly and deliberately give up your ability to dictate the UX. If you have visions for a beautiful, tasteful product, and you want to control the journeys that your users go through when using your protocol, this isn't the approach for you. If the bulk of your conceptual work is in your protocol, and the frontend is merely being used as an interface, then maybe you could consider adding an incentive structure for hosting it.

Centralized Hosting

Finally, then, we should evaluate a centralized approach. This is, essentially, no different from hosting any other website. You are responsible for the hosting technology choices, its uptime, or whether you'd like to hand over this responsibility to some hosting platform. Services like Vercel and Heroku make this easy, since you're just hosting an application like any other. Cloud hosting platforms such as AWS, Azure, and Google Cloud Platform give you more flexibility, configurability, programmability, and choice. Or, in simple cases, you can throw it up on a static host such as GitHub pages.

There are obvious benefits to centralized hosting. Firstly, *it's a well-known problem*. We've been hosting websites on centralized servers for as long as the Web has been around. Almost all the categories of tooling – servers, infrastructure as code, and CI/CD pipelines, to name a few – assume a centralized hosting approach. It's a straightforward and legible set of problems with lots of talent and documentation aimed at getting it right.

Secondly, and crucially, *centralized hosts support dynamic code*. If hosting on a centralized server, it's straightforward to add a server-side component. You can run a server-side language, such as Ruby, Python, PHP, or whatever else; you can serve your frontend via a mixed framework such as Next.js; you can even run an AWS Lambda function or use another "serverless" technology to power your backend. If you need to run a small indexing node, or a database, or provide integrations with some third-party web2 service, or even perform server-side rendering, this can be done with minimal fuss.

The disadvantages to centralized hosting are, essentially, the disadvantages of centralization. Your site won't be censorship resistant. There will be single points of failure, unless you architect your system carefully. You'll need to keep paying for your hosting bills and keep your domain names renewed. And it's also, in an important sense, contrary to the stated longer-term goals of the crypto movement: if your company goes under, then the interface to your protocol – which is likely to continue running – will become unavailable. Hosting on a centralized platform means that the buck stops squarely with you, for as long as people can expect to use your platform.

Another important thing to consider: A centralized hosting platform that you control does mean that you are responsible for your security posture. This is a blessing and a curse. A curse: Your responsibilities are higher, and you need to secure your own site security deployment processes. You may wish to have your frontend and hosting setup audited and will want to monitor deploys and changes closely. A blessing: You have one place to concentrate your security efforts. You don't have to worry about verifying the frontend code that other people are running. The security parameters you need are within your control: you, your company, and your brand are responsible for maintaining the Principle of Trust, not other, unknown, people.

Of course, your security posture is always something you are responsible for, and the decentralized approaches we've sketched out earlier are no different in that respect. There will still be security vulnerabilities when using them, and these will still be attached to your brand, well within the purview of your commercial and moral responsibility.

For one final time, our rubric is as follows:

- **User experience**: There are no trade-offs here, other than the possibility that your servers go offline. You host and serve your site as you would any other.

- **Developer experience**: You can use robust infrastructure-as-code practices to consolidate your hosting environment into something replicable and well structured, or you can throw the files into a GitHub repository and host via GitHub pages. Different hosting platforms will have different developer experience constraints. Centralized hosting gives you all the same choices that you have with web2 applications.

- **Operational complexity**: Similarly, this is mostly a question of how sophisticated your setup needs to be. But, again, it is a well-known set of problems, and not something unique or idiosyncratic that the constraints of web3 place upon us.

- **Decentralization**: There is, of course, no decentralization in this approach. You can get some of the benefits by serving your site via a CDN such as AWS CloudFront or Cloudflare or hosting it on a platform that provides high reliability via separated availability zones.

So the centralized approach is what it says on the tin: the exact same way you host anything else. There's nothing distinctively crypto about this, because there doesn't need to be. If you're not looking for censorship resistance at the level of your frontend, and you are willing to take responsibility – for the availability and security posture – through hosting as you would normally, then there are no good reasons to not do what already works.

Final Considerations

We've evaluated four different approaches here, three decentralized and one centralized. Judging by the performance on our rubric, the most viable decentralized approach is to integrate a competitive frontend mechanism into your protocol or host on IPFS using a centralized pinning system like Fleek. In both cases, your ability to run custom backend code *that you control* is severely compromised. You could merge the approaches by hosting a centralized API that the static, decentralized frontends can interact with, but this neuters the decentralization benefits: at that point, you might as well run the entire thing. If you want to control your user's experience, build a beautiful, tasteful product, and be able to run any sort of off-chain code, it looks as your best approach is usually to host it yourself and forego decentralization at the frontend.

I'll argue in more general terms, in the next chapter, that decentralization of frontends often isn't worth it. But I hope this section has illustrated that there are options available, and if it is a priority, it is possible to do so. There are significant trade-offs to doing so, and this becomes clear when you consider that many of the best responses to "how do I host my site easily on IPFS?" are of the form "use some centralized service X." The existing Internet has inherently centralized points: DNS servers, hosting providers, and browser vendors all have some greater or lesser degree of centralized control over the infrastructure that makes the Internet work.

The important question to ask, again, is "is decentralization worth it?" As I'll argue in Chapter 6, there are times when the answer to that question is a resounding *yes*, but there are also many, many times when the answer is *hell no*. Does a decentralized host make your user's experience better? Does it help them solve their problems better, easier, more efficiently, with less friction? In my opinion, if the answer to those questions is "no," the benefits have a very high bar to clear.

Fragility and Antifragility

Fragile systems suffer due to disorder, robust systems do not, and antifragile systems benefit from it. Crypto is full of disorder. Disorder emerges because of the properties of decentralized networks, constant innovation, the composability of protocols, the hostile environment, uncertain regulation, and cultural shifts. Products can be made more robust by considering robustness during development cycles. Centralized systems are typically more robust than decentralized systems, although that isn't always the case. Products can be made antifragile by analyzing customer behavior and by constantly changing and adapting the product as the environment shifts. You are a part of the system.

In his 2012 book *Antifragile: Things That Gain from Disorder*, the heterodox economist and philosopher Nassim Nicholas Taleb asks what the opposite of "fragile" is:

> *Almost all people answer that the opposite of 'fragile' is 'robust,' 'resilient,' 'solid,' or something of the sort. But the resilient, robust (and company) are items that neither break nor improve … Logically, the exact opposite of a 'fragile' parcel would be a package on which one has written 'please mishandle' or 'please handle carelessly.' Its contents would not just be unbreakable, but would benefit from shocks and a wide array of trauma. The fragile is the package that would be at best unharmed, the robust would be at best and at worst unharmed. And the opposite of fragile is therefore what is at worst unharmed.*

This paragraph – and the rest of this excellent book – offers three different levels of fragility that a system might exhibit:

- **Fragility**: The system suffers due to disorder.

- **Robustness**: The system does not suffer due to disorder.

- **Antifragility**: The system improves due to disorder.

This chapter has been discussing various infrastructure questions about Ethereum products: How do we test our products? How can they be hosted? What sorts of constraints does decentralization place on potential answers to these questions? But infrastructure is about the set of services and facilities needed to allow a system to endure. This includes your development processes, and so this seems like a good place to consider the notion of fragility in crypto. Since this is a book about products, we'll be thinking about fragility, robustness, and antifragility in terms of the products you build on top of Ethereum, but we'll also gesture toward how this might affect the protocol layer too and the other technical and socioeconomic layers that turn the product from a bunch of code to a constellation of services and value-creating behaviors.

Sources of Disorder and Fragility

Before we can consider how to make our systems robust and, ideally, antifragile, we must first understand what makes them fragile. Fragility, in my gloss of Taleb, refers to the property of a system such that it suffers within environments of disorder. Crypto is an environment of disorder, from the lowest technical level to the culture that permeates its development and marketing cycles. In what ways does this disorder emerge; what are the sources of a crypto product's potential fragility?

Let's look first at some sources of disorder that we've already discussed:

- **A user's interface – their wallet software as well as their browser – is not something that the product can control.** Wallet software is a highly competitive and changing space, and different vendors take different approaches to solving for different user flows. Disorder emerges at the interface between the app and the wallet and at the moment the user is taken away from your environment to sign transactions. Furthermore, this interface is changing over time, as wallets become more advanced.

- Ethereum smart contracts are run on a decentralized network, where **requests to compute are evaluated against competing requests** in a dynamic market and where **the results of these requests can be challenged and take time to be confirmed**. These network dynamics exhibit disorder because it is close to impossible to predict how long a given request will take to emerge into a state of consensus.

- Contracts are often built by composing on top of one another. This means that **the contracts that underlie your product could change**, or **their state could be modified in some way that your product doesn't expect**.

- **Gas prices are dynamic** in a way that makes pricing transaction costs ahead of time rather difficult. If your product is relying on high volumes of transactions, then small changes in gas prices might present severe disincentives, changing your user's behaviors. Can your business model sustain a prolonged period of network congestion and high transaction costs?

- **Indexing layers present another level of abstraction to worry about**: Does your data arrive in time to meet your frontend's render cycle? Is it fresh enough to make your system useful/not a violator of the Principle of Trust?

- **Decentralized hosting services complicate and compound the uncertainty** in your deployment processes and the user's connection to your application, but also reduce a single point of failure.

In the previous four chapters, we've seen how some of these sorts of constraints can enmesh your application in webs of uncertainty, and we've explored the trade-offs that you can make to reduce it. But there are many other technical sources of disorder that Ethereum products must reckon with. Some examples are as follows:

- **Hacks and smart contract vulnerabilities can force protocols to be paused** or their state – for example, values such as TVL, expected interest rates – to move out of predictable ranges.[16]

- **There are infrequent hard forks of blockchains** such as Ethereum, and sometimes – for example, after the recent Proof of Stake upgrade – it means that your product may have to handle new networks or tokens that you hadn't expected.

- **Some transactions can be subject to race conditions**, where the ordering of how those transactions are included within blocks – something you can't control – can matter hugely.

As well as some other, nontechnical sources of disorder

---

[16] This specific problem bit an old colleague of mine recently. When the Audius Project halted the contracts in response to a vulnerability (`https://twitter.com/AudiusProject/status/1551026771838914560`), they turned off all functions, including `balanceOf`. My colleague's internal script had assumed that this function was always available, which, when it wasn't, broke his system.

- **Market movements**: The composability of crypto means every token will eventually become a market. And introducing market dynamics to a system that doesn't expect them will change how that token is bought, sold, and therefore used. We'll see how this corrupts the governance aspects of product building in crypto in the next chapter. But this affects products directly, too: if the price of ETH goes up quickly or crashes by 80%, your product may need to handle sudden spikes in load or a different set of usage patterns.

- **Regulatory changes**: New laws – or new interpretations of old laws – could affect how your users onboard, the range of actions they are able to perform, or the sorts of compliance requirements that you need to implement in order to run your product legally or increase the costs of building or using it in some other way.

- **Cultural changes or meme shifts** can change how your users use and conceive of your product in sudden and often violent ways. In the summer of 2020, Uniswap faced a "vampire attack" from a newly competing protocol, SushiSwap, which dragged huge amounts of liquidity away from the former and forced Uniswap to change their product road map and launch the UNI token to stem the tide.[17]

In a world of composable, trustless protocols, a set of norms that encourage innovation, and a hostile environment, every new change can present a form of disorder. Much of this is impossible to predict or build around; at least some of it is inevitable. But there are things you can do to build robustness, and perhaps even antifragility, into your product.

Robust Systems

There are some general approaches to buttressing the robustness of your products, giving them greater facility in dealing with these many and varied sources of disorder. Some of these will be familiar from both our discussions in this book and from your experiences in web2:

---

[17] See https://phemex.com/blogs/what-are-vampire-attacks-in-crypto for more on vampire attacks.

- **Write lots of tests!** Structure your code in a way to make it easily testable, from automated unit tests of core functionality through to a wide range of manual testing scenarios. Run your tests at different times and upon different states of the blockchain.

- **Expect unanticipated user input** and therefore validate and handle this input. Understand the values that your smart contract API requires, supports, and disallows; and understand what is an *appropriate* range of values. Use warnings and errors to guide the user toward input that you can handle. Be paranoid.

- **Build for flexibility**, so that it's possible (and ideally easy) to change how your product works as the underlying context changes. Use feature flags to allow you to switch parts of your product on and off and roll features out to users incrementally.

- **Use best practices around techniques like caching.** Ensure you can readily expire caches and that you keep an eye out for data drift. Always be ready to rebuild your caches (including your indexes) from scratch.

- **Don't trust code you didn't write**, including the API – the protocol – that you're integrating with. Parse its error messages, read its code, format its inputs, and put layers between the contract's surface area (the smart contract calls you make) and the user's surface area (your UI). Third-party APIs could rate-limit or even switch off access from your application. You'll need to decide whether that is an acceptable trade-off to make in exchange for reduced code complexity. To help with this decision, consider how the incentives are aligned: Are you paying somebody for a continued service?

These approaches, taken together and applied broadly, will get you fairly close to a robust system. But there are crypto-specific problems you'll need to address, too, with their own concomitant approaches to robustness:

- **Rely on community standards** when dealing with crypto infrastructure (but don't trust wallet software, nodes, or any other participants to follow them). We'll discuss standards more in the next chapter, but the takeaway here is to use them, follow them, promote them, and suggest improvements. Standards making is a community activity.

- **Implement UI and rely on UX patterns to stabilize the user's experience** across the various forms of network uncertainty, guiding them through it while minimizing assumptions about processing time, finality, and similar concepts. Where possible, reduce the number of decisions the user needs to make, and build UI that is able to abstract away that uncertainty and render it certain.

- **Spend time with the protocol team** and ask questions about what sorts of black swan events your protocol code – and the economic system it models – will be vulnerable to. If you can build around these vulnerabilities in your product, even better; but just understanding them will give you a leg up when the problems begin.

- **Cultivate a sense of purpose**, both within your team and your broader community. Focus on building a product that solves a user's problem, rather than just getting a notoriously fickle and self-serving hostile environment excited for a hot second. If you are adding value to your user's lives in a sustained and legible way, you can weather many changes in fashion and shifts in norms.

Finally, consider how decentralization can affect your robustness, especially with respect to regulatory changes. If you centralize some of your business processes and have some centralized control over your product, you're more likely to be able to move quickly, be flexible, and have a clearer regulatory starting point. (There are reasons to disagree with this take, but it's ultimately a question of how much risk you'd like to expose yourself to, and centralizing your basic legal entity and basic product development and deployment procedures does seem to give you more optionality to adjust to a changing regulatory regime.)[18]

Robustness, then, is something that you work toward through good development practices. It's something you need to think about before and during your product build; it deserves time spent in the hammock, not just time spent at the terminal. It's something that you can engineer through paranoid programming and rigorous testing. It's a property of your processes as well as your product. And it's something that you will have to cultivate. Crypto will force robustness upon you, or you will die.

Antifragile Systems

We have done a quick survey of the sources of the disorder your product might have to endure and some ways to make your product robust to this disorder. But Taleb's trichotomy goes one step further: antifragile systems are more than robust. They benefit from variability. When disorder occurs, *they get better*.

We can apply similar thinking to product engineering on Ethereum. What sort of characteristics does an antifragile Ethereum product have?

- **A robust and improving interface** that gets better when it's used in unconventional ways. You can achieve this via an explicit goal of multiple frontends that we incentivize for, as in the case of this chapter's "Competitive Frontends" section – and then let the market develop frontends for your ever-growing use cases. Or it can be something that we can encourage more gently: publishing our ABIs and core data model as an npm package, as we discussed in Chapter 4; standardizing the basic transaction flow; coding basic user

---

[18] You could, of course, follow the crypto-libertarian meme of "become ungovernable": decentralize your product maximally and remove the ability of a regulatory body to censor your product. But this approach is unlikely to be sustainable forever. As Matt Clifford says, the physical is stubbornly persistent; you, the nodes you rely on, the servers that validate your blocks and serve your frontends, the fiat on-ramps that provide the ecosystem with liquidity, and the pipes that connect them altogether need to be located *somewhere*. Until the nation state looks very different, you'd be wise to remember that. You can also exploit the differences in competing regulatory regimes: if a particular polity has a more stable or flexible relationship to crypto, you could consider basing your operations there; regulatory arbitrage! Regardless, none of this is legal advice.

flows around our core functionality and then exposing, perhaps via an "expert mode" toggle (as, e.g., we discussed in Chapter 2), whatever configuration options are required.

- **Feedback loops that nudge demand around relative to supply.** Consider the problem of network congestion. An antifragile system could alert the user that the network is congested and, where appropriate, advise them to submit their transaction later (turning the disorder of network congestion into a trust-preserving property of your product).

- **Independence**: An antifragile Ethereum application is characterized by its independence from other parts of the ecosystem; it protects users against changes to the protocol layer, to the lower transaction layer interfaces, to the hosting environment, and to the wallets they use. It is composed of a set of loosely coupled components that can be upgraded, replaced, or reused as needed, with minimal disruption. It uses simple abstractions built upon minimal assumptions.

- **Transparency**: An antifragile Ethereum product benefits from the public nature of the blockchain by allowing the user's data to be readable and exportable in a transparent way. If a use case emerges, or some disorder creates access problems, the basic mechanisms of accounting and the data required to recreate them are available outside of the product.

What is common about these characteristics is that in order for the system to improve, its developers need to be monitoring its usage, adjusting and revising the interface. There should always be a *human in the loop*. It's much too easy to treat an interface as a wrapper around a set of known behaviors of a protocol: the protocol lays out how it can be used, and you build an interface around those behaviors.

But this is not the way to build an antifragile product. Instead, you should be observing how your users interact with the protocol. Use analytics to track in-app user behavior, keep an eye on the pieces of dependent on-chain state, and wrap them up into a feedback loop that helps drive your product road map.

The hashtag is a helpful example of this sort of feedback loop in action. The hashtag emerged organically out of user behavior: originally, Twitter did not support hashtags in any meaningful way. Users began to include them as a way of categorizing content (and, subsequently, as a mechanism for comedy and meme creation). As they became more popular, third-party developers began to implement tools that could read and track these tags' usage. Over time, first-class support for hashtags was introduced into the Twitter UI. This helped drive more usage of hashtags, which brought more power to the third-party tooling, which incentivized Twitter to increase its native support. A virtuous cycle formed until the variability of usage started to stabilize. Ahead of time, it would have been hard to predict that users would add strings of characters to the pound symbol ("#") and that this would become a way to add structure to tweets. But it happened, and the Twitter team was then nimble enough to understand and respond to this emergent use case.

Because crypto protocols are much easier to access and can be built upon by third-party developers – that is, they are *permissionless* and *composable* – you can expect to see such emergent behavior from your own users. If your protocol provides value, and if it is being used by any serious number of people, you will see patterns of behavior and custom integrations that you would never have expected, often in a very short time from launch. Adapt and change your frontend as such behaviors emerge. Even if your product doesn't give rise to hashtag-like pieces of emergent user behavior, the system in which your product sits – the Ethereum ecosystem – is sufficiently chaotic that you will benefit from being on top of all this, and being ready to adjust, even if that means killing your more sacred cows.

Your product, in short, should be a living, breathing thing, something that not only permits users to interact with the protocol but informs, shapes, and sometimes limits how the protocol can change. Your system can only be antifragile if you are a part of it. You will need to be there to change, sometimes radically, course-correct, or otherwise adapt. But even if you aim for antifragility, miss, and hit robustness, it was still a successful process. You've built something to weather the storm. And, if you're building in crypto, you can be sure that a storm is coming.

Summary

At the beginning of this chapter, we looked at testing. I gave a description of how I like to design and test my Ethereum code, by building up lots of small, discrete, pure functions to encode business logic (which can then be tested via standard unit tests) and then a set of end-to-end test scenarios supported by setup scripts.

We then talked a little bit about hosting. We explored some approaches to decentralized hosting, including IPFS, and saw how decentralized hosting forces us to incur various costs and restrictions. We compared this against a centralized hosting approach, which comes across rather favorably (if we don't feel the need to decentralize our frontend, that is).

We concluded in the last section by looking at how our products might exhibit fragility and where the sources of that fragility might come from. We looked at Nassim Nicholas Taleb's notions of robustness and antifragility and considered how our products might exhibit these properties.

In the next chapter, our final chapter before the conclusion, we'll start to bring all these threads together. We'll evaluate decentralization properly, exploring it as a spectrum. And we'll think about standards and how they affect Ethereum development over time. Once that's done, we're nearly home.

CHAPTER 6

Decentralization

By now, we've seen how Ethereum's idiosyncratic execution model presents challenges for people trying to build products. A lot of these idiosyncrasies come from the decentralized nature of the Ethereum blockchain. And a lot of these idiosyncrasies do not serve the best interests of our companies, our products, and most importantly our customers. We need to rethink what decentralization means in practice, face some harsh truths, and be more flexible and open to centralization where it is suitable and useful and aligned with our goals. In this chapter, we'll step away from the technical focus of previous chapters and instead consider how decentralization affects building with Ethereum.

Decentralization Is a Fetish

Crypto-skeptics and crypto-fanatics tend to use an implicit assumption of maximal decentralization. Most people don't actually want decentralization; their goals are prior to decentralization. Decentralization is therefore a helpful meme, but ultimately a fetish, born from confusing the ends with the means. Decentralization is a spectrum, not a binary, and a multidimensional spectrum at that. The network, computation, data, indexing, and the rest of the application layer can all be more or less decentralized. Decentralization at the network level is good. The fact of potential decentralization can be powerful too; counterfactual decentralization is an important property. Decentralization can therefore be a backstop against some of the larger problems with centralized systems, without forcing us to be centralized where it is unnecessary.

When you ask a crypto-skeptic what decentralization means, they offer these sorts of properties:

1. **Many nodes are run across many jurisdictions**; products run in a way that can't ever be shut down or censored.

© Jamie Rumbelow 2023
J. Rumbelow, *Building With Ethereum*, https://doi.org/10.1007/978-1-4842-9045-3_6

2.   **Individuals can access the system for whatever nefarious purposes**[1] **they wish**, without the need for AML/KYC checks.

3.   **Power is completely diffused** rather than concentrated in any one party; therefore, no individual party is responsible, legally speaking.

These sorts of conditions refer to what I'll call *maximal decentralization*. Maximal decentralization is a description of a system such that that system is maximally decentralized in every way possible (up to whatever point of diminishing marginal returns seems appropriate). It is *a point on the decentralization spectrum*. Decentralization itself is a property of a system such that the system can have more or less participation, more or less accessibility, and more or less diffused power.

This might seem like a meaningless semantic distinction, but of course not all semantic distinctions are meaningless, and some are indeed important. How we define our terms matters, because it determines the shape of what we build and gives us criteria against which we evaluate our success. Moreover, if we disagree over what we mean by a term like "decentralization," we end up arguing fruitlessly. We exchange claims and both sides miss the point. So we should define our terms!

A lot of crypto-fanatics also believe, somewhat reflexively, that we should be aiming for maximal decentralization. The worst crypto-fanatics are just as ideological as the worst crypto-skeptics. This is a problem. People shouldn't be fanatical.

For almost every category, maximalism is bad. It ties you into a priori commitments, which reduce your optionality and cripple your ability to adjust to new facts. Strong beliefs are important, but they should generally be held weakly. It also makes you much more likely to act tribally. Humans are tribal, and "decentralize everything" can become a rallying cry, a standard around which troops array for battle. It makes technical questions political, and politics is the mind-killer.[2]

Crypto people shouldn't be fanatical, because computing is the art of the science of trade-offs, and "decentralization" gives us a lot more room for maneuver than either its critics or fanatics seem to allow. Trade-offs are useful, and understanding the trade-off space is most of the work.

I suspect that crypto people don't actually want decentralization *per se*, because when you ask *why decentralization matters*, you get answers like

---

[1] https://twitter.com/SGBarbour/status/1528432799941808130
[2] www.lesswrong.com/posts/9weLK2AJ9JEt2Tt8f/politics-is-the-mind-killer

It makes the technology more accessible and more censor-resistant. It gives broader access to more people, especially those less well-served by existing financial infrastructure.

This means that their motivations are *prior to decentralization*. They want accessibility, not decentralization. They want censorship resistance and greater equality of opportunity, not decentralization. Decentralization is the means to achieve these goals, not the goal itself.

We also want other things. Decentralization means more competition, and more competition means more innovation: diversity is good – let a thousand flowers bloom! The ideas being generated and built upon by the crypto community are not commodities: they are meaningfully new contributions to a meaningfully new technology stack; we get more ideas when we have a more competitive space, and we get more competition when people are able to use the technology and gain access to the liquidity needed to prove the new ideas out within a real market.

So what we want is better, more accessible technology. Technology that is able to iterate faster and benefit from the combinatorial effects of an open and often open source development model. Technology that is not gate-kept and can be used and built upon by anybody who wants to do so.

This reveals a kind of fetish held by many in the crypto community, an error of thought caused by confusing the ends with the means. This is *the fetish of decentralization*: the belief that we want decentralization for its own sake, not because it gives us an environment in which we can achieve the goals we actually care about, but because it matters simpliciter.

In the Ethereum community, decentralization is as much a *cultural* phenomenon as it is a technological decision. But this cultural commitment to maximal decentralization is restrictive. It forces us to make significant trade-offs in product quality and encourages us to reason about our products in technical terms, rather than in terms of our users and their goals. It precludes many sensible design decisions, increases the operational costs, and, in many cases, makes the broader experience worse. And because it's deeply rooted in the cultural substrate of the technology, it is a hard thing to change.

In order to break away from this fetish, we need to think about decentralization in a more flexible, yielding way. We need to reconceive of decentralization as a set of trade-offs that are made in support of our *actual* goals – accessibility, censorship resistance, competition, composability; most of all solving problems for users – without holding ourselves hostage to its demands. We need to give ourselves more flexibility, on the one hand; and, on the other, stop giving our opponents a stick with which they can beat us.

Decentralization Is Multidimensional

Decentralization isn't a binary state. Systems can be more or less decentralized. When we have arguments about whether a system is decentralized, what we're actually arguing over is whether a system is decentralized *enough*.

But this raises a really important question: Decentralized enough for what?

There isn't a single answer to this question. It depends entirely on what kind of an application we're trying to build and what sorts of problems we're trying to solve for our users. We are building products, not technology, and these products have different audiences and aims. The technological decisions we make, the properties we're going to optimize for, are a function of our product goals, not the other way around. In order to understand the decentralization spectrum, then, we first need to think about what we actually want. What are we building? What sorts of properties do we want our product to have?

Once we have a clear idea of our product priorities, we can then decide where on the decentralization spectrum we wish to sit. But in order to do *that*, we need a better idea of what sorts of decentralization we can choose between. What are the dimensions of decentralization?

Dimensions of Decentralization

There are different dimensions of decentralization, different layers of the product and technical stack that can be more or less decentralized. As this book, I hope, has made clear, there are lots of ways to decentralize your product, some valuable, some unimportant, and all conditional on your product and commercial priorities.

The first, and an obvious dimension of decentralization, is a *decentralization of computation*. Much of this we get "for free" by choosing to base our application on Ethereum. We may, in some instances, wish to move some computation off-chain. If we are building a complicated trading strategy, for instance, we might perform quite a lot of the computation off-chain and only flush the results of that computation on-chain when we actually wish to trade. What are the trade-offs here? Speed, since the EVM is not a fast execution platform, and gas costs, since the more computation we put on-chain, the more we'll have to pay for it and, depending on market conditions, the less assurance we'll have that there will be space in the current block. Perhaps also some developer concerns: Writing complicated mathematics in good quality Solidity, for instance, is a fundamentally more challenging task than writing it in an off-chain language, since every line of on-chain code needs to be audited and optimized and the library ecosystem is less mature.

There are also considerations that affect the product more directly: there are certain values and APIs that we'll need to pull from an off-chain source. We could place an oracle on-chain, run some off-chain code to keep it updated, and put as much computation in our contracts as possible, but someone would still need to manage the oracle. If our API was private, or we wanted to filter some values before, that someone would have to be us. We also might want to push values out to off-chain APIs (such as push notifications).

All in all, then, we should think sensibly about how our product goals and our technical capabilities relate to what gets computed on-chain and what gets computed off-chain. There are for sure benefits to computing things on-chain where possible, the biggest of which is reliable composability over time. If you need to run off-chain processes to make your product work, then this increases the risk for others using your protocol. There are also significant transparency benefits: on-chain computation can be verified through the standard Ethereum consensus mechanism, and it very well may increase the trust that your (more technical) users have in your product.

The second dimension of decentralization is *network decentralization*. I won't labor this point very much, since this is a book about product, rather than about Ethereum itself. There are strong community norms to keep the network decentralized, and this is where some of the most impressive innovations keep happening: the Proof of Stake merge, upcoming sharding improvements, and even the EVM itself are a testament to the time and energy spent ensuring the decentralization of the network. And this is unequivocally a good thing: if the network isn't decentralized, then nothing else above it is, and what we are building ceases to inherit its benefits.

There's another dimension of decentralization that matters: the *decentralization of data*. This is different from computation, and the underlying network, since it's about where the state lies, rather than what is processing it. If you are performing computation off-chain, then you should generally try to move the results of these computations on-chain. You get some of the composability and transparency benefits of decentralized computation, but you also get a lot more flexibility *around* your product, since you can always reconstruct the current state of your system from what is on-chain; you can build a new frontend without having to worry about rewriting the data storage layer. Moreover, others can build frontends for your system – or tooling, or analysis, or extensions to functionality – without any work on your part. And the decentralization of data has other public benefits that we'll discuss shortly.

But notice that all these different sorts of decentralization don't in any serious way preclude you from being more centralized at the product level. You can index your product data in a centralized way without compromising the underlying decentralization of data. You can host your product in a centralized way without compromising the underlying decentralization of the network. And you can centralize your product development *process* – how you build and manage your product – without compromising the underlying layers of decentralization: network, data, and computation. Decentralization is multidimensional, and being decentralized on one dimension does not usually necessitate being decentralized on the others.

Decentralization As a Backstop

A moment ago, I said that there are public benefits to certain forms of decentralization that are important parts of the evaluation space. We must realize that often *just the ability to decentralize means that the goals of decentralization can be achieved.* Centralized parts of a decentralized system don't make the system totally centralized; it's not a binary!

Consider RPC node hosts. We've mentioned a few in this book already, and while, for example, companies like Alchemy do enjoy some dominance in the market, *it is reasonably easy to run a node* and would not be especially capital intensive to start a competitor. And there are clear incentives to do so: you can build a good business building pickaxes for an inchoate industry. We know this is true, since there *actually are* lots of competitors. This gives the larger teams such as Alchemy a very good reason to not abuse their power. If they did, it would be extremely easy for their customers to leave. The fact that the computation layer and its implementation – for example, the geth codebase – is permissionlessly accessible means that there are downstream pressures on people who use those implementations to not abuse their power.

Being "counterfactually decentralized" is a real thing, even if the actual distribution of control is skewed to one or a few parties. The fact that there *could* be competition and that the costs to launch new competitors are low creates a natural pressure away from the inevitable monopolistic tendencies of having that control.

Given my evaluation of various trade-offs in previous chapters, it might seem as though I'm strictly antidecentralization. That is not at all the case, as I hope I've shown here. There are many benefits to decentralizing parts of your technology stack. Acknowledging trade-offs goes in both directions.

In the interests of intellectual honesty, then, let's make them more explicit.

What are some of the problems with centralization? It can, and does, impose various sorts of risks and externalities that decentralizing parts of the stack can help mitigate:

- Centralized systems can **curtail innovation**, by enforcing permissioned access to the platform at the expense of unforeseen and potentially valuable new ideas. The incentives of the platform owner can conflict with the shared benefits; innovation, in this sense, is a public good that might impose private costs.

- Centralized systems **amplify weaknesses**. If a certain piece of code has a bug or a particular needed feature hasn't been implemented, centralization can increase the impact that these shortcomings have on the community. More decentralization of implementation means more diversity and fewer systemic weaknesses and more variation in the meme pool.

- Centralized systems **tend toward more centralization**. Having control over resources and data creates a flywheel of growth and increased power, which makes competition more difficult.

Decentralized systems help undercut the ability of centralizing parties to gain full control, by encouraging competition, which drives innovation and widens access. The composability of smart contracts, like the composability of open source software, accelerates innovation even further.

The key point here is that the problems centralization causes are global problems: they apply at the system level. For any individual, responding to predictable incentives, more centralization is usually a benefit: it's better to get more power, customers, money, etc., than less, and centralizing can make this easier and more attractive. But for the system as a whole, more centralization can lead us into suboptimal equilibria.

So if we care about avoiding these suboptimal equilibria, decentralization needs to be embedded at *the system level*. The underlying technology needs to provide a *backstop*, a mechanism for preventing too much centralization from creeping in.

But this doesn't change the incentives for individual teams. *Centralization is often the right choice for your team, product, and users.* The trade-off space for you is different from the trade-off space for the community at large. We've seen plenty of examples in this book how this decentralization fetish can have direct consequences on the quality of your products.

What we need is a backstop: a way of ensuring decentralization on the dimensions it matters. Fortunately, the system design of Ethereum provides this backstop. It acts as a form of regulation, limiting the ability of a single party to have so much power that competition is impossible and monopoly rents can be extracted.

This means that you may, and indeed will, make centralizing choices. And this is okay. It should be considered to be okay. It should be expected. And the community can be safe knowing that your gaudier excesses are limited by the decentralization in the underlying platform.

Practically, what does this look like?

- We can be **free to make centralizing choices** with our frontends. Indexers don't need to be decentralized nor do our web hosts. We can use centralized infrastructure providers. We can make use of centralized data stores. We can run our products on centralized web hosts. We can avoid the complexities and costs of decentralization by *simply not indulging the fetish.*

- We can **move some computation off-chain** if that makes our products better. Putting all computation on-chain is a recipe for slow, expensive, and cumbersome protocols with inelegant user experiences. In many cases, for instance, data processing, computing the results off-chain and then committing its results on-chain is a much more sensible approach that benefits the user without losing many of the benefits of a public and auditable blockchain. However, we need to weigh this against the future composability of our protocols: Is this something that matters to you? Will it matter to your users?

- **We can ask for, and rely on, user-identifiable information.** Some use cases won't need this, but we shouldn't be afraid to do so if ours does. Being able to provide email or push notifications is valuable. And charging users via Stripe or other standard payment mechanisms also will require some kind of off-chain user info. If your business model is better off cast in the SaaS mold, that's fine!

- We can be free to **use analytics** to track and monitor our users, feeding this information back into our commercial models and product design processes. We can be free to use cookies and other browser-side tracking technologies to make our products more functional and user-friendly. Pseudonymity is not the same thing as anonymity, and there is no reasonable expectation of complete privacy when using products built by centralized companies.

In short, we don't need to play to the gallery, "performing" decentralization, in order to curry favor along a unidimensional community norm. Use decentralized technologies where appropriate; use centralized technologies when appropriate. And, crucially, always with an eye on whether what we're building is actually usable and will actually be used. We'll pick up this theme again in the conclusion.

Standards

Standards are a form of implicit coordination. Who sets the standards matter, since standards have path-dependent effects on the sorts of products we can build in the future. If we increase standardization at the application layer, then we can improve product quality, improve product interoperability, and save us all a lot of time. Three examples where this seems pertinent are error messages, security and verification, *and* authorization. *Standards enable composability. Product engineers can, and should, be more involved in the protocol* and *standards design process. Finally, if we don't codify standards, that doesn't mean we don't have them: it just means that our standards, like our histories, are written by the victors.*

We've mentioned various standards in passing throughout this book. Standards and decentralization are very deeply linked in some important ways. Better understanding these links is essential for the future success and robustness of the Ethereum community, and studying them can provide responses to some of the worries we might have about the current state of Ethereum product engineering.

To that end, in this section, I'm going to make two major points:

1. **Standards matter**, a lot, and they matter in ways that are not initially obvious.

2. We should **make greater use of them**.

I'll start by arguing for the first claim, expanding on the notion of a standard and justifying why and how standards can be important. With this developed notion of a standard in hand, I'll move to the second claim, defending it by exploring some ways in which standards could be applied to meaningfully improve, in particular, the user experience of Ethereum applications. I'll then draw some practical lessons for those of us building with Ethereum.

What Are Standards?

We'll begin by exploring what "standards" means.

Some Etymology

I obliquely referenced the dictionary definition of "standard" earlier. Let's make it explicit. The word *standard* flows into English from the Old French *estandart*, meaning a battle flag or a rallying place.

This is etymologically interesting, because it suggests two senses. The first is an active sense: troops on the battlefield, rallying around a battle flag, which gives us the sense of active coordination, pride, and centralized focus. The second has the tone of something slightly more passive: a gathering place. Why do I say more passive? Because people gather naturally. One of Schelling's great insights was that there exist points at which agents will converge naturally in the absence of coordination. If it is a warm, sunny day, people gather on the beach, naturally, passively, no flag needed.

This reading, this more passive sense, also suggests an interesting definition of standard, one that I think captures something important about the essence of the term and one that I will be taking with us as a base for the rest of this section:

A standard is a form of implicit coordination.

For crypto, the word "implicit" is important. Why? Because its semantics imply decentralization. Coordinating explicitly means coordinating in a centralized manner, with all of the responsibilities and gate-keeping privileges that that can entail.

In a slightly weaker sense, implicit forms of coordination seem much less likely to be coercive. There are certainly forms of implicit coercion, but built into the notion of implicit coordination is the idea that individual agents are choosing to follow a specific path, and that path converges naturally with others'.

This doesn't mean the standard *itself* needs to be implicit: many standards are codified, written down explicitly and shared as a standard. But on this definition, standards give us a mechanism for coordinating implicitly, without needing to rely on a central authority to organize us. *The fact that the standard exists is enough.*

Slightly more practically, this means that standards are

- **Opt-in**, in the sense they're not forced upon you by the underlying technology.

- **Generally popular**, or at least followed reliably (more than 50% of the time).

- **Often codified**, but subject to revision, in the sense that the codification is a lagging indicator. If the community moves, so does the standard. (More on this point later.)

This serves as a good starting point for our discussion.

Who Sets the Standards?

If we think about standards in these terms – opt-in, popularly followed, and often codified – then we're left with a notion that seems *central* to how we build software on decentralized platforms. This centrality means that standards can be powerful, which raises the question: Who gets to set the standards? How are standards decided upon?

One obvious place to start is the mechanisms of community governance.

In Ethereum, this means most prominently the EIP/ERC infrastructure. ERCs, in particular, are good examples of this form of standards as implicit coordination, since nobody is compelled to follow them – they are opt-in – some of them are generally popular, and they are codified in documents and interfaces (with available mechanisms for amendment). They allow smart contract engineers to coordinate implicitly around shared behavior and expectations.

229

ERC-20 is perhaps the most famous example. It provides a basic interface that defines the notion of a "token" and therefore is foundational to most of crypto and all of DeFi. We looked at the ERC-20 standard in some detail in Chapter 2's "Accounts and Wallets" section.

It provides a primitive, but *only insofar as it is standardized*. This is an excellent illustration of why standards like these can be so powerful: if nobody followed ERC-20, it's unlikely we would have a common, composable notion of a token. Representations of on-chain value – what the standard provides for – would be semantically fragmented between applications. Its status as a primitive is due to the fact that people use it to coordinate. Standards yield primitives.

A more recent case is ERC-4626, a tokenized vault standard spearheaded by Joey Santoro, then at Fei Labs.[3] It provides a standard for wrapping an ERC-20 token in some form of vault or yield-bearing instrument. By standardizing, the designers hope to provide compatibility and fungibility between different encapsulations of the same token or even different encapsulations of different tokens, allowing you to swap between them in a generic way. The details of how it works are interesting,[4] but not relevant here. Why it is a useful example is because it illustrates how standards, as we have defined them, can *themselves* be composed into new primitives. You can take standards and combine them with other ideas to create new primitives.

A third and final example of a standard formed by community governance is ERC-2612, which allows for signed rather than transacted ERC-20 approvals. This is a case of taking a primitive and *improving* it, adjusting future behavior after learning lessons from the past. The fact that the standard is codified means that *there is some canonical representation*, and thus it can be upgraded.

So the mechanisms of community governance clearly give us plenty of examples of standards.

But there are others who get to set standards. One important group are those who build developer tooling. The JavaScript ecosystem provides an illustrative example. Before npm was released, package management in node (and across JavaScript more broadly) was this big fragmented messy thing, with the notion of a JavaScript package ill-defined and the mechanism to distribute it left up to the developer. npm set the standard for more than just the distribution mechanism: its popularity led developers to use

---

[3] https://eips.ethereum.org/EIPS/eip-4626

[4] See, for instance, Joey's discussion on the Solidity Fridays YouTube channel: www.youtube.com/watch?v=L8dijE5qhTg

`package.json` files to describe and define codebases in JavaScript. Usage of the tool for its specific use case – defining and reading dependencies – has led to a form of implicit coordination around an approach to describing a much broader structure of metadata. Now, `npm` is used as a script runner and setting for configuration of third-party tools, as well as a way to identify a package and its dependencies.

Tooling is, in fact, a specific instance of a much more general source of standards. *Standards are written by whoever builds the interfaces that the majority of people use.*

Another JavaScript example: If you study the 1990s browser wars and how their impact ricocheted into the early 2000s, you realize very quickly that the entire shape of frontend development, and with it much of the Web, was determined by a handful of businesses: namely, whoever was building the browsers at the time.[5] There is a nearby timeline in which we're all still using Flash!

What's the parallel here for crypto? One springs to mind: MetaMask. While it's true that the majority of crypto *holders* use centralized exchanges, the majority of crypto *users* use MetaMask: at the time of writing, it's still overwhelmingly the most popular self-custody active crypto wallet, which means that MetaMask gets to set the standards for how dapp frontends interact with wallets. You see this already: the ubiquitous `window.ethereum` object with which all dapps integrate – via second-order tooling, such as *ethers.js* – and with which all competitor wallets have to remain compatible is something that MetaMask gets to control. If you want your dapp to be usable by a majority of users, then it has to work with MetaMask. MetaMask's dominance means they get to decide, broadly, how the dapp/wallet interface behaves.[6]

Thus, those with priorly existing resources find themselves at the apex of power, able to dictate the terms of coordination for all other parties. This puts us at risk of a form of "standard capture."

---

[5] It was only when Mozilla launched Firefox and started to gain market share that JavaScript took off seriously. Even then, it nearly ended up being scrapped in favor of ActionScript, but because Microsoft didn't want to collaborate with Macromedia, the attempts to standardize around ActionScript fell through. It was really only the period between the AJAX whitepaper in 2005 and the release of Chrome and codification of ECMAScript 5 in 2009 that JavaScript became indispensable, for better or worse, to the web experience.

[6] EIP-1193 (`https://eips.ethereum.org/EIPS/eip-1193`) aims to codify this interface, and the wallets are more or less good at following it. But the point still stands: if they wanted to, MetaMask could deviate from it, and most dapps would have to deviate in turn.

Standard Capture and Path Dependence

In a broadly market-based system, a community will converge upon some solution or another based on the competition between multiple options in conceptual and implementation space. Firms compete to solve a problem by offering different versions of solutions. The better solutions, we hope, rise to the top.

However, it's rarely this clean in practice. The solution the market chooses is often *not* the *optimal* solution. A lot of technological choices we make are path dependent: the fact that a solution has already been chosen "locks in" that solution's eventual success, since an individual consumer's preferences are often irrational or inelastic or underspecified relative to their longer-term needs or wants.

"Lock in" is an especially severe problem when developing smart contracts. Major contract changes are very difficult, especially when large amounts of liquidity are involved and need to be moved from one contract to another. The risks go up, and the velocity of changes goes down, locking in prior behavior.

When your priority is shipping – which, by the way, it usually should be! – "good enough for now" is often the best heuristic to use. But central to this heuristic is the fact that we're often explicitly and implicitly making trade-offs!

So technological choices we make today implicate those trade-offs. My decisions today might

- Render impossible future features

- Make it much more difficult to compose my functionality with other participants

- Set psychological and cultural expectations of how things *ought* to work in the future

- Shape what problems and behaviors are most *salient*

Any one of which can have important downstream effects on what gets built, what gets funded, and what gets used. The effects can also be commercial: if we allow "standard capture," then we may be handing monopoly power to early ecosystem participants simply because they're early, not because it's necessarily the right or desired thing.[7] Technological choices are path dependent, and this path dependence matters to our products.

We can once more look outside of crypto to see a great example of how the path dependence of standards affects our products.

Let's consider the use of the RSS standard for distributing podcasts. Using RSS saves the developers of podcast players lots of time: they don't need to worry about the distribution mechanism of the podcasts themselves and can focus on other parts of their application, such as the interface and branding. Their apps inherit all of the existing podcasts, which helps solve the cold-start problem. Standardizing on RSS has meant that many more podcast players were launched that would have been otherwise. But standardizing on RSS has also meant that a key part of the podcast experience – how audio content gets from the producer to the listener – is ossified and cannot easily be changed. So the choice of using RSS to distribute podcasts has both enabled much of the growth in the podcasting medium *and* limited its technical capabilities.

This path dependence means that we can't rest on our laurels. We need to be proactive and thoughtful about the standards we set and aim to do so in an explicit, codified, and community-driven way, rather than allow the standards to emerge based on who happens to have power or what happens to be the right immediate technological choice to make.

The Case for Greater Standardization

My defense of this second claim is mostly a defense by example: I've come up with three areas where I think good standardization could meaningfully improve the user experience of DeFi and where it could do so precisely by aligning behaviors between the various constituencies – protocol, product, platform engineering, as well as wallet designers and core developers – that we've been discussing throughout this book. But my broad point is that there is a much greater design space for application-level

---

[7] A good example here is Apple: their App Store system had huge benefits for developers in the early years of apps, giving them a common platform to develop upon and bootstrapping the ecosystem thanks to the success of the iPhone. But that has had the effect of giving large amounts of control, to a single organization, over a big part of the software economy. See, e.g., www.hey.com/apple/iap/ for an instance of how this can (arguably) go wrong. For further reading on the economics of the App Store, I recommend the excellent Stratechery: https://stratechery.com/2022/data-and-definitions/

standardization than we typically see in Ethereum. Most EIP standards are concerned, understandably, with underlying network behaviors. Product engineers should rise to this challenge.

Error Messages

We've spoken a little already about how error messages are a fundamentally broken part of the product engineering experience in Ethereum. Many smart contracts return unstructured strings; some smart contracts return objects, which are machine readable but not standardized in any meaningful way; some smart contracts don't even revert with any error message. This makes parsing, formatting, and suggesting remedies inside products much more difficult.

By standardizing error messages at the smart contract level, we can give a both more consistent and more localizable experience – for, at least, the 80% use case, which would give us at least some coverage over the sorts of applications that we care about – and allow more general tooling to be built that could reduce product engineering time. It could also reduce *protocol* engineering time, because fewer decisions would need to be made, and testing libraries could be written around asserting against a well-known set of errors.

There has been an attempt at standardizing error messages before. The EIP-1066 standard is a solid, and pretty extensible, attempt to standardize error messages, built on the HTTP status code model. Unfortunately, for reasons I'm unable to figure out, it has gone stagnant.[8]

There are even farther-reaching benefits of a popular and codified error message standard. Beyond just informing the user something has gone wrong, a standard would allow us to make suggestions about how to fix it. We can embed predictable and familiar *retry logic* into our applications and wallet software.

A good analog here, which might help illustrate what I'm suggesting, can be found in much web2 developer tooling. Lots of IDEs pick up on syntactic or semantic errors and make suggestions inline, as in Figure 6-1.

---

[8] https://eips.ethereum.org/EIPS/eip-1066; my suspicion, which might be uncharitable, is that it has gone stagnant because not enough of the people working on Ethereum standards care very much about the application layer or, at least, don't spend much of their time working there. Yet another reason why raising the status of the product engineer is important: Standards affect products, and so product engineers should be helping to shape and inform those standards.

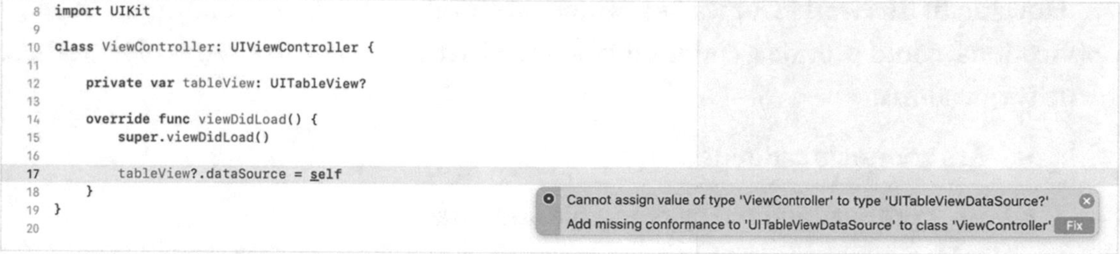

```
 8  import UIKit
 9
10  class ViewController: UIViewController {
11
12      private var tableView: UITableView?
13
14      override func viewDidLoad() {
15          super.viewDidLoad()
16
17          tableView?.dataSource = self
18      }
19  }
20
```

○ Cannot assign value of type 'ViewController' to type 'UITableViewDataSource?'   ⊗
  Add missing conformance to 'UITableViewDataSource' to class 'ViewController'   Fix

Figure 6-1. *Xcode provides a "fix" button when it detects a fixable syntax or semantic error in the user's code*

Clicking "Fix" causes the IDE to change the code and fix the syntax error. It makes writing code easier, allows developers to use more esoteric syntax arrangements, and adds to the learning value of time spent in the IDE.

We can imagine similar "fix" logic built into wallet software or the frontend apps that they interact with. If a user makes a trade on a decentralized exchange that reverts because of slippage concerns, the contract could report this error in a standardized way and suggest a new price. Or, if the contract reverts due to insufficient gas allocation, the wallet could resubmit the transaction with a higher limit. An error standard gives us the chance to provide rich, helpful user experiences that would smoothen over the rougher edges of our applications and delight our users – something that, without such a standard, would not be possible.

More generally, in at least some cases, a contract can revert with enough information to inform the wallet how to correct the error without the user having to reason about it too closely. Just like in the IDE example (Figure 6-1), we can give users a faster, easier, and more robust experience, but only with a standard to power it.

Security and Verification

As we've said time and again in these pages, the Principle of Trust is extremely important. Our applications and our wallet software can better adhere to it when there are standards that allow it to do so. We should strive to increase the *safety* of what we're building, and a set of standards around application-level contract verification would be a good first step toward doing so.

How might this work? Our wallets, which are developed independently from our applications, could provide a community-sourced set of answers to a series of important security questions:

- Are contracts audited?

- Are contracts audited by reputable auditors?

- Are contracts audited by several different auditors?

- Have the most recent changes to a contract been audited?

- Is there a bug bounty program?

- Has the frontend been audited?

- Are there contingency plans and processes in place for handling hacks and other malicious events?

- Are deposits to the protocol insured or guaranteed in some other way?

Providing answers to these sorts of questions could allow wallets to increase safety and nudge users away from bad actors, enhancing trust. It would also be an important symbol for the products themselves to advertise: as with meeting various industry standards in web2 – PCI DSS compliance comes to mind – or with publishing the artifacts of contract audits, having a standardized way of signaling secure practices could allow us to increase trust and automate some verification.

This alone would be a good feature for a wallet developer to build unilaterally. Argent, for instance, provides a whitelist of trusted contracts that increases the rigor of the transaction flow. But whitelists are limited, and a community-driven standards approach could benefit *all* honest actors in the ecosystem: if the mechanisms to indicate contract trustworthiness are standardized, we can rely on broader community norms rather than gatekeepers to signal trust.

Authorization

In order to build richer user experiences around contracts, we need to know who can access or transact with what in what ways at what time. If we have a standard way for protocols to report permissioning levels, then we can build systems that provide an interface to several contracts at once.

There have been some steps toward this with ERC-173[9] – a standard for contract ownership – but this hasn't, in my opinion, gone nearly far enough. A smart contract authorization standard – perhaps based on the OpenZeppelin role model[10] – could meaningfully enhance the authorization flows we can build in our products.

Authorization is an area where there is a lot of plumbing that needs to be rebuilt for each contract: if we standardized some authorization behaviors at the contract level, we'd be able to write tooling, component libraries, and interface checks that could be used, reused, secured, and tested, but only with a standard.

There is also some precedent for this general approach: teams such as Tally and Sybil have built frontends over the popular Compound Governance Bravo interfaces, which represent DAO governance contracts. But these interfaces are standardized via the "standard capture" approach: they happened to be used a fair amount over the past few years, so many protocol teams have continued to use them. A codified, popular standard could improve the average quality bar higher.

Some Lessons

So we've discussed what standards are and why they matter and explored some possibilities as to how we might rely on them more in the future. These examples, I hope, have shown how powerful standards can be when designed in a community- and application-first spirit. We'll now tie these two points together and consider some of the lessons that they suggest.

Firstly, it tells us something about *composability*. Composability is a property of smart contract to smart contract interfaces, but it's also a property of interfaces between smart contracts and wallets, wallets and applications, and smart contracts and applications. In fact, it's a property of every component of the application layer. And this composability, which has many great virtues, is only possible because of implicit coordination: the very essence of a standard.

Secondly, another important lesson that we've driven home throughout this book is for *product engineers to be more involved in the protocol design process*. Protocol engineers should think deeply about the layer of applications that sit above your contracts: wallets, other contracts, frontends, and tooling. But many protocol engineers

---

[9] https://eips.ethereum.org/EIPS/eip-173
[10] https://docs.openzeppelin.com/contracts/3.x/access-control

are busy, or deeply technical, or otherwise unfamiliar with the UX consequences of their decisions. You, the product engineer, should be in the room, asking questions like "How can we design this contract to make rich user experiences easier?"

Thirdly, and building on the second point, *product engineers should be more involved in the standards design process.* Sensible and standardized events, sensible and standardized return values, and sensible and standardized errors each make protocols easier to integrate with and permit higher-order user experiences that simply wouldn't be possible otherwise. (They also save the protocol engineers some time and mean fewer conversations between the protocol and the product are necessary.) Lots of great ideas and opportunities to standardize, such as EIP-1066, end up stagnant. We should all be excited about any opportunity to standardize what we build from scratch right now, if only because it frees us up to work on the parts of our applications that drive actual value: solving user problems. There should be product engineer standard working groups, all-hands sessions for product engineers to discuss these issues with protocol engineers, and a wholesale increase in the status of products in the culture that is the Ethereum application sphere. Our products will be higher quality and our users will be grateful.

Finally, the most important lesson of all, if we don't standardize more in a community-driven way, *we still end up with standards.* It's just that we end up with standards designed by specific people for specific use cases. And, at the limit case, we hand the power to standardize to for-profit teams who are responding to their own cluster of noncommunitarian incentives.

Standards are public goods. They are integral to how we gain the benefits of decentralization without overindexing on it as a moral virtue. And we shouldn't allow our public goods to be angled toward wherever immediate importance – or venture capital money – happens to be pointing.

Summary

We began this chapter by exploring decentralization in more detail, arguing that it is a substantially more subtle set of trade-offs than it might seem. Most discussion of decentralization is unidimensional: you're either decentralized or you're not. This, it seems, is deeply unhelpful and doesn't help us reason in a smart way about our products. We then discussed standards, which help us codify and shape our relationship to decentralization. We also looked at where more standards could be applied at the application level, improving product quality, improving our practices, and creating more value for our users.

As we approach the end of this book, we'll turn next to the conclusion, where I'll take the basic ideas that we've been discussing and present some more speculative claims about the future of building products with Ethereum.

CHAPTER 7

Conclusion

In this book, I've argued for two main points:

1. **Product engineering on Ethereum is a distinct discipline**, with its own set of challenges and constraints that make it an interesting and worthwhile endeavor – and one worthy of higher status than it currently enjoys.

2. **Decentralization involves trade-offs**, and sometimes these are trade-offs that aren't worth making.

As we come to a close, it's worth stepping back and considering what crypto promises, what the future might hold for the industry, as well as what the world might look like if crypto's promise is fulfilled.

I don't expect everybody to agree with me on this. In fact, I don't expect *anybody* to agree with me: the ideas I present here are controversial, speculative, and informed only by my own experiences. Lots of very smart people won't believe a word I say. But, if I can't convince you to agree with me, I hope I can at least convince you that this vision is plausible, not crazy, not unrealistic, and perhaps not even undesirable.

Crypto Futurism (Without the Hyperbole)

One way of thinking about companies – that I find frequently useful – is to reason about *value creation* and *value accrual*. Value creation is the process of providing value to your users: What can they do now that they couldn't before? How does your solution resolve their problem in a more efficient or otherwise more desirable way? Value accrual is how your company captures some of the value that it creates. If you capture too much of it, you might simply take away any value you create – in economists' terms, you might erode your customer's *consumer surplus* – or you might make it too easy for a competitor to come along and undercut you. If you capture too little of it, you might not be able to build a sustainable business.

© Jamie Rumbelow 2023

J. Rumbelow, *Building With Ethereum*, https://doi.org/10.1007/978-1-4842-9045-3_7

If we're trying to understand how crypto evolves, then it's worth asking: Where is value likely to be created by crypto, and where is this value likely to accrue?

Value Creation

Understanding how value is created by crypto is partly about understanding traditional finance, partly about understanding the *skeuomorphic links*[1] between traditional finance and decentralized finance, partly about understanding what is native to and novel in crypto.[2]

We can start with traditional finance. This won't come as news to anybody: there is something deeply wrong with the traditional financial system. In many important respects, it is overregulated or, at least, regulated incorrectly. The regulations are designed to prevent fraud, or mismanagement of risk, or other socially bad things. But empirically a lot of these checks don't seem to work very well, and they also add a huge amount of *friction*.

Let's take AML (Anti-Money Laundering) regulations, for instance. If the priority is to prevent money laundering, reduce the funding of illicit transactions, and choke the funding sources of bad agents, then AML mechanisms can largely be considered a failure.[3] In fact, roughly 2–5% of the traditional finance system is used to fund or

---

[1] Take two successive paradigms, A and B. The people building B are likely to first look to A to see what can be done. They find these older use cases from A and adapt them in various ways to fit into B. When implementing these use cases in B, they may need to change some things. But in order to make these use cases *legible* and *natural*, they want to preserve some parts of A, so they create skeuomorphic links between the new thing in B and the old thing in A. For instance, "desktop" and "trash can" and "file" provide skeuomorphic links between an old office desk (paradigm A) and a computer UI (paradigm B).

[2] ...and partly about how Ponzi schemes work. We'll ignore the obvious Ponzi scheme economics of a lot of current protocols, not because it isn't an important criticism of crypto that I think needs attention, but mostly because this book is already much longer than I was expecting it to be.

[3] "[T]he anti-money laundering policy intervention has less than 0.1 percent impact on criminal finances, compliance costs exceed recovered criminal funds more than a hundred times over, and banks, taxpayers and ordinary citizens are penalized more than criminal enterprises"; www.tandfonline.com/doi/full/10.1080/25741292.2020.1725366. Even if the studies this paper relies on are not entirely methodologically sound, or if the data is noisy, it only has to be directionally correct in order for its results to be important.

distribute the funds of crime; Bitcoin is roughly 1.26% over five years.[4] And these ineffective checks come at a significant cost: the paper cited in footnote 3 suggests that some $304 billion worth of money is spent on compliance costs,[5] and other studies suggest the numbers are higher still. These compliance costs get built into the transaction fees of normal transactions; we're all paying a tax for a service that doesn't seem to work very well.

So all this friction makes it more difficult for financial institutions to innovate, and the costs get passed on to us. And there's also a cultural phenomenon at play here: financial institutions are *financial* institutions and typically aren't populated with technologists. Their servers are written in ugly, old, grown-up languages like COBOL. Their data is siloed and difficult to access. Their process documents read like the unabridged *Ulysses*. It's very likely that there are much better ways of structuring the finance world that we simply won't be able to *try* unless smart technologists come along and break things and experiment. Experimentation is good, and crypto gives us an opportunity to do it. It's much, much easier to write a novel financial mechanism in a smart contract than it is to do so in traditional finance, for path-dependent, historically contingent reasons, as much as for "good" reasons, like fighting crime or preventing systemic financial meltdowns (which, as 2008 demonstrates, the traditional financial system isn't *that* great at either).

Secondly, there are still a lot of big opportunities for value creation in tokenizing real-world assets. This opens up the possibility of using these assets as leverage, in a flexible way.[6] It also opens up the possibility of securing the provenance of these assets, allowing their ownership history to be tracked, at least with what's available on-chain. Lots of assets like art and wine need to be tracked to ensure they've been looked after well, kept in the right conditions, sold to reputable dealers, etc. If we can find a way to make various real-world claims about these assets representable and verifiable

---

[4] Traditional finance: www.unodc.org/unodc/en/money-laundering/overview.html. Bitcoin: Taking the average of 2017–2021, inclusive, from data provided by https://blog.chainalysis.com/reports/2022-crypto-crime-report-introduction/

[5] ~0.38% GDP; or 15% of the higher estimate of 5% of traditional finance money laundering (fn. 2).

[6] A common example here is housing: an NFT that represents your house could be used as collateral to borrow against without having to go through a traditional mortgage broker or, as is more likely, without having to go through the *current* mortgage system. There are obviously lots of ways this can go wrong. And it'll also require a deeper relationship between the off-chain legal system of property rights – i.e., the system that lets you call the police and say "somebody I don't want to be there is living in my house" – and the on-chain claims. But the idea is interesting and worth exploring properly.

on-chain, then tokenizing the assets themselves becomes quite powerful or, less speculatively, tokenizing stocks, allowing you to do all the cool stuff that rich people do with stocks (like borrowing money against them) without having to get on your knees and beg somebody at J. P. Morgan to let you.

And, thirdly, there are lots of things that crypto lets us do that aren't really possible in noncrypto environments. Flashloans allow arbitrage traders to pull *the entire liquidity available in a pool out*, perform their trade, and return it within the same transaction, without affecting any of the rest of the market. That's a level of computerized very short-term lending that is essentially impossible to do in normal markets and becomes even more difficult to do as the numbers get bigger. Alchemix has developed a protocol for self-repaying loans – loans that siphon off the required amount to keep the loan solvent without ever needing to issue a margin call on the collateral – which is something that can *probably* be structured in a traditional way, but will be difficult and will require the phone number of an expensive banker. And, of course, it's all automated and accessible to anybody.

I've given examples from the finance world here, mostly because it's the space I understand the best and also because it's the area where Ethereum alternatives to traditional systems seem most developed. But it's also a good example of where I think crypto is going, because, abstractly, it seems like an extremely *good* use of crypto. Most of modern finance is just a system of rules around processing entries in a database table, at a high level. At some point, these entries bottom out in real-world assets, but that's only after a lot of levels of abstraction have been stripped away. And it's also a good example for my current argument because these are all areas where crypto can show *actual value creation* for the very sorts of people who are most interested in value creation and are therefore most likely to pay for that surplus value created.

So I think it's quite possible that crypto's killer features will not be those aimed at consumers, but rather at businesses, particularly finance businesses. We've already spoken about the troubles with trying to educate users about crypto terminology and the intricacies of the technology; I've already shown my cards, suggesting that the successful crypto applications will be ones that abstract away these intricacies and solve object-level problems with these abstractions. This suggests that crypto can form the basis, but not the vocabulary, of modern finance.

All these examples help illustrate a larger point, which is that we should treat financial infrastructure as a product that *can and should be iterated upon*, rather than as a presupposed foundation. The traditional finance system has emerged over hundreds of years, in a contingent, path-dependent way. The constraints that held true in Renaissance Florence and 18th-century London *may no longer constrain us* – but the existing finance system and the financial regulation that supports it are often not flexible enough to remove these constraints. Composability, standards-driven integration, open access of data, and open access of developers allow us most of all to test and experiment, rather than flounder. If crypto can provide a platform for this testing and experimentation, then it can create a lot of value indeed.

Value Accrual

We've discussed value creation: how crypto might create value for users. Now we should ask how – and, importantly, *where* – that value accrues. My suspicion is that it will accrue much more to services with elements of centralization, rather than decentralized protocols.

Decentralization involves lots of trade-offs. As we've seen, it is often easier to make higher-quality products, reduce user friction, and add value to users by opting for centralized technologies. In at least some cases, the product that is marginally better is likely to be the one that is marginally more centralized. And this means that companies with a touch more confidence in centralizing are likely to do better, at least on the margin.[7]

And these trade-offs go beyond the product trade-offs we've discussed in this book. There are also business model trade-offs: tokenomics is an inexact and incomplete science, and it's not clear to me how protocols can ensure they are able to build profitable and defensible businesses around composable pieces of protocol infrastructure. Using tokens for utility pricing is a good start, but in many cases I suspect it's much easier to build a business with a standard centralized billing structure than with a freely trading token subject to speculative price fluctuations.

If crypto adoption grows in the future, it will grow because of companies building at the intersection of web2 and web3: fintech organizations allowing financing products that bridge on- and off-chain; tech and social media companies adopting crypto as

---

[7] There are some great examples of companies that show how well this can work in practice. The perpetual protocol, dYdX (https://dydx.exchange), builds an excellent and popular product that is decentralized in spirit, but is willing to centralize parts of their stack where appropriate.

underlying incentives mechanisms; tokenizing real-world assets, perhaps; etc. These companies will be working in regulated industries with traditional corporate structures and will inevitably have a higher level of centralization.

It's also worth asking about the base rate here: In which previous cases has value accrued to protocols? I suspect it isn't very high. SMTP didn't capture the value of email, Outlook and Gmail did. HTTP didn't capture the value of the Web, Google and Facebook did. Historically, the *applications layer* is typically where the value ends up accruing, and if I'm right about application trends, then these applications are likely to have aspects of centralization built into their structure. Of course, there are important differences between Ethereum protocols and the other protocols I've mentioned. For one thing, Ethereum protocols exhibit features of applications too. For another, the notion of value is built into them directly, via tokenization. It's possible that Ethereum protocols are disanalogous from traditional networking protocols enough so that value can accrue to these protocols. Today's DeFi is full of examples of protocols trying to figure out how to get value to accrue to them. Some of these examples have been fairly successful. But it remains to be seen whether they are scalably, reliably, persistently so. There are many more experiments to be run.

And then, of course, there's regulation. Even those companies with a deep cultural commitment to decentralization will have to centralize aspects of their organizational structure in order to work within this new world. The details are unknown, the legal framework is nascent, and we're not especially close to having a robust set of rules to follow. We're all still trying to figure this out. But regulation is coming, and it will be a forcing function. Maximal decentralization within the boundaries of this regulation will not be possible. Many important companies – Uber and Stripe, to name two noncrypto examples – have come from entrepreneurs pushing these boundaries. And a huge amount of the innovation in crypto has been possible because of the lack of regulatory clarity and, until recently, the lack of mainstream attention. (Indeed, that was kind of the point!) That, however, was a moment in time that I suspect has passed. If you're dealing with other people's money, there will eventually come a time when you need to deal with the government, operate in a safe and auditable way (or, at least, a way that signals to the government that you're safe and auditable), abide by the rules, and, hopefully, improve them.

You might disagree with any of the preceding points. It's possible that decentralized teams develop new technologies and resolve the computer science puzzles that cause the major usability and performance issues we've discussed in this book. It's possible that crypto will discover a critical mass of crypto-native use cases that don't rely on intersecting with the centralized world. It's possible that crypto regulation will falter and fail, or that it will be unenforced, or that heroic lobbying efforts will carve out a greater space for decentralization within it, or that it will simply be ignored. And it's possible that tokenization mechanics are a meaningful step forward for protocol value accrual. In short, it *is* possible that this time it's different.

But crypto teams shouldn't expect it to be easy. All the way along the timeline of technological development, the trade-offs will be used as a – very justifiable – reason to *not choose the decentralized option this time*. Until decentralized and centralized platforms are at a parity in terms of value creation for actual users, any growth the decentralized platforms experience will necessarily be curtailed.

Finally, many of the innovations that the crypto community develops won't *actually* rely on decentralization. It is possible to imagine a remittance system that is much simpler and cheaper for the user than the old guard Western Union shops: companies like Wise are doing it already. It is possible to imagine an online payment mechanism that is much more enjoyable for developers to integrate and handles the flows in a digitally native way: companies like Stripe are doing it already. While crypto may *pioneer* new innovations at the intersection of finance, technology, and culture, there will be companies freed from the constraints of decentralization that can *copy and rebuild* these ideas in a centralized way. Indeed, there is already some evidence that the success of crypto is creating pressure in traditional finance to liberalize existing companies' regulation, allowing new products that embody some of the benefits of crypto, without the difficulties of decentralization.[8] The ideas are new and impressive, but many of them are possible without crypto.

Final Thoughts

As I was writing this conclusion, the news broke that the centralized exchange FTX had become insolvent and was going into bankruptcy, evaporating the $32 billion company's value into nothing, over some 36 hours. The short version is that FTX used customer

---

[8] https://ec.europa.eu/commission/presscorner/detail/en/IP_22_6272

funds as a backstop for their trading firm, Alameda, when the latter suffered large losses.[9] It has given the crypto community a large shock, and the long-term consequences are still not well understood.

Some people, very reasonably, have argued that it's a sign we need more decentralization, more self-custody. And they're right: if FTX depositors had control over their tokens, and they weren't being lent out in an overleveraged way, then the exchange might not have collapsed quite as spectacularly, and the many, many retail investors who have lost money would be okay. If all the transactions and trades and accounting were rendered publicly on a blockchain – or if all the accounting logic was automated and executed on Ethereum – then this never would have happened. But, of course, this involves trade-offs: FTX wouldn't have been able to grow as quickly; there are many products it simply wouldn't have been able to sell; and, most importantly, it would have severely increased the smart contract risk exposure of its depositors.

The FTX debacle is also a demonstration of how quickly access to large amounts of capital in an unregulated market can go awry; and it's an example of hubris and, as it turns out, downright fraud.[10] So it should also be a reason to *welcome* some more regulation. This was a failure of process and risk management, and regulation is designed (more or less effectively) to force good process and risk management on financial institutions. If crypto is ever going to handle the level of transaction volume that traditional finance does – global payment volume alone is measured in the tens of trillions – it's going to need to integrate with the existing financial system, and that means regulation. You can't build stable systems without checks and balances and without mechanisms for effective regulatory compliance.[11]

We should also think about the culture that made FTX, and the many frauds and mistakes that came before it, possible. Crypto, and tech in general, lionized FTX's success and the young, high-IQ, maverick status of its founder. Crypto has been in a remarkably *defensive* posture, creating self-protective feedback loops that drive our mental models away from reality. We need to change some of the memes that drive this culture. Telling opponents that they're "ngmi" ("not gonna make it") is not just

---

[9] For the longer version, see the always-excellent Matt Levine's column, "FTX Had a Death Spiral," Nov 9, 2022, *Bloomberg*, and Levine's later columns on the same subject.

[10] `www.strangeloopcanon.com/p/reality-strikes-back`

[11] One of the ironies is that FTX made lots of noise about their compliance processes and how they were welcoming of regulation, because they were one of the good ones. Compliance theater, alas, is not compliance.

incendiary and funny, it's also counterproductive: it creates tribal dynamics, and that hurts the in-group as well as the out-group. It makes us less resilient to mismanagement and fraudulent behavior and less able to spot it when it happens. Even optimizing for goals such as *permissionlessness* isn't obviously a good thing if we want crypto to be used by people who, more or less, don't mind that certain trades are illegal or certain sources of money should be blocked. A more productive, and softer, version of the same goal is something like "widespread access," and that's something that is both in keeping with the more attractive visions for crypto's future – as a system for democratizing access to finance – and with the inevitable integration of crypto into the rest of the world.

So we need to grow up a bit. Crypto technologies have been wrapped up in a culture war, a culture war that crypto itself has birthed and sustained. Wrapping up your technological choices into cultures – antagonistic, aggressively self-assured cultures – might be helpful to help maintain a committed core of contributors, but it quickly becomes a burden. A shift away from the current memes of petty in-group tub-thumping and toward a set of memes based on solid moral and intellectual grounding and a spirit of sensible pragmatism won't resolve these culture wars, or placate crypto's fiercest skeptics, but it will at least refocus our energies on building technologies that ultimately serve customers.

All in all, there could still be an exciting future for crypto ahead. There are still lots of very smart people who believe in the technology; my team at Fei Labs were exceptional and also far from the exception. There are strong commercial and moral reasons to believe that the financial world needs remolding. Crypto is *interesting*: the problems are new, and the design space is still so wide open. The culture is idiosyncratic, cultish, self-reflexive, fast-changing, and changeable. If the value of crypto goes to zero in six months' time – aside from hurting my book sales – the experience and insight into the relationship between technology and the current cultural moment is invaluable. And, finally, crypto and DeFi's promises are so extraordinarily huge that, on an expected value basis, the probability of the world actually turning out to be this way can be very low, and it will still be worth dedicating resources to.

Right now, it seems like crypto could still be anything: a roaring success, a colossal failure, something in between. It could die with a bang, exploded by its own giddy excesses, crippled by a sudden change in regulation, floored by a crashing market. It could die with a whimper, the best ideas being annexed by web2, the smartest contributors leaving in dribs and drabs. It could flourish and grow, sustainably, safely, and be the technological substrate of much of the next generation of finance and ownership. It could rush into dominance, supplanting failed nation states[12] and supporting free markets.

Any outcome would be interesting, worth studying for anthropological reasons as well as technological and economic. Any outcome would cause damage, collateral or direct. Any outcome would liberate and harm, displacing some forms of privilege and creating others.

Our responsibilities as technologists, then, are to consider how our decisions align with our personal values and what we can do to increase freedom and prosperity and autonomy as we build the future; to take each other in terms of good faith; to see the best in what we can build and to reduce the harms (or, at least, think deeply about whether the harms are worth the benefits); to respect the user; to respect one another; to understand that technology is so often a force for good, the main driver of human progress, that it needs to be protected from enemies outside and within; to understand that history contains many examples of technology being used for great evil, causing great pain; to understand these trade-offs; to look to the future without forgetting the past; and to never succumb to hopelessness.

---

[12] https://thenetworkstate.com

Index

© Jamie Rumbelow 2023
J. Rumbelow, *Building With Ethereum*, https://doi.org/10.1007/978-1-4842-9045-3

Printed in the United States
by Baker & Taylor Publisher Services